Therapeutic Communities
for Children and Young People

Community, Culture and Change

(formerly Therapeutic Communities)
Series editors: Rex Haigh and Jan Lees

Community, Culture and Change encompasses a wide range of ideas and theoretical models related to communities and cultures as a whole, embracing key Therapeutic Community concepts such as collective responsibility, citizenship and empowerment, as well as multidisciplinary ways of working and the social origins of distress. The ways in which our social and therapeutic worlds are changing are illustrated by the innovative and creative work described in these books.

other books in the series

Therapeutic Communities for Children and Young People

*Edited by Adrian Ward, Kajetan Kasinski,
Jane Pooley and Alan Worthington*

Therapeutic Communities 10

Jessica Kingsley Publishers
London and Philadelphia

First published in the United Kingdom in 2003
by Jessica Kingsley Publishers
116 Pentonville Road
London N1 9JB, UK
and
400 Market Street, Suite 400
Philadelphia, PA 19106, USA

www.jkp.com

Copyright © Jessica Kingsley Publishers 2003
Printed digitally since 2007

Library of Congress Cataloging in Publication Data
A CIP catalog record for this book is available from the Library of Congress

British Library Cataloguing in Publication Data
A CIP catalogue record for this book is available from the British Library

ISBN 978 1 84310 096 6

Contents

Part II Practice

Part III Management and Development

Part IV Applications and the Future

Conclusion

Acknowledgements

This book arose out of our own work as (at various times) practitioners, managers, trainers, educators, and consultants in relation to therapeutic communities for young people. More immediately it has arisen from our connection with the Charterhouse Group of Therapeutic Communities, an association of some of the longest-established communities in the UK – but also now including a number of much 'younger' and more diverse units. We are grateful to this Group for the support and encouragement which it has given us throughout the project. We are also grateful to Rex Haigh and Jan Lees, the series editors, for their interest in and enthusiasm for the project – without which it might never have got off the ground in the first place.

We have all learned enormously from the young people and their families with whom we have worked, and have hoped to stay mindful throughout the project of the urgent and serious needs of young people who have suffered the sorts of experiences and deprivations described at various points throughout the book, but who have also had the amazing resilience and courage to work through these experiences in the therapeutic communities. A similar tribute is due to the staff of the communities, whose task is unremittingly demanding, although also uniquely rewarding and valuable. Our friends, families and employers have allowed us the space and time to engage in the time-consuming business of editing this book, and will be as pleased and relieved as we are when it finally appears. We have had financial support from the Charterhouse Group, the Peper Harow Foundation, Barnet Healthcare Trust and the Northgate Clinic for some of the expenses incurred in preparing the book, for which we are very grateful. Last but not least, we owe a particular vote of thanks to Julia Warner, who undertook (with her usual equanimity, good humour and thoroughness) the painstaking work of translating the raw documents into finished and polished texts for publication.

CHAPTER 1

Introduction

This is a book about trying to hold things together – which is sometimes known in a very specific sense as 'containment' or 'holding'. It is not just about holding 'things' together, however – although it does include some of what this phrase might imply, in the sense both of managing difficult situations and of keeping a whole team or organisation on the road despite the many diversions and pitfalls which it may encounter. It is also, more importantly, about holding *people* together, and especially about holding individual young people who may never have experienced that sort of caring, supportive and integrative 'holding' which every human being needs in order to grow onwards from a safe beginning. We will be looking at the extremely difficult and challenging task of providing this sort of healthy new beginning for some of the most traumatised and in some cases the most dangerous (either to themselves or to others) young people, within the collective setting which is known as the therapeutic community approach. We will aim to create a picture of this approach: its history, its theoretical base and its practice as well as the planning, management and further development and other applications of this sort of practice. We hope this picture will help practitioners and others to gain some 'purchase' on a task which can feel immensely complicated and at times elusive or even impossible to achieve.

Sometimes in the general field of child welfare, as people get frustrated with the apparent impossibility of bringing about real change and improvement in young people's lives and conditions, they talk despairingly of their services being 'at best just a holding operation'. What they seem to mean by this phrase is that all of their efforts and stress and resources don't seem to be effecting any real progress, but are just preventing further instances of the disintegration of families, or the emotional breakdown of individuals, or even the total collapse of teams, arrangements or whole organisations. These are entirely understandable anxieties, which we have all felt at times in the course of such work. Indeed these anxieties often represent in themselves our own personal struggle to come to terms with the reality that, whatever combination of personal, moral or other motivations may have driven us to come into this sort of work in the first place, we are sometimes rowing against a huge tide of destructive influences and impulses in humanity itself, and that apparent reverse or failure will always be an integral part of such work.

However, what each of the four of us as editors has long recognised, both in our own direct practice with young people and their families, and in our other work with staff teams, students and organisations, is that even enabling a 'holding operation' may sometimes be a fantastic achievement and one which may ultimately make an enormous and long-lasting difference to the lives of those we have been trying to help. Holding together individuals, families and groups who may otherwise be on the very brink of self-destruction (and here we are using 'holding together' in the sense of stabilising and introducing some coherence and consistency to them) may not usually be identified as the main goal of child care services, but it may nevertheless be usefully recognised as a necessary precondition or perhaps a 'base camp' from which any further achievements can then be attempted.

This is not to say that this book is only about stabilising the incipient chaos in some children and families. It is also and primarily about those further achievements hinted at above: promoting positive emotional change and growth in very troubled people; the releasing of young people's true potential which may hitherto have been blighted or hidden by years of abuse, neglect or other trauma; and the reversal of the cycles of emotional and other deprivation and despair into which these young people may have been born. These kinds of achievement may sound idealistic, and indeed it is probably true that we are in part going to be writing about the planting of hope and idealism in what often feels like the most barren and poisoned of grounds. It is not wild or inappropriate idealism that we are advocating, however, but a principled and disciplined striving towards genuine change and maturity.

The sort of 'holding' that we are going to describe relates directly to what the paediatrician and psychoanalyst Donald Winnicott called the 'holding environment' – the provision of understanding and toleration but also firm boundaries as well as the establishment of the ability to communicate and relate – which he argued is an essential task both of the early mother-child relationship and (through different means) of the relationship between therapist and patient, and in our case between therapeutic community and young person. It is from this experience of being 'held' that both the infant and the child in treatment can begin to feel stability and security, which leads to the establishment of a sense of self, and of identity, and ultimately to a secure ability to relate and to grow on into mature, responsible and productive adulthood.

Our focus will be on a specific way of working, which might be thought of as a very specialised context and method through which this holding experience can be created. The book contains several variations on the definition of the therapeutic community approach, and indeed the whole book might be thought of as embodying the struggle towards pinning down a full and accurate account of this method. We feel we have gone some way towards achieving that account, although as will be seen later, there is still a long way to go. It is an approach, and a practice context, of huge complexity and subtlety, although in practice it must nevertheless boil down to a set of experiences which will make sense to the most troubled and difficult of young people, which means that somehow all of this subtlety and complexity needs to be presented to the young person in as straightforward and down-to-earth a manner as possible. Part of our task in writing and editing this book, therefore, has been to manage the tension between complexity (concepts and language which may appear 'difficult' or even excluding) and simplicity (everyday experiences in residential care which must ultimately be experienced by the young people as making sense and being genuinely helpful). This is not an easy balance to achieve, and we are sure we have not always got it right.

The therapeutic community for young people

There is much misunderstanding and confusion as to what is meant by describing a place as a therapeutic community for young people, and as we have already said, this book includes several attempts at definitions. For the purposes of introducing the book to the wide range of potential readership, however, we will offer a working definition here.

When we use the term therapeutic community in this book we mean it to refer to a specialised unit for children, usually residential and often incorporating education as well as care, and usually organised on the basis of offering planned therapeutic help and support over a period of perhaps two or three years. At the heart of this work will be a recognition of the need to understand and address the impact on children of traumatic early experience (for example of serious loss, neglect, abuse or extreme attachment difficulties). Such experiences are likely to have had severe consequences for the child's capacity to be looked after, to make friends or be part of a group, to learn and be taught, or just to respond appropriately to everyday interactions. The view which will be taken of these difficulties is that they are unlikely to improve without intensive and skilled psychotherapeutically informed help on a 24-hour -a-day basis.

The underlying theory base will be explicitly psychodynamic, though other perspectives may also be included, and this theory base will be used to understand staff dynamics and the management of relationships in the whole place, as well as to explicate the difficulties facing the children and their families. The staff will normally be well trained and supported themselves, with regular opportunities for both supervision and consultation, and with a full programme of daily and weekly staff meetings.

The place will be arranged so as to offer intensive levels of support to young people both individually and in groups, and in scheduled sessions as well as in the course of the ordinary interactions of everyday life. The life of the place will be focused on regular weekly (and in many places daily) 'community meetings' in which young people and staff will discuss and resolve issues arising in daily life as well as other matters of concern.

The method of working in therapeutic communities for young people bears a strong similarity to that used in many of the therapeutic communities for adults, including principles such as democratization and reality confrontation (Rapoport 1960), and especially incorporating the principles that it is the whole experience of the community of children and adults which is therapeutic, and that all members of the community can and do contribute to each other's growth and development. In the child care setting, however, the therapeutic community approach also includes something very different as well, because here the care is for young people rather than adults, and these young people have immediate needs for the ordinary nurturing and loving care which any young person needs. The community has to find a way to provide this 'intensive care', even though these very troubled youngsters may find it extremely difficult at times to acknowledge that they have such needs at all, and may indeed reject the offer of it with great rage, confusion and even violence, as we shall see later in the book. The aim will also usually be to promote children's awareness of each other's needs for this sort of care as well as their own needs, and to develop a culture in which it will be possible for young people to understand, support and help each other – and thereby also to help themselves and mature towards responsible adulthood. The therapeutic community for young people is much more than just the sum of these various components of practice, however. Its task is holistic and integrative, in the sense of holding together all the disparate and often conflicting elements in the lives and minds of a group of very troubled children and the staff aiming to support them, and seeking to create a single culture of understanding, learning and even loving within the whole community. Although therapeutic communities operate mainly in residential care settings, the range of applications is wide, including psychiatric care, special education, family centres and young offenders' institutes. These differing contexts will necessarily influence the structure and boundaries of the work in each place, but the primary focus on understanding and responding to children's deepest needs in a group or institutional setting remains the same.

It will be evident from the above comments that, for the staff, this is a way of working which is extremely demanding but also hugely rewarding. In today's 'evidence-based' terms its effectiveness is still technically unproven, even though the best-known places of this sort have impressive track records of successful help to children and their families stretching back well over fifty years in some cases. Each place of this kind is highly individual and yet each is also instantly recognisable for its therapeutic community approach. Not all are as successful or as long-established as this, or not as consistently so, and one of the difficulties is that it is a way of working which, because it relies so heavily upon the resilience and resourcefulness of the staff working closely with the most disturbed and confused young people in the country, may go through considerable variations over time. Thus even the best of places are likely to go through cycles of greater and lesser effectiveness. One of the ways in which therapeutic communities aim to keep themselves on track, and to keep the staff team sane, creative and productive as a group, is through sound leadership and drawing upon regular advice and support from external consultants, who may meet with either senior management or with the whole team at times.

The practice demands skill and patience, and yet it is notoriously difficult to describe in objective terms – indeed some of the best texts in this field are those written in highly subjective terms by the charismatic and even at times wildly egocentric characters who have often been the most successful leaders of such communities. Nevertheless it seems extremely important to attempt some clearer description of the details of practice in all their complexity, so that those who wish to work in this way can have something more reliable to go on than simply an individual's personal account.

Elsewhere in the book will be found various attempts at defining the practice – sometimes by listing examples of what is involved, sometimes by trying to capture the spirit of it or by explaining the theory-base. Perhaps the best way to learn the practice, however, is to spend some time working in such a place, or to join a learning community on a training course, with others engaged in similar work, in which the methods can be experienced for oneself, as described later in the book. Learning by 'doing and being' and by reflecting, is part of the business for everyone involved in therapeutic communities.

The structure of the book

What we have assembled is a collection of chapters which, taken together, build up a composite and powerful picture of the theory and practice of therapeutic community work with young people. It is not quite the first book to do so, as others have covered some of the same ground, but none has attempted quite the same span or depth of coverage that we have undertaken here. We hope it will therefore stand as a reference point for those working in or with this field of practice, as well as for those in other professions or disciplines who may wish to learn something about this approach to practice. We also hope that this book will lead on to other collections, which will not only address some of the gaps which we have recognised, but will also allow for some of the topics covered here to be explored in much fuller depth.

After this introduction, we begin with Part I: Ideas and Origins, in which we aim to establish the context for the subsequent chapters by focusing not only on the historical development and precedents of this approach to practice, but also on the location of the theory-base for practice in terms of the other professions and disciplines to which it has connections We have called this 'the core framework of theory for practice in therapeutic communities'. We continue this theoretical exploration in the next three chapters, where we bring together three necessary perspectives or types of thinking – the individual, the group, and the systemic – which seem to us to underpin the practice of therapeutic community work with young people. It is important to recognise that each of these, taken together with the chapter on the Core Framework, must be 'held together' in practice, so that no single model or theoretical assumption takes precedence over any other.

In Part II we have assembled a number of chapters covering everyday practice in therapeutic communities from many different angles and perspectives. Our focus here has been on trying to answer as specifically as possible the question 'Where's the therapy in therapeutic community work?' For example, we address the ways in which everyday interactions between staff and young people can be harnessed into the overall therapeutic endeavour, the ways in which the ordinary living experiences of young people are planned for and managed to enhance their value, and the ways in which the 'key' relationships between staff and young people are thought about. Since therapeutic communities have moved on a very long way from the days in which they may have been (perhaps unfairly) stereotyped as remote from those other powerful realities of children's lives to which they would eventually and inevitably return, we have included chapters on two essential ways in which these realities are addressed. Thus, there is a chapter on the educational task – a case study of the way in which one institution developed and expanded its educational provision and tied this in to the external demands of the broader educational system. There is also a chapter on the inclusion of working with children's families as part of the task of the therapeutic community, in this case including a number of examples from different communities of the many different ways in which this task can be achieved.

In Part III we have a number of chapters on the management and development of the therapeutic community, focusing first on the central task of leadership. This chapter offers a reflective account by the former leader of one of the most influential therapeutic communities in the UK. The other chapters in this section include an account of the processes of staff supervision and consultation, and of staff development and training: these chapters each recognise in different ways the reality that by far the most important resource in the therapeutic community method is the staff themselves – their personal as well as their professional selves, both individually and collectively. It is a truism, of course, that the staff themselves can only provide the necessary caring and 'holding' for the young people if they themselves are properly cared for and 'held', but again these are not easy tasks to achieve, and these two chapters provide valuable insights into what is involved. There is also a chapter on research here, in which the authors focus on the sharper end of 'what works' and what is known about or can be proved about what works in this field. The answers are understandably constrained, which of course does not mean that we should not be continuing with this approach, but that we need research methods and philosophies of a similar subtlety and complexity to the way of working itself.

The final part takes our focus outside the boundaries of the traditional therapeutic community itself, as we consider the other contexts in which this approach has been undertaken, or at least attempted. So we have a chapter on the local authority context, in which the focus is on the development of therapeutic resources and understanding within local authority children's homes. Another chapter covers a range of applications in other settings, as diverse as field social work, foster care and residential care for children with autism – this chapter also addresses the essential question of how the types and levels of understanding inherent within the therapeutic community approach can be disseminated and taken up within other settings, in these cases through a multi-disciplinary training course for senior staff. Finally we have an example of one of the central methods used in the therapeutic community, the 'Community Meeting', being applied in the very different context of a secure unit for adolescents.

Editing as holding

We return now briefly to the theme of holding. Our own experience in bringing this book together has involved another form of holding, including at times that awfully familiar anxiety that the whole project was about to fail either by flying apart in a thousand directions, by the sudden appearance of huge and irreparable gaps, or simply by our own difficulty in keeping the whole project going in the teeth of a tearing wind (the demands of our other jobs and commitments). We have not been able to include all that we would have wanted to, and indeed we are painfully aware that some of those huge gaps are still there, although we have had to reassure ourselves that nevertheless what is included is valuable and worthwhile in its own right. In particular we would have liked to include more material on issues such as:

- the detail of the challenges and strategies involved in managing individual relationships between staff and young people

- the quality of the physical environment, including a full recognition of its potential symbolic meanings to young people

- the moral and ethical dilemmas which arise both in everyday life and in the overall planning and delivery of therapeutic work with groups of young people

- questions of the cultural, ethnic and gender identities of children and families, and the ways in which therapeutic communities can address these issues

- the organisational complexities involved in managing a therapeutic resource for young people.

Some of the above chapters we had planned to include but for various personal, organisational or other reasons they did not get written (or in some cases not in time or in the right form for inclusion in the book); others we recognised early on that we simply would not have space for; and others again we would like to have commissioned or written ourselves but did not manage to do so. We have had to learn to forgive ourselves these gaps, failings and frustrations and so we hope that you, the reader, will do likewise.

Part I

Ideas and Origins

Introduction

It will be clear from Chapter 1 that we cannot realistically talk about 'the' therapeutic community for young people, as if there were one single blueprint or model of practice used everywhere. In contrast, the reality is that there are many different types and models of practice, each with its own line of descent from its forerunners (and the same is true of therapeutic communities for adults). In current practice in the UK, as we will see in Chapter 3, some communities have been designed to follow a particular model of practice, others are deliberately eclectic in their use of a range of different approaches, while others again have gradually evolved and developed their own practice, fairly separate from other places. It is only since the late 1980s that there has been a coming together, within the Charterhouse Group, of this wide diversity of practice, although there had of course previously been many informal contacts between places and between individuals from these places. Throughout this book we will be drawing upon examples from across this wide range of practice: we will often be saying 'Here's how it is done in this place, while elsewhere it may be done differently'. That is part of our aim in this book – to survey the field, and to draw out the common points as well as the distinctive practices of particular places which others might be able to adapt to their own circumstances.

In this part, on 'ideas and origins' our aim is to outline and illustrate the main concepts upon which the practice is based. Since practice is so diverse, this may be quite a challenge – both for the writers and the readers of the coming chapters! Chapter 2 presents an overall framework - to which we will return later in this brief introduction. In Chapter 3 Kajetan Kasinski traces some of the ideas and methods used in therapeutic community work back to their origins and antecedents, as a way of exploring the roots and underlying themes in the work. In Chapter 4 Monica Lanyado will start this process by looking at the children and young people themselves: who are they, what are their social, emotional and other needs, and most importantly why and how have they become like this? She will be drawing upon attachment theory and other developmental models to explain the nature and impact of the sorts of traumatic experiences which these young people may have had, and to indicate what sorts of help they may need. In Chapter 5 Philip Stokoe focuses on what we have called 'group thinking', looking at why living in groups can make a difference to these young people, and how this may work. He defines some key terms and concepts in the psychodynamic approach to working in groups, and then looks at children's therapeutic experiences in both small and large groups, including not only the formal group meetings which character-ise many therapeutic communities, but also the informal everyday groupings which emerge and dissolve again throughout the day in such a place. Finally in this section, in Chapter 6, Colette Richardson takes a wider view, to look at children in the context of the 'systems' in which they have lived and grown: what has been the ongoing pattern of these children's relationships with their family and other networks, and how have these relationships contributed to their difficulties – and again, what does this tell us about how they might be helped?

Our aim in grouping these chapters together has been to show how each element or perspective – the individual, the family and the group, as well as the historical perspective – tells us something different but essential about children's experiences and about how they may be helped. We want to emphasise strongly that no one of these elements should be prioritised above any other, as they all need to be in place and fully understood if the work is to be really effective. This means, however, that we also need some overarching (or perhaps underpinning) framework if we are to hold all these perspectives together, both in theory and in practice. In daily practice, this is where the central principles of the therapeutic community can help, because they focus on how the 'whole' can hold together and how each single element or person involved in the work relates to each other element or person. Since this is how best practice operates, we also need to be able to explain and analyse it in this theoretical context, and it is for this reason that we will be focusing in Chapter 2 on the 'core framework' of the therapeutic community. The aim here will be to show what is at the heart of this approach to practice, by looking at a number of elements, some version of each of which will probably be found in most therapeutic communities for young people. (It is hard to be more pre-scriptive than this, since the reality is that some communities will be much stronger on some of these aspects than others.) We will also be trying to show the ways in which this model reflects but also differs from the model of the therapeutic community which is used in adult services.

CHAPTER 2

The Core Framework

Adrian Ward

Introduction

When Hillary Clinton quoted the African proverb that 'it takes a whole village to raise a child' she was not, of course, thinking about therapeutic child care (she was actually scoring political points) (Clinton 1996). Nevertheless, we may find some relevance in this idea of a child thriving on the concern, love and active contribution of a whole community in order to grow, develop, learn, and in our case also to be helped and restored. There are important differences, of course, because in the therapeutic community we are not starting from the same place as the average village or neighbourhood. In particular, whereas the ordinary child in his or her home community is growing into that community from what is, we hope, a secure home (i.e. family) base, the young people whom we have in mind in the therapeutic community setting are likely to have experienced multiple breakdowns, losses and other traumas in their family before they even join us, and are likely to be suffering greatly as a consequence of these experiences. At the beginning, therefore, these children will probably have *no* sense of a secure base from which to grow, which means that what the therapeutic community has to provide for them is both the security of a primary individual relationship and the broader base of a community of relationships with others (children and adults) who will share in the give and take of learning and developing together.

In this chapter I shall be looking at some of the key ideas underlying therapeutic community practice, in order to establish some 'first principles' as a basis from which the rest of the book can proceed. The function of this chapter is therefore to set the scene for the material which follows, and especially for the next three chapters, which focus in turn on the individual, the group and the systemic dynamics of therapeutic community practice. Beyond these theoretical chapters, the book moves into the more detailed consideration of a wide range of elements of practice, but since part of the ethos of the therapeutic community is that everything should work together towards the same aim, several of those chapters will also be presaged here in this account of what we are calling the 'core framework' of therapeutic community practice. The scope is ambitious, which means that this chapter may appear rather dense at times, but the intention is that it can be used as a reference point or clearing house for the other chapters, so that readers can use it to refer to and fro.

First principles

Returning to the metaphor of the village, what theory needs to do for us is to explain *how* the village raises the child, or in our case, how the whole therapeutic community can be made to work to help and heal the child (and family!). We need to know this because, whereas in most cases a village or neighbourhood can be left to get on with raising its children, the therapeutic community cannot be left to chance. It has to be planned, managed and monitored, and its work has to be set in the context of moral and ethical principles. We have to know how to help people do this planning, managing and monitoring so that therapeutic communities can carry out this difficult work successfully, which means that we need ways of understanding and explaining such matters as:

- how individual traumatised children can be helped in a group setting

- how this help can be connected to active support for the child's family and plans for the child's future

- how a group of such children can be enabled to support, help and learn from each other

- how a staff team can be enabled to work closely together to support both the group and the individuals

- how the whole enterprise can be kept focused on its own task and yet also connected to the rest of the world.

This is not an exhaustive list, but they are all necessary items. Equally, the theory base which I want to use is fairly broad. This is a complex field of practice, and we will need to draw on a wide range of ideas to encompass the whole field.

I shall in fact be using 'theory' in a number of different ways, as people do in practice. In the first section of the chapter, I shall be using the concept of 'group care' as a way of delineating the broad field of practice within which therapeutic community work can be located. In this sense 'theory' is being used to provide an overall framework for describing and analysing what I am calling the 'mode of practice'. In the second section theory is used differently: here we look at some aspects of psychodynamic theory in particular, using this as an underpinning set of ideas to help us explain the ways in which people behave, and the links between thinking, feeling and acting. We then look at the specific concept of the therapeutic community, which in effect brings together the group care context and the psychodynamic theory to give us a detailed model of practice. However, these two uses of theory are not quite enough for what is needed, and we turn next to 'systems theory' as a way of helping to trace and explain the connections between the various elements. Finally there is some attempt to outline the moral and ethical principles which must underpin the whole enterprise. It should also be added that, although this is a chapter about the use of theory in practice, it is not in itself a heavily theoretical chapter: it is perhaps an aerial view or street map of the village rather than an escorted walk around all the byways – the finer detail of both the exposition and the application of theory comes later, throughout the rest of the book.

1 Group care as the mode of practice

My starting point is to think about what I call the 'mode of practice' – in other words, what sort of work is this? The answer is that it is not the same as what is usually thought of as social work, in the sense of fieldwork (visiting individuals or families), or 'care management' (assessing people for 'packages of care'), but neither is it 'pure' clinical work in the sense of a sequence of individual or group sessions for children from an expert, although it does has some affinities with all of the above. It is much more appropriately located within what has been called 'group care', i.e. residential and day care, which involves using a group of staff in a specific building over a period of time to work closely with a group of people needing help. Group care is a very broad category, though, since it includes settings as diverse as family centres, 'drop-in centres', homes for older people, small group living settings for people with learning disabilities and so on, and whereas therapeutic communities have some broad elements in common with places such as these, they also have some important distinctive elements of their own. My argument, therefore, is that therapeutic communities are a specialised and finely-tuned version of group care.

I have argued elsewhere (Ward 1993) that what is distinctive about group care as a mode of practice can be seen in terms of its emphasis on the following items:

1. the network of relationships between the team and the group of service-users (i.e. the children)

2. the close interdependence required of the team

3. the public or semi-public nature of much of the work

4. 'opportunity-led work': using opportunities for useful work in the informal everyday life of the centre

5. the co-ordinated use of time (e.g. the use of routines for daily living, the planning of regular events such as mealtimes and bedtimes, the impact of staff rotas, etc.)

6. the planned use of space and the physical environment (the quality of the building and of each room, plus its location, etc.).

Some of these elements will feature more strongly in some group care settings than in others, and some (such as the interdependent team) may also occur in many other settings such as the clinical and fieldwork teams mentioned above. The argument here, however, is that, *when taken together,* these elements add up to a quite distinctive mode of practice, involving groups of staff and of clients – in this case children – working together closely over time towards a clear aim. I am not going to discuss all of these elements here, as many of them will be explored in more detail in other parts of the book – for example, 'Opportunity-led work' is the focus of Chapter 7, the use of space and of the 'environment' of the therapeutic community is touched upon in Chapter 8, and the co-ordinated use of time features strongly in Chapter 10. What I want to draw attention to here is the 'group-ness' of group care – which means exploring the implications of the fact that there are groups not only of children but also of staff, as well as a 'whole group' of both children and staff.

I have referred above to the 'network of relationships' between the staff and the children as a key feature of the work. By this I mean that, whereas in some clinical and other settings each worker focuses separately on a number of individual children, and each child relates primarily to just one or two staff (and sometimes to a small group of other children), in a group care setting, by contrast, all of the children in a group, and all of the staff, interact with each other and affect each other's work and progress more or less directly. There are enormous implications here for the workers in terms of the necessary awareness of the way these groups may interact and influence each other for better and for worse. The group is the greatest resource in any group care setting, yet it is often under-used because people do not fully recognise its strengths or know how to harness them. There are also implications for the ways in which the work needs to be organised, and for how the team needs to be able to work together to support each other.

The additional element in group care of the 'public or semi-public nature of the work' is significant here, because it indicates that this network of relationships operates largely in the open, rather than in individual consulting or interview rooms. The implications are obvious: colleagues witness each other's practice as they work alongside each other, and the children (and sometimes their relatives and other visitors) will also be aware of how other children's needs, rights and wishes are responded to, and of how staff relate with each other. This is not to say that all the work of a therapeutic community is or should be conducted in a fully public forum. Indeed there are many aspects of the work which demand meticulous attention to confidentiality. But confidentiality is not always the same thing as privacy, and certainly not the same as secrecy – for many young people, secrets are potentially very painful things. What this all means is that the issue of what is public and what is private is a constant dilemma in therapeutic communities, and is rarely straightforward to handle.

I have also referred to the 'interdependent team', by which I mean that in the group care context teamwork typically means that workers need to be able to rely directly upon each other in their everyday work with service users, by contrast with those other settings in which teamwork may simply mean the occasional meeting for the allocation of new work or for consultation on future plans. Thus, for example, in the interdependent team of a therapeutic community one person can only focus fully on a planned individual session with a child if she knows that someone else is with the rest of the group, while the person supervising that group may herself be dependent on an administrator in the office to 'field' phone calls and visitors. Under pressure, or in a crisis, people may have to leave what they are doing to help each other out – although they will need to be clear about how priorities should be decided in such cases (for instance, in most cases, a planned individual session is sacrosanct whereas the supervision of a group watching television may allow for more flexibility).

This interdependency applies not just in terms of the planned sessions but also in terms of all the other events and informal activities of the day, where people may need to call upon each other's support or intervention at a moment's notice. This means that workers need to cultivate the ability to know what each of their colleagues is doing at any given time, to know who they can call upon for support if there is a crisis or some unexpected event in the unit, and to have a sense as to who may need support following a difficult incident, and so on. They need to know how to work with each other collaboratively and flexibly, moving rapidly between, for example, a planned group meeting and a conflict between two young people arising from the everyday interactions in the unit. See Dockar-Drysdale (1968) for an excellent discussion of these issues of 'role and function'.

This sort of ability may seem to come naturally to some people (particularly those who have grown up in large families!), but it certainly does not do so for everyone, and it often needs to be learned by people new to the work or new to this particular approach, especially those who may have previously worked in more rigid and defended organisations. Without it the 'knitting together' of the fabric of the place soon becomes unravelled. Again this factor has widespread implications for the management of the unit, for instance in terms of the appropriate arrangements for staff meetings and supervision.

I have spelled out some of these typical features of the group care mode of practice to emphasise the extent to which awareness of both group and individual dynamics – and of the interactions between the group and individual – is needed. These features will be found to some extent in most group care places, from the drop-in centre for people with learning disabilities to the residential home for older people with mental health problems, although they naturally arise in different ways in each place. Taken together, they form the backdrop or context of the work, and here I am using them to provide the 'first base' or foundation for this examination of the theory base for therapeutic community practice.

2 Psychodynamics as an underpinning theory

Whereas the group care framework offers an approach to thinking about practice, it does not in itself presuppose any particular theoretical underpinning. I emphasise this point because there are group care settings which use all sorts of different theoretical perspectives, as well as some which do not appear to use any explicit theory base. Since our focus in this book is on therapeutic practice, we will need a more precise frame of theoretical reference for this, and it will probably be evident by now that the preferred theory base in most therapeutic communities for young people is the psychodynamic one. This is primarily because within the extensive literature on psychodynamic thinking about individuals, families and organisations there is a large amount of work which can be applied very productively to the work of therapeutic communities. It is not my intention here, however, to explain what psychodynamic thinking consists of, since more of that will be found in later chapters, but rather to set the tone for the book by showing how this thinking connects with other elements in the theory base of therapeutic community practice.

Relationships and attachments

The most obvious of these connections (and perhaps the most familiar for staff in therapeutic communities for young people) is probably found in the work of Winnicott and others on the relationships between mothers, fathers and children and on the consequences for children of early disturbances in these relationships (Winnicott 1965). Winnicott was a paediatrician and psychoanalyst who studied early developmental processes in infancy. He focused especially on those processes and developing relationships through which children are helped by their parent(s) to move from their earliest state of absolute dependency towards becoming relatively independent physically and emotionally, and able to function as autonomous beings. He talked about the 'holding function' which (usually) the mother provides, by which he meant both literal physical holding and the metaphorical holding of the child's powerful feelings, and he argued that it is through this holding that the child is enabled gradually to establish itself as a person in relationship with others. In parallel with this approach, John Bowlby focused on the instinctual processes of attachment through which the relationship between child and mother becomes established (Bowlby 1984). More recently, the burgeoning literature on attachment provides both the research evidence to flesh out the theoretical work of Winnicott (1965) and others and some fairly clear lessons for practice in terms of both the assessment and the treatment aspects of therapeutic community work, (see Chapter 4 for fuller discussion). Psychodynamic thinking of this sort can also provide workers with the means towards understanding the sometimes enormously complicated patterns of relationship and conflict within families. This provides a 'way in' to begin helping children and their families to resolve their difficulties (see Chapter 12 on family work), since what children bring with them to therapeutic communities is not just their own troubled inner worlds but also their often distorted and disturbed relationships with their families and others.

It is important to add here that the really critical element which psychodynamic thinking introduces is the existence of the unconscious. In other words, we are not just looking at what happens consciously and explicitly between people (whether between mother and infant, child and peer group, or residential staff and their manager), but also at what happens unconsciously – that element in our relationships which is instinctual and not easily known about but which nevertheless may affect all our interactions with others as well as our own 'inner world'. The interplay between the conscious and the unconscious elements in communication gives rise to much of the most challenging but also the most productive work in therapeutic communities, and we will see examples of this throughout the book.

It should also be emphasised that when we are thinking about relationships and attachments we are not only focusing on the one-to-one key relationships between the child and its mother or perhaps between the child and its keyworker: we are also focusing on that whole 'network of relationships' which was identified in the previous section.

Staff dynamics and anxiety

Beyond the detail of the work with individual children and their families, then, psychodynamic thinking can also help us in many other ways. For example, it can enable us to unravel and explain some of the staff dynamics involved, by highlighting the ways in which, for instance, unconscious anxiety may impinge upon the work of individuals or whole teams. Here the work of authors such as Isobel Menzies-Lyth (1988) is helpful in tracing the connections between the task of an organisation and the anxieties which that task may generate in the staff. Menzies-Lyth argues that these anxieties may influence the whole operation of an organisation (such as a therapeutic community), because individual staff tend unconsciously to pool their anxieties into what is known as a 'collective defence', which then disrupts or inhibits the work.

In the case of a therapeutic community, the task of the organisation might, for example, be defined in some cases as 'to help children who have been seriously traumatised and cannot cope with family or school life to become children who can cope with family and/or school life'. When we reflect on the reality of a task such as this, we start to realise how fraught with anxiety it may be, with all its connotations of violence, disturbance and distorted relationships. Anxieties such as these may find especially fertile ground, of course, in particular staff members, bearing in mind the sorts of motivations which people may inevitably have for doing this sort of work (such as the unconscious need to re-work their own traumas or other disturbances from their own childhood).

The risk to the organisation is that, if unacknowledged, such anxieties may come to predominate in people's attitudes to their work in general and/or to the children in particular. If individual staff members are excessively anxious about the sorts of issue outlined above, or if these understandable worries are not sufficiently contained, they may start instinctively to protect themselves against the anxiety by, for example, avoiding too much direct contact or emotional involvement with the young people, or perhaps by feeling unconsciously compelled to plunge themselves into the deepest traumas of individual children to 'rescue' them, but thereby losing the necessary detachment actually to help the children.

For individuals to handle their anxieties in this way would be problematic enough, but the more serious scenario is when a whole team or organisation adopts a collective defence of this sort. Such a situation is not that uncommon, in fact, since the anxieties are real and people do need some defences, and are likely instinctively to seek some form of group cohesion under pressure. One example of this phenomenon in a therapeutic community happened when the atmosphere in the unit became extremely tense and volatile, apparently in reaction to some members of the team becoming very much more controlling and punitive than usual in their responses to the young people. During the course of team consultancy with an external consultant, this 'crack-down' itself turned out to be related to unspoken but nevertheless powerful anxiety among some team members that the children might literally become 'riotous' and destroy the building, just as had recently happened in a much-publicised prison riot and fire. The irony, of course, was that, because it was all conducted at a less-than-conscious level, the action of the staff was counter-productive and almost self-fulfilling, as it seemed for a while very likely to provoke the very rebellion which it was unconsciously designed to prevent. This example illustrates how unconscious anxiety in a team may unwittingly lead to a sub-version of or diversion from the real task of the work, but similar defensive anxieties can also operate at other levels, including the broader organisational level.

What is needed to address and counteract these collective defences against anxiety is a mechanism by which the team or organisation can become collectively aware of such tendencies and then find more productive ways of dealing with the anxieties – such as acknowledging them and reflecting on them together, usually with the help of supervision or consultancy. In fact, it can be argued that this sort of support and developmental learning is needed on a regular basis by all teams engaged in work of this sort, if they are to prevent the slide into over-defensive or anxiety-driven practice, and to remain truly focused on their task. The later chapters in this book cover this area from different angles, including management and leadership (Chapter 13), consultancy and supervision (Chapter 14) and staff development and training (Chapter 15), but all draw on a psychodynamic perspective to underpin this work.

The holding environment

We have moved in the above discussion from looking at how parents provide 'holding' for their children to enable them to develop a healthy personality and an ability to relate with others, to focusing on staff anxiety and how it needs to be contained through supervision and consultancy. These two themes might appear to be quite unconnected, but they are in fact directly linked through the concept of the 'holding environment'. This is the term which Winnicott originally used to refer to the totality of the mother's provision for her young child, and here it was intended to convey that 'holding' goes well beyond literal physical holding and beyond the immediate reassurance which a warm cuddle can provide to a distressed child. It refers rather to the whole quality and importance of the human context in which the young child begins his or her developmental journey.

The link with professional practice is one which Winnicott himself made in two ways: first by drawing a direct parallel between what the mother provides for her infant and what a therapist may need to provide at an unconscious level for his or her patient, and second by drawing a further parallel with the sort of 'holding' of a staff team and its anxieties which we saw above. In the context of individual therapy, this 'emotional holding' (Greenhalgh 1994) is provided by the therapist through the medium of deeply attentive listening plus the offering of insightful and well-timed responses which convey to the patient the sense of being understood without being intruded upon. At the broader level of an organisation with therapeutic aims, Winnicott extended the metaphor to incorporate the total treatment 'environment', or the whole human and physical context in which care and treatment is provided in a range of settings – including, in our case, therapeutic communities.

What needs 'holding' in these settings, then, is not only the individual child and his or her distress, but also the groups of children and their interactions with each other and with the staff, as well as the group of staff themselves, whose own strong feelings both as individuals and as team members will be aroused through working with the children and their families. Since the staff need to provide emotional holding for the children, they will also need some element of holding in their own right if they are to feel sufficiently secure and resilient to provide for the children, and if (as we saw above) the anxieties inherent in the task are not to overwhelm or divert them.

To be more specific, the aspect of 'holding' in each of these contexts will consist of a number of elements, including the following:

- providing suitable boundaries for behaviour and the expression of emotion so that strong feelings can be expressed but do not get 'out of hand'

- meanwhile also providing an element of 'giving' and tolerance in relationships, so that people will feel genuinely cared for and, where appropriate, looked after; this 'giving' in the relationship may also include some degree of interpretation or at least 'reaching out' in communication

- the appropriate containment of anxiety (see above, and Bion 1962), which might mean communicating to the other person – 'Let's think about that anxiety together until you can find a way or an opportunity to manage it for yourself'

- working towards complete clarity in communication, by aiming to clarify and resolve any misunderstandings or confusions as soon as possible – people under extreme stress are highly likely to interpret things in quite distorted ways, and for those prone to feeling 'unheld' these distortions will often consist of variations on the theme of being persecuted or in other ways undervalued.

Providing a holding environment for a group of troubled children will therefore be a complicated task, involving a mixture of conscious and unconscious elements; and when we also take into account the provision of appropriate 'holding' for the staff team who are themselves engaged in the holding process, it will become evident why the role of leadership in such settings is such a complex and demanding one. Eric Miller offers two related thoughts in this context:

> (i) The quality of the holding environment of staff is the main determinant of the quality of the holding environment that they can provide for clients.

> (ii) The quality of the holding environment of staff is mainly created by the form of organisation and by the process of management.

> (Miller 1993, p.3)

Providing an appropriate holding environment for staff can therefore be seen as the overall framework within which therapeutic care is provided for children and their families. In practice, the holding environment in a therapeutic community will be provided through the whole pattern of arrangements for one-to-one, group and inter-group relationships, as well as through the containment of these relationships through a network of arrangements for supervision, staff meetings, consultancy and management (see Ward 1995). In addition, 'holding' will be conveyed through less tangible means such as the 'atmosphere' of the place and the spirit in which the work is conducted, as well as through those more tangible means such as the quality of the physical environment. In everyday life in group care settings, there is sometimes a real and difficult challenge to be met in trying to maintain the quality of 'atmosphere' in the face of the diversionary and even subversive interventions which may come both from troubled children and from anxious or exhausted staff. Here again we see the absolute need for good leadership.

This outlining of the part which psychodynamic thinking contributes to the theory base for therapeutic community work has been necessarily brief, and readers will find more detail elsewhere, especially in Chapters 4, 5 and 6. My intention here has been to show that this thinking applies not only to our understanding of the individual children and their families, and to the interactions of groups of children and of staff, but also to the whole ethos of containment and communication which is summed up in the concept of the 'holding environment'.

3 The therapeutic community as a model for practice

The concept of the 'holding environment' provides a theoretical foundation upon which practice can be built, although it might be objected that it is still couched in rather vague terms, and that it is not yet clear exactly what such an approach would look like in practice. To some extent this is inevitable, and our aim is that the remaining chapters of this book will help to illustrate how this approach is applied in practice. Underpinning all these chapters, however, will be an assumption that, in the context of group care for children and young people, the most powerful model for making operational the concept of the holding environment is that of the therapeutic community.

The therapeutic community model is one which is based on a long tradition in the fields of both adult psychiatric care and the residential care, education and treatment of children, as we shall see in Chapter 3. In fact it might be said that the history of therapeutic community practice goes back to long before they were actually called therapeutic communities, and just to confuse matters more, some therapeutic units which would be very recognisable to readers of this book as therapeutic communities do not necessarily call themselves that! Others have used terms such as 'planned environment therapy', and the 'therapeutic milieu', and it was probably only in the last years of the twentieth century in the UK that such places called themselves therapeutic communities. They did so perhaps partly as a way of forming alliances with the adult therapeutic community movement, but also in some cases as a way of specifically acknowledging one of the key components of the adult therapeutic community, the concept that it is the *whole community* itself which is therapeutic, rather than it just being a place in which 'expert' staff perform therapy on patients or clients.

Some readers may have rather negative assumptions about therapeutic communities. Some people, for example, retain an impression of the therapeutic community as somewhere between the imagined 'let it all hang out' ethos of an encounter group and the unbounded and charismatic permissiveness of some religious cults. By contrast with such stereotypes, however, the therapeutic community model of practice is actually very clear and disciplined. It is also a model which fits well within the 'group care' approach, since it focuses very much on the nature and quality of interactions between the various groups and groupings in the place.

What is meant by the therapeutic community model is one in which the 'whole is greater than the sum of its parts', and one which places great emphasis on establishing a 'culture of enquiry' (Main 1990). This means that all members of the community, whether staff or 'clients', work together on understanding and resolving whatever difficulties and conflicts may arise, whether for individuals, for groups or for the community as a whole. The aim is that at every level within the organisation, practice will be conducted in a spirit of open and equal endeavour, and expressed through a system of regular and frequent 'community meetings' of everybody involved. If this starts to sound rather idealistic, there may be some truth in that, and what is probably closer to reality is that many places do adopt a 'therapeutic community approach' (see below) although they may not all meet every characteristic of the ideal model. In this context it is worth reading the 'audit checklist' developed by Kennard and Lees (2001) for an overview of these characteristics in the adult therapeutic communities, and the standards developed by Gatiss (2001) for a different approach to the application of standards to the child care context.

In truth, there is no such thing as *the* therapeutic community. What there is, is a set of ideals, beliefs and working practices which (like the group care characteristics, but in this case in much fuller detail) can be identified as typical of the therapeutic community approach. The central principle of this approach is the belief that all members of the community (children as well as staff) can give as well as take in therapeutic exchanges and indeed that it is *the community itself* which is therapeutic, rather than (as is more traditional in clinical work) that it is primarily only the staff who engage in therapeutic endeavour. The focus of the work thus becomes the task of enabling people to realise and apply their own ability to help as well as to be helped. Put more succinctly, the focus of the staff is on enabling the community to become and remain therapeutic. While these principles have been frequently articulated in respect of therapeutic communities for adults with mental health problems, they have been less fully developed and explored in relation to therapeutic communities for young people – which is part of what motivated us to produce this book.

In general terms, the ways in which the principles of the therapeutic community are applied in practice include the following:

- an emphasis on the value of *groupwork* as a medium both for therapeutic work and in some places for decision-making with the young people

- a specific commitment to the use of the daily *community meeting* as a medium for both practical and therapeutic business between young people and staff

- within this group context, a willingness on the part of staff to commit themselves to medium/long-term *individual therapeutic relationships* with young people

- an emphasis on the potential for therapeutic communication between staff and young people to arise from *everyday interactions* in daily 'living alongside' each other (i.e. opportunity-led work)

- in daily practice, a commitment to a *personal* and involved style of working, in which the quality of the relationships between young people and staff is seen as playing a central role in the treatment process

- a commitment to the value of the physical and personal *'environment'* for its contribution to the therapeutic task

- engagement with the *other key systems* in the young person's life, including their family and other personal networks, as well as with their educational, health and other developmental needs

- the use of *psychodynamic* rather than solely behavioural or cognitive theoretical frameworks to underpin the treatment philosophy, and of *systemic* thinking to interpret connections between people, events and feelings

- in internal management structures, an emphasis on each person's role and *potential contribution* to the agreed task and philosophy rather than mainly on status, rank and formal titles
- a commitment to the value of a full system of staff support and supervision, including the use of *consultancy* for senior managers.

(adapted from Ward and McMahon 1998)

None of these working practices is offered as a perfect ideal, however, and in reality even the longest-established therapeutic communities are continually adapting them to manage the constant tensions between ideals and reality. For many children's residential units it may be more appropriate to explore the use of the 'therapeutic community approach' rather than aiming to become what has been called a 'therapeutic community proper'. In terms of the unfolding argument of this chapter, the therapeutic community approach can be seen as an example of how the concept of the 'holding environment' can be applied in practice, and as one version of how psychodynamic thinking can inform therapeutic practice in a group care setting.

At this point it should also be acknowledged that the therapeutic community approach is not the sole reserve of the residential setting, and that there have been many other applications of some of the above working practices in settings as diverse as family centres, schools, and psychiatric day units. Several examples of these broader applications are outlined and discussed in Chapter 17.

Systems thinking as a model for holding the whole thing together

Since the aim of this chapter is to provide theoretical frameworks which will help practitioners to hold together the complexities of therapeutic practice, it seems appropriate to move at this stage to thinking about systems theory. Indeed the principal value of taking a systems approach to practice is that it encourages us always to think about 'the interconnectedness of things'. In fact we have already encountered one application of systems thinking earlier in the chapter, in the material on task and anxiety in organisations. Fuller discussion of some aspects of systems theory, with practice applications, will also be found in Chapter 6.

The basic premise of the systems approach is that every human organisation, such as a family, team, or indeed a therapeutic community as a whole, may be envisaged as a 'system' consisting of many parts. All of these parts or 'sub-systems' not only have characteristics and patterns of their own, but are also interconnected and affect each other (although sometimes in unexpected ways); in addition, the whole system is viewed as being in some senses greater than the sum of its parts, and can also be said to have its own characteristics and patterns. One of the images which has sometimes been offered as a concrete example of a system is that of a central heating system: while the separate components of a central heating system may function well internally, they are not much use by themselves until they are properly connected-up and functioning together, when they become an effective system for heating a house.

Systems thinking focuses on such properties as the boundaries and connections between sub-systems, and on the extent to which a system is 'open' or 'closed' to interaction across these boundaries. A further characteristic of systems relates to the issue of change. The systems approach is based on the view that since all the parts of a system are connected, change in any one part is likely to affect all other parts. The implications of this simple idea are enormous, especially in therapeutic communities, where change is usually a central preoccupation. At the same time, systems are seen as naturally tending towards homeostasis, or maintaining a steady and unchanging state. Thus all systems are said to be inherently geared towards preserving themselves intact by keeping their various parts in a state of balance. Taking these last two characteristics together may help us to explain, for example, why an attempt to change a whole system (such as a troubled family, or an unhappy staff team) by 'pushing' all the parts at the same time may fail, whereas by contrast a well-aimed 'nudge' at one small part or sub-system may set in motion much greater changes in the system as a whole.

Straightforward examples of the systems and sub-systems in a therapeutic community include: the place as a whole (all the people within it); the staff team; the group of children; the family system of any given child; etc. The systems approach can help to explain the ways in which 'systems' such as these operate both within themselves and in interaction with each other.

The connections between the parts of a system, and the ways in which these parts influence each other, can all be studied within the systems approach, although the approach itself does not presuppose any single theoretical basis for the connections. In fact, it is an approach which allows for the use of many different theories, and is not really a theory in its own right at all, more a way of looking at the world: it will not in itself provide answers, but it may provide a more productive way of framing the questions.

There are therefore many different ways in which systems thinking can be applied to therapeutic community work. In Chapter 6 we will see one approach to the use of systems thinking to underpin certain clinical aspects of the work, such as planned work with individual young people, while in

Chapter 12 there are several different examples of the application of systems thinking to work with the families of children in therapeutic communities. There is an extensive literature on family systems and family therapy to draw upon, and some units do explicitly make this the basis for their practice, although perhaps not many have fully trained family therapists on their staff team. A third area in which systems thinking can be directly drawn upon is in terms of the dynamics within the group of young people, and the strategies which staff can use in order to engage with them in everyday life and to respond appropriately to events and challenges. Here systems thinking encourages us to look at the ways in which members of the group of young people may affect each other's thinking and emotions, and the ways in which staff efforts may best be directed to influence these effects.

Systems theory can also be applied to help our understanding of the ways in which other sub-systems of a therapeutic community interact, for example in looking at how the group of young people and the group of staff may be affecting each other, or at the relationships between different groups of staff such as 'domestic' and 'professional' staff. Likewise, we can look at the relationship between the therapeutic community as a whole and other systems with which it interacts, such as key organisations in the local community, or the 'parent' organisation which funds or oversees the unit.

In fact it is perhaps in terms of these relationships between the therapeutic community and its organisational and societal context that systems theory can make its most useful contribution. We saw earlier how writers such as Eric Miller (1993) and Isobel Menzies-Lyth (1988) use an 'open systems' approach to address the primary task of organisations. This model can be summarised into a few key concepts, as follows: any organisation is viewed as an 'open system' with one central or primary task, this task being achieved through a number of co-ordinated 'systems of activity', or sets of arrangements for carrying out the various functions of the unit (Miller and Gwynne 1972). Clarity about the primary task is seen as essential to the proper operation – and indeed the survival – of the system.

The concept of the 'open system', on which this model is based, simply represents the fact that most organisations function by being 'open' to their surroundings: they take in or 'import' materials at one end, 'process' or 'transform' them, then send them out or 'export' them again at the other end. The term 'materials' is used metaphorically, since in a group care organisation it is people (young people in this case) rather than inanimate materials who come in at one end and go out again at the other: this is obviously an important difference between group care organisations and other kinds of human organisation – factories, insurance companies, etc. A 'closed' system, by contrast, would be one in which nothing comes in or goes out – the stereotype of a monastery is very nearly a closed system, although it has been pointed out that 'there is no perfect closed system, because there is nothing that is not affected by influences from outside' (Bruggen and O'Brien 1987, p.56).

Applying this framework to the problem of defining the task of a unit such as a therapeutic community, the open systems approach proposes that the central or primary task of the unit should be expressed in terms of the 'throughput of materials' – i.e. the 'process' of each child's stay at the unit, from admission through to departure. It is in relation to this process that the primary task is seen as 'the task which the enterprise must perform in order to survive' (Rice 1963) – in other words, the primary task is that which it must be seen to be achieving if it is not to lose its supply of referrals or even to be closed down.

What this approach highlights is both the need to be absolutely clear about the task of the therapeutic community, and the difficulty of doing so, since so many competing expectations often have to be met. For example, what children's families may want from the unit may differ in subtle but significant ways from what the external managers or the employing agency may expect, and both of these may differ again from what any given referring professional may hope for. One hypothetical example of the primary task of a therapeutic community was offered above, but for any given unit the primary task cannot usually be lifted 'off the shelf', it has to be thought through and negotiated. It will usually be the responsibility of the manager, in consultation with all parties, to negotiate and renegotiate the task in order to keep the work of the unit properly focused, and to be aware of the ways in which the anxieties inherent in the task can affect its achievement. Like most welfare organisations, many therapeutic communities struggle to be clear about their primary task, and it often happens that the organisation drifts off task or becomes preoccupied with secondary or even apparently trivial aspects of the task (Menzies-Lyth 1988). For further discussion of this theme, see the chapters on organisation and consultancy (chapters 13 and 14).

4 Values in therapeutic community practice

Beyond the uses of theory which have been covered so far in this chapter, there is one further essential element: the use of theory to inform and explicate the value systems which underpin practice. Whilst there will not be space here to engage in a full exploration of the value base of therapeutic community practice, it seems especially important to recognise this value base of practice at this stage, since the discussion so far has proceeded as if all of this theory and all of the practice is somehow 'neutral' in terms of value systems. In reality nothing could be further from the truth, since at every moment in therapeutic community work with young people we are forced to reflect on our own personal value systems and how they may coincide with or differ from the professional values which we need to uphold. To what extent and on what grounds, for example, are we entitled to restrict young people's self-determination? What are the proper boundaries of confidentiality in a working method which relies in part upon young people's ability to disclose and reflect upon their innermost thoughts and feelings in a group setting? How can a method focusing mainly on 'inner world' disturbances and trauma also help young people to cope with the many forms of 'real world' oppression or discrimination which they and their families may have experienced, such as the effects of racism, and the stigma of poverty and of mental health difficulties?

One way of addressing such questions is to argue that therapeutic community principles and methods may in themselves be interpreted as involving the implementation of familiar moral and professional values such as 'respect for persons' and 'user self-determination', which have often been articulated in respect of professional practice in fields such as counselling and social work (e.g. Banks 2000). In those contexts, however, such values are usually applied to the individual one-to-one relationships between staff and clients whereas, as we have seen, therapeutic community practice involves a much more complex set of interconnecting relationships. Here it often raises difficulties in terms, for example, of the impact on one young person of upholding another young person's rights or wish for self-determination.

In practice, many of the struggles in daily life in therapeutic communities, and many of the fiercer debates which can emerge in community meetings, involve some battle around just these sorts of moral and ethical dilemmas. How far, for example, can one individual's self-determination be allowed to impinge on another or on the group as a whole, or how can the confidentiality of an individual resident be fully respected when something currently happening in their family of origin is disturbing them so greatly that their behaviour is having a dramatic effect on all the other residents? Not only is it proper that such questions of appropriateness and principle should be discussed with young people in open meetings, but these discussions may also in themselves be seen as contributing to the moral development of the residents – although to make such a statement invites a further question as to how far we are entitled to see our task of moral development: are we not there, after all, simply to look after them, 'cure' them, and help them on to their next placement, rather than to engage in their 'moral development'? If we think we can avoid such moral questions, however, we are deluding ourselves and will do the young people a disservice by under-recognising and under-valuing the (admittedly contentious) moral element in our practice. This moral element is in fact a central component in the tasks of parenting, education and psychotherapeutic treatment – the boundaries of which tasks therapeutic community practice straddles.

There are other aspects of practice which raise issues of value and principle, especially in relation to matters of challenging discrimination and oppression. It can be helpful to approach these issues by thinking in terms of power and prejudice, since these are issues which directly affect all of us, and especially all of the young people in therapeutic communities. Most of the young people who arrive at therapeutic communities will have been on the receiving end of other people's arbitrary or unfair use of power in some form. If they have been physically or sexually abused they will have thereby experienced the most extreme forms of personal disempowerment. They are also likely to have been excluded from school and often from other social institutions – even from family life itself – and thus, it might be argued, from the very heart of what it means to be a member of society. In addition, if they are from a minority ethnic group, they are likely to have experienced racism in both a personal and an institutional context, and to have registered these experiences at both conscious and unconscious levels.

Therapeutic communities have not always been seen as addressing issues of racism very effectively, although the requirements of the legislation and official guidance have increasingly contributed to improvements in this area. However, it can be argued that the therapeutic community approach is centrally concerned with addressing issues of personal power, and the experience of racism is certainly one of being on the wrong end of other people's abuse and perversion of power. The aim of treatment can be formulated in terms of enabling young people to rediscover their own potential for relationships, intimacy and development, all of which involve being able to handle issues of power appropriately, and to confront experiences of powerlessness appropriately. What is starting to develop in therapeutic communities for young people is a fuller awareness of the ways in which conscious and unconscious experiences of racism may compound the other difficulties and trauma which they may have experienced. The whole therapeutic community environment, including the network of relationships between adults and young people, needs to be designed and managed to allow for the sensitive handling of such experiences, by ensuring that practice is driven by an informed and aware value base, including a full commitment to anti-racist practice.

The therapeutic community working method involves not only the nego-tiation and mediation of personal power, but also the understanding of the role which the unconscious plays in the experience of power. This latter element complicates the situation enormously, since it means that many of the interactions between adults and young people in daily life may evoke memories of deeply wounding or anxiety-provoking earlier experiences (including elements of racism) of which the young person may not be fully aware at a conscious level, but which may yet engender an unconscious reaction which will emerge very powerfully in the present. Where this is happening, it is not uncommon for the adults themselves suddenly to feel powerless (because this reaction, which actually belongs with the young person, has been projected into them) and even panicky, and then to make mistakes or poor judgements which can complicate the situation even more. This may all be played out in the sometimes heated exchanges of everyday life as well as in the dilemmas of individual relationships and therapeutic endeavour. Therapeutic community workers therefore need all their ethical 'wits' about them (as well as their collective antennae for unconscious commu-nications) if they are to handle the issues of personal power and prejudice in everyday life.

Conclusion

Many practitioners may approach the topic of 'theory' with caution and reluc-tance, and perhaps another indication of this caution is that many people prefer to describe their approach as 'eclectic' rather than being tied to any one particular framework. Eclecticism, meaning judicious choice from within a range of ideas, is certainly a valid approach, so long as we are clear about why and how we are choosing the approaches which we do, and the approaches which we select actually complement rather than contradict each other. The aim of this chapter has been to outline a range of ideas which can be used for different purposes, and which do appear to complement each other well:

- group care for its account of the overall context and mode of practice
- psychodynamic thinking as an underpinning theory, with the concepts of the holding environment and of the therapeutic com-munity as increasingly specific models of practice
- systems thinking as a way of holding the whole thing together.

I would not wish to be prescriptive about which particular blend of ideas any staff team should draw upon, but I would argue that such choices should be made explicitly and on the basis of clear judgements about what will work best in the given context. It will be the responsibility of the staff team as a whole to aim to be clear, informed and explicit as well as eclectic in drawing on different frameworks for different purposes.

CHAPTER 3

The Roots of the Work:
Definitions, Origins and Influences

Kajetan Kasinski

Introduction

There is a group of psychologically damaged children and young people whose condition is such that they are seemingly unable to tolerate being cared for in families in the community. They are thus not amenable to most of the commonly available forms of supportive or reparative work. One treatment for such children is through the therapeutic community approach. The task of this chapter is to place this approach in context, both in terms of its origins and its history, and in its relationship to other services dealing with such clients.

Although therapeutic community work with children and young people goes back at least 150 years it is only over the last 30 years that it has acquired its present name and identity. Therefore much of its history involves looking at how a number of separate projects and individuals working at various times and in different contexts attempted to work in a particular way with a specific group of children and young people. While they may have been travelling in the same direction, they were not necessarily following the same path, using the same map, or even defining their goal in the same language. What linked these various endeavours to each other and to present-day therapeutic community work with children was a number of commonly held beliefs and practices.

These included *beliefs* that:

1. the problem behaviours of such children were often the result of the experience of severe and repeated traumas or deprivations, especially in terms of their parenting or care

2. to effect lasting change it was therefore necessary actively to attend to and repair the particular nature of their relationships with others

and

3. that this was not generally possible through mainstream provision for these children

and *practices* which:

1. placed an emphasis on the attention given to the detail of common everyday interactions in a consciously designed, usually residential, setting

2. did so openly, through a group process involving all staff and clients/patients as much as possible

and

3. attempted to address the multiplicity of each child's needs in an integrated way.

Some of these 'core features' have been explored in more depth in the previous chapter.

The approach was rooted in several disciplines, including education, care, reform, and mental health. It also drew on a variety of different ideas and philosophies to support and direct its practice. Thus the process through which the approach developed has of necessity involved a resolution or synthesis of several different contexts, outlooks or positions. Two major catalysts in this were the emergence first of psychoanalysis in the early years of the twentieth century and second of the actual concept of therapeutic community in the 1940s. Psychoanalysis 'made it possible to put relationships and emotions under the microscope in ways that were impossible before' (Holmes 2002). The concept of therapeutic community provided a link between psychodynamic thinking and institutional practice.

Looking at the history of the approach therefore involves consideration of both changes over time in the way the client group has been recognised, understood and responded to, and developments in the way various projects fitting the above criteria worked with such children. This chapter will therefore start by defining the client group, and will then explore its history. It will move on to the approach itself, first in terms of what influenced and moulded its development at different times, and second through considering some of the actual projects and individuals involved. There is inevitably something arbitrary in selecting some of these over others, especially as I have chosen to limit myself to the UK. I have done so partly to simplify an already complex story, and partly to restrict myself to projects that demonstrate a particular strand of the approach or a key stage in its development. Whether and how the history of the approach has any value in informing present-day work in the field will be touched on in the conclusion.

The client group

Today

The group of children and young people I wish to describe is one that today is familiar to most professionals in the field from individual cases, high profile in terms of needs and presentation, and yet one which is not widely recognised as having a single group identity. It is not the task of this chapter to propose this group for inclusion as a new diagnostic category, partly because of the degree of social drift involved in trying to define it, and partly because of the risk of tautology inherent in such a claim. Likewise, I am neither proposing that all such children can be helped by therapeutic communities, nor that this is the only form of treatment to which they could respond. Rather I would suggest that the value of considering this group as a distinct entity is to help refine understanding of their aetiology, pathology and prognosis, and so to stimulate ideas about possible forms of intervention or treatment.

The defining characteristics of this group are threefold. The first is a seeming inability to tolerate the experience of being cared for in families in the community; this is often associated with a history of neglect, abuse, or disruption in the biological family. The second is a resultant case complexity, as defined by factors such as duration of difficulties, range of needs, and degree of multi-service involvement; this is often associated with a high profile presentation and a variety of 'at risk' behaviours in evidence. The last characteristic is the relative absence of those resilience factors (e.g. peer group support, capacity to self-reflect, etc.) that would enable other children and young people in similar circumstances to survive.

Most, but by no means all, of the children in this group would be 'looked-after children', i.e. in the care of local authorities. In the last few years it has been increasingly recognised that such children are significantly disadvantaged in their development from childhood to adulthood. In terms of care they are likely to suffer further neglect and disruption (25% of all looked-after children have had over ten placements in total, 19% more than three in the past year. See Polnay and Ward 2000). In terms of relationships with others, they both lack a stable peer group and are more likely to be involved in brief and inappropriate relationships and early, unplanned sexual activity (15% of girls leaving care are either pregnant or already mothers, Acheson 1998). In terms of education their schooling is often inadequate and interrupted (30% of looked-after children are not receiving education, Kraemer 1999). Finally there is an increased likelihood of associated physical or psychiatric illness (68% of looked-after children have a psychiatric disorder, rising to 96% of those in residential care, McCann, James, Wilson and Dunn 1996) with resultant poor self care, poor self esteem, risk of drug or alcohol abuse and/or impulsive violent or self harming behaviours. Not surprisingly the prognosis is also very poor: 75 per cent leave care with no qualifications, 50 per cent are unemployed a year after leaving care. One third of those in prison and one third of the homeless have a history of being in care (Utting 1998). Perhaps even more worrying is the prognosis for the next generation, for the future children of these children.

The above statistics mainly refer to the whole group of looked-after children. They make even more depressing reading for the sub-group I described earlier, for that small but significant minority of such children who seem unable to be adequately 'parented' by the various systems and resources in place for this purpose.

It is worth considering why, even though individual cases may be acknowledged, the group is not widely recognised as a discrete entity in its own right. First, it lacks a commonly known or used name. Conditions such as autism, dyslexia, and depression have undoubtedly benefited (in terms of publicity and resources) from a recognisable 'brand image'. Terms that might be applied to this group, such as 'attachment disorder' or 'incipient personality disorder' are inadequate in that they are respectively either little used outside professional circles and/or carry undesirable stigma when applied to children or adolescents. Probably the best 'official' description of this condition is in *The ICD10 Classification of Mental and Behavioural Disorders* (listed as category 94 – Disorder of Social Functioning with Onset Specific to Childhood and Adolescence):

> While the existence of this category is well recognised and accepted, there is uncertainty regarding defining diagnostic criteria, and disagreement about the most appropriate classification. The category is nevertheless included because of the public health importance of the syndrome,

because there is no doubt as to its existence, and because serious environ-mental distortions and/or privations are crucial in the aetiology. (ICD10 1992)

A second reason may lie in the relationship between children in this group and the professional systems involved with them. In many ways they are defined by their needs, or at least in the way these needs are presented and in who responds to them. They fall across the services provided by health, social services and education agencies. Attempts by any single service independ-ently to address the issues which fall within its remit tend to flounder rapidly with the realisation that it is impossible to do so without attending to related issues outside of that remit. At best this results in a sense of frustration and helplessness among the professionals involved. At worst it leads to a culture of scapegoating or blaming other services, or of a covert relinquishing of respon-sibility. Therefore, unless the involved agencies are prepared to invest the time, energy and commitment necessary for establishing real working partnerships with each other, these children's needs are not met and the children them-selves slip through the net. Unfortunately there is also often a reluctance (albeit an understandable one) for an individual service to 'take the lead' in such cases. Furthermore the children themselves seem to find and exploit or amplify any divisions in the system around them.

A final reason is to do with the children themselves. Contact with them can overwhelm, hurt or provoke distancing among involved professionals. It is often difficult to face such a child openly, difficult to look them in the eye, without assuming either a falsely reassuring omnipotence or an unhelpful despair. This is strikingly similar to professional attitudes towards adults with personality disorder, who are often regarded as manipulative, attention seeking, irritating and difficult and frustrating to manage (Lewis and Appleby 1988). The reluctance to acknowledge personality disorders in adults as 'real' mental disorders, and the suggestion that this could change with the identifi-cation of an apparently effective treatment approach (Kendell 2002) seems very actual and relevant to the group of children I have been describing.

In the past

In order to place the origins of the therapeutic community approach in context it is useful to look at how such 'difficult' children were recognised and managed in the past. This involves taking into account not only the evolution of concepts like childcare, education and development, but also what systems existed at different times with both authority and resources sufficient for the task.

Aries (1962) proposed that the concept of childhood did not exist at all in Western Europe before the late seventeenth century. His work has subsequently been criticised, both on grounds of methodology and on the premises on which it was based. Nevertheless its value is to suggest that our present-day concept of childhood is a relatively recent one. This concept sees childhood as a state distinct from adulthood, and having an increasingly particular significance and being longer lasting than previously thought.

It now seems likely that before the seventeenth century emotional disturbance in individual children was recognised, possible causes considered, and the beneficial effects of reparative experiences acknowledged (Shahar 1990). However there was no infrastructure in place for implementing such ideas and practices more widely.

Following the break-up of feudal economic and social structures and the changes in organised religion, the state increasingly took over responsibility for the management of those, including children, at the edges of society. Initially this was through the Poor Law tradition. Though a small number of severely disturbed children could be admitted to asylums, or sometimes even treated in their doctors' own homes (Wardle 1991), up to the start of the nineteenth century the majority were dealt with through the courts. How they fared was largely a matter of local circumstance and provision.

Over the next 150 years there were three developments that changed the way in which such children were recognised and managed. These were:

1. revisions to the law relating to young people

2. the introduction of universal education

3. the development of specialised social work and mental health services for children and young people.

At the start of the nineteenth century courts had little option but to sentence a child convicted of vagrancy, beggary, stealing or the like to prison or the workhouse. Over the next 100 years a growing recognition of the need to treat child offenders differently from adults led to reforms in the law. This was supported by a growing understanding that delinquency or 'moral insanity' could be the result of underlying distress or deprivation. Initially these reforms involved creating alternatives to prison, such as reformatories or industrial schools. Later changes recognised the need for a separate legal process for young people. These culminated in the establishment of Juvenile Courts in 1908.

Alongside this came the introduction of education for all children below a certain age. This was driven by an unusual alliance of political pragmatism and liberal philanthropy. Social and demographic changes accompanying the Industrial Revolution had led to a significant increase in the number of unemployed and unoccupied children and young people for whom school would be a useful alternative to 'roaming the streets'. The Education Act of 1870 established free, universal, and compulsory education, initially only up to the age of 11. An unforeseen consequence of this was the discovery of a sub-group of children who, for a variety of reasons, could not be contained at school. Subsequent Acts acknowledged and made provision for different categories of 'unschoolable' children, including some of those initially described as 'morally handicapped' (1921 Education Act), later to be termed 'maladjusted' (1945 Education Act). This promoted the development of remedial or therapeutic education, of finding acceptable and suitable ways to allow such children access to the education that was now their right. An early attempt to formalise inter-agency initiatives came with the creation of Approved Schools in 1933, residential schools to which children could be sent by order of the Juvenile Court.

A pattern similar to that whereby the provision of compulsory education revealed the existence of a sub-group of 'unschoolable' children was repeated at the start of the Second World War with evacuee children. The policy of moving children from the cities to the countryside uncovered the existence of a group who were unable to tolerate the accommodation made available to the majority. As these 'unbilletable' children were neither primarily criminal nor unschoolable, assessment of their needs was undertaken by the relatively fledgling mental health and social work services. Surveys of evacuees (such as those involving John Bowlby in Cambridge, and Donald Winnicott in Oxfordshire) suggested that 2 per cent of evacuated children (15,000 in total) required specialised residential treatment (see Bridgeland 1971). As a result various specialist 'hostels' were established, each receiving input from a range of professionals.

The wartime experience had several consequences. One was the rapid post-war growth of child mental health and social work services. This included the tripling in the number of Child Guidance Units in the immediate post-war years, and the setting up of inpatient psychiatric units for children and adolescents. Another was the acknowledgement of a group of children who required specialist residential care which incorporated a treatment element. The 1944 Education Act and the 1948 Children Act aimed to correct the inadequate care of both looked-after children in general, and the most disturbed or deprived ones in particular. Local authorities were encouraged to set up their own specialist schools and units, as well as being given power to inspect, recognise, and support existing establishments.

Though not connected to the work with evacuees, the origins of therapeutic community work with adults were another consequence of the war. Apart from the coining of the term itself (Main 1946) the significance for work with children was in locating this particular approach in the category of treatment, and in providing a source of directly related ideas and practices.

The last 50 years have seen a gradual consolidation of the changes effected over the previous one and a half centuries. The profile of children concerned has been raised by developments like the 'discovery' of child physical abuse in the 1960s, sexual abuse in the 1980s and, most recently, abuse in children's homes. The 1989 Children Act, particularly in its acknowledgement of the rights, responsibilities, and needs of 'at risk' children and their parents, continued the process. Nevertheless it is salutary to recall the Government report that preceded the 1948 Children Act; while not condemning individual bodies, such as the Home Office, Health, or Education, it warned that the lack of inter-agency co-operation could mean that the needs of the most needy children would continue to be overlooked (Curtis Report 1946).

It is interesting to consider the range of labels that has been used over time to describe the group of children being considered. These include criminal, delinquent, morally insane, deprived, damaged, maladjusted, emotionally 'frozen', disorganisedly attached. There are overlaps and distinctions among these labels; not all delinquents are maladjusted or deprived, and not all 'damaged' children break the law. These names reflect themes in the history of how such children are managed and understood. They provide evidence of how different agencies with different remits approach the task of dealing with problem children from different directions. A consequence is the present day complexity of involved 'languages' and networks. The names indicated the influences of models like psychoanalysis or educational theory and the meaning given to particular behaviours. They also suggest the process whereby the concept of a group of children at the edges of society has become increasingly refined, with various constituent sub-groups being identified. One of these sub-groups is the one I described earlier, the one consisting of children seemingly beyond control, education, care or treatment in the community.

The approach

Historical overview

Alongside changes in the way that difficult children who 'didn't fit in' were recognised and understood came the development of various (mainly residential) projects which explored alternatives to mainstream provision for their management. It is among these projects that the roots of the therapeutic community approach are found. Though they may have fitted many of the defining criteria outlined at the start of the chapter, they would have used their own ways of describing what they were trying to do, and how and why they were doing it.

In the nineteenth century such initiatives were largely driven by a loose mixture of Christian philanthropy and a growing awareness of a link between deprivation and vagrancy or delinquency. Many of the founders of such projects made use of Christian language or terminology in their writing. Though this language has largely been replaced by that of psychology or psychoanalysis, there is a sense that the ideas behind it have not been entirely superseded. Carpenter (1851) and, later on, Wills (1945; 1960) (see next section) wrote passionately about the importance of love in the work, squarely in the tradition of St Paul's Letter to the Corinthians. As acknowledged briefly in a document on standards produced by the Charterhouse Group, there are striking parallels between the Christian monastic tradition (especially as outlined in the rule of St Benedict) and therapeutic community work. These include the way in which the daily work of the community is seen as a vehicle for its primary task, and the emphasis on the involvement of the whole community in decision-making. Another link is between the therapeutic community approach and the medieval Christian tradition of pilgrimage. This acknowledged that the attention paid to the details of the journey was as important as arrival at the destination. It also involved a journey to a place where previously rigid divisions could be temporarily loosened, and the existence of alternative realities considered (Brown 1981). Those processes are all ones that can be seen to take place in a therapeutic community.

The emergence of psychoanalysis in the early years of the twentieth century was the next major influence on this line of work. This is evident in the work of pioneers such as Lane, Neill, and Wills in the UK and later, Bettelheim in the US. In addition to allowing a new way of looking at emotions and relationships, it provided ideas about the psychopathology of development, and a framework for understanding the behaviours of disturbed, delinquent, or maladjusted children. It also enabled some of the practices which were almost 'instinctively' considered central to the approach (e.g. an emphasis on how young people's relationships with authority were negotiated through practices such as democracy or consensus in decision-making) to be understood and articulated in terms of a wider body of theory and knowledge (e.g. using Erikson's ideas about adolescent stages of development).

Psychoanalytic ideas and practices were initially sometimes applied in a rather rudimentary manner, with enthusiasm outweighing thought about possible consequences or limitations (see section on Homer Lane, later in this chapter). This was tempered over time and through experience, and, through the 1940s, first by developments and discoveries in child psychotherapy, and second by the emergence of the concept of a therapeutic community. The former allowed a more considered and relevant developmental dimension to be introduced in work with children. The establishment of the therapeutic community model through the pioneering work of Bion and Foulkes at Northfield, Jones at Mill Hill and later at The Henderson, and Main at The Cassell has been very well documented elsewhere. (Campling and Haigh 1999). (Incidentally it is worth noting that one of the subsequent developments at The Cassell was the establishment of specialist sub-units working in the overall context of 'hospital as therapeutic community'; these included one for adolescents, and another for families with children.) Kennard (1983) distinguishes three ways in which psychoanalysis was central to therapeutic community work: through the practice of individual therapy itself; as a way of making sense of the swirl of the various emotions and feelings that can arise between individuals and sub-groups in the community; and through a framework for looking at the institutional processes involved. As in adult therapeutic communities the way such ideas were put into practice in settings working with children fell along a continuum, from institutions where each patient received an intensive individual therapy, to ones where therapy was confined exclusively to the group. However, a shared belief was that psychoanalysis had to be 'not just done, but lived' in daily events and interactions.

Nevertheless the therapeutic community approach with young people was not just an invention or by-product either of psychoanalysis or of the adult therapeutic community movement itself. It is more accurate to see the approach making use of developing ideas and practices to articulate and refine what was already happening. Kennard (1999) suggests it is more useful to see the therapeutic community approach in general as a modality of treatment into which a variety of theoretical models can be fitted. In the case of work with children the models will also have to include group analysis, systemic family therapy and, most recently, cognitive therapy.

There are several other reasons why the approach should not be considered to have developed as a unified movement or as a single model of treatment. Reference has already been made to the wide range of settings, age groups and disciplines involved. Many of the early endeavours were largely dependent on the leadership or charisma of a particular person, and often failed to survive that person's departure. There was little evidence for a commonly held philosophy; in most cases theory followed practice, with ideas evolving out of solutions to specific difficulties or problems (Bridgeland 1971). To this can be added a diversity of commissioning agencies, modes of referral, and funding arrangements. All of this resulted in different emphases being placed on various aspects of the work by different projects and by those who led their development.

Another reason lay in the fact that many such projects served as a counter-point, or experimental alternative to 'mainstream' provision for this group of children. There was an inevitable tension between approaches that concentrated on controlling or minimising undesirable or antisocial behaviours, and ones that saw in such behaviours clues to understanding the reasons for them, and to developing from these an approach for treatment. This tension was evident in the ambivalence of government bodies towards such projects. On the one hand was the wish to protect society against the antisocial activities of children and young people, on the other a recognition that custodial training establishments were not only unsuitable, but often did not produce the desired results. This ambivalence was shown in the way support for and encouragement of innovative work was tempered by unease, suspicion and anxiety about public opinion, which could result in sudden censure or withdrawal of recognition or funding. One result was that at least until the 1950s most of these institutions were dealt with by statutory agencies on an individual basis, and so were viewed and functioned largely as independent of each other.

However, that was also not the whole picture. The various projects were neither completely isolated nor ignorant of each other. Several of the early 'founding fathers/mothers' met together regularly. Equally important were the ways by which particular projects made themselves known or accessible. Chance visits or contacts proved an important way by which the earlier projects influenced the direction of the later ones. Bridgeland (1971) uses the term 'pioneer' for many of the individuals involved. Their achievement lay in creating a story or a myth that inspired others to follow them; as important as what they actually did was how this was communicated to the outside world.

In order to do justice to the development of the approach it is helpful to look at some individual examples of how it was applied. Each has been chosen to highlight one of the themes inherent in the approach, or a particular stage in its development.

Precursors: Ragged Schools and Mary Carpenter

The first mention of an approach that consisted of more than relatively unrecognised and discrete local initiatives was in the mid-nineteenth century with the growth of specialised day schools for delinquent and unschoolable children. These included 'Ragged Schools' and 'Industrial Schools'. There are several reasons why these can be considered as the precursors of therapeutic communities for children and young people. In many ways they were ahead of their time. For the first time there was an open acknowledgement of the need to address all factors (physical, psychological, emotional, familial and environmental) that would affect needy children. It was common practice among teachers at these schools to visit children at their own homes. The need for such teachers to be more highly trained and capable of greater flexibility in their practice than those working in ordinary schools was also recognised. The value for society in general of enabling such children to escape their hopeless conditions was acknowledged. In Aberdeen in the 1840s, where attendance at industrial schools was made compulsory for all children found guilty of begging or vagrancy, complete success was claimed 'both in rehabilitating quasi-delinquents, and in freeing Aberdeen from their activities' (Carpenter 1851).

The Ragged School movement also attracted the attention of certain individuals capable of influencing State provision and legislation for this group of children. Mary Carpenter, in many ways a typical representative of the tradition of Victorian philanthropy, was perhaps the most significant. It was her writing and lobbying which contributed to the 1854 Youthful Attenders Act, which made private Reform Schools eligible for Government funding and inspection, and the subsequent Industrial Schools Act (1857; 1861; 1866) which did the same for Industrial Schools. Her belief that there was 'no essential distinction between delinquency and other forms of disturbance which postulate the need for childcare' (Bridgeland 1971) foreshadowed later developments.

However, these schools also suffered from disadvantages that they were not able to overcome, and which led to the eventual demise of the movement. These included difficulties in securing the children's regular attendance for a sufficiently long period, overdependence on the tenuous goodwill of local magistrates and public and above all the persistent negative effects of the children's deprived home circumstances. As a result many subsequent projects were residential ones, deliberately sited away from these children's places of origin.

Experimenting with authority: The Little Commonwealth and Homer Lane

The most well known and influential of the early pioneers was undoubtedly Homer Lane, founder and director of The Little Commonwealth. This was a residential community of around 50 adolescents and adults based in Dorset. Its referrals came mainly from the newly created Juvenile Courts.

Lane was an American woodwork teacher, whose success at running residential institutions for juvenile offenders in his own country led to an invitation to advise on the setting up and running of a similar venture in the UK, an invitation which resulted in his becoming its first and only 'Superintendent' in 1913. He had worked in America in one of several so-called 'Junior Republics', whose rationale was that using a form of internal self-government, modelled on the American Constitution, would have a beneficial effect per se.

At The Little Commonwealth, Lane took this idea further, placing greater emphasis on the community being both self-sufficient and independent from outside society (which he thought was potentially alienating). He believed that sharing with young people authority usually held by adults would enable them to see that these particular adults were on their side, working with them rather than against them. He developed the ideas of the Junior Republics, and evolved an elaborate system of self-government, including both economic and judiciary functions. 'Citizens' (all staff and patients over the age of 14 had equal voting rights) lived in 'families' housed in three cottages on site. Each 'family' was responsible to the Commonwealth as a whole for the consequences of the behaviour of each of its members.

The Little Commonwealth closed in 1918, when allegations about Lane's inappropriate behaviour with young women residents led to Home Office Certification (and therefore funding) being withdrawn. Though it seems that Lane did indeed act imprudently, it is likely that official unease about the project rather than evidence for any abuse or misdeed was the main reason for its closure.

The Little Commonwealth is significant for several reasons. It was the first establishment formally to give equal weight to the voices of staff and patients in a treatment setting. Several commentators have suggested that Lane should be acknowledged as the founding father of the whole therapeutic community movement (Farquharson 1991; Kennard 1983) even though the term was not coined until 20 years after his death. The venture attracted a great deal of attention and publicity. Lane was a charismatic figure and attracted support from a wide range of individuals and official bodies. Perhaps his greatest contribution was in inspiring others to take his ideas further and apply them to other settings dealing with troubled children.

Meeting multiple needs in a single setting: The Caldecott Community and Leila Rendell

Leila Rendell, the founder of The Caldecott Community, was, together with Homer Lane, a member of a small group of individuals working with destitute and delinquent young people that met regularly in the years preceding the First World War.

Her origins, like Mary Carpenter's, are in the Victorian philanthropic tradition; she saw her task as providing an environment that would enable underprivileged, deprived and needy children to reach their full potential. Though she shared Lane's ideas, perhaps her most important contributions were in her attempts to bring together care, education and treatment in one setting, and in her capacity to recognise the need for flexibility and adaptability when working with such children.

For example, Rendell's policy of not restricting routes of admission into The Caldecott from its inception implicitly recognised that it was not only children who come to the attention of Courts or Welfare Services who are distressed or damaged by being deprived of a secure family environment. Through allowing herself to remain open to new ideas and practices she was able to acknowledge the limitations of the approach perhaps more than any of her contemporaries; thus she was both prepared to acknowledge its inadequacies and, if appropriate, to recommend alternative forms of treatment.

These attributes are reflected in the history of The Caldecott Community itself. It started as a nursery school in London in 1915, became a residential establishment two years later and survived three further moves before arriving at its present home in Kent in 1945. 'Difficult' children were accepted from the early 1920s. It was recognised by the Department of Health as a 'Special' School in 1938, for those children whose behaviour had led to their exclusion from normal schools. By the 1960s the proportion of such children in The Caldecott had grown to almost two thirds of the total, and by the start of the new millennium it was changing again, moving into smaller units in a variety of locations. The capacity of The Caldecott to negotiate such changes, both internal and external ones, and not be 'frightened into a static security' (Bridgeland 1971) is a reflection of the personality of its founder.

Alternatives in education: Summerhill and A. S. Neill

A. S. Neill is probably the most widely known of those individuals inspired by Lane, and the one most directly influenced by him. Neill described his own visit to The Little Commonwealth as 'the most important milestone in my life' (Neill 1960). He later went on to become Lane's 'patient', when the latter became a psychotherapist, while in between times teaching Lane's son at King Alfred's School in London. As the founder and headteacher of Summerhill School, Neill took Lane's ideas and applied them to education. Though the actual model of Summerhill, where lessons were not compulsory and where all rules were decided at the weekly council meetings of the whole school in which children would outnumber adults, were not widely replicated, Neill's influence in provoking thought about attitudes and practices in teaching has been and still is enormous. Partly because of its innovative practices and partly because it did initially accept a proportion of 'problem' children, Summerhill also had a significant impact on other pioneering projects in remedial education, and on individuals involved with them. Two such individuals were Otto Shaw and John Aitkenhead.

Shaw, a petroleum engineer, had a 'Damascus experience' on reading one of Neill's books, and in 1934 set up Red Hill School, a co-educational establishment for secondary age maladjusted children. His significance lies in his recognising the importance of documentation of the outcomes of such work (admittedly in his case mainly in terms of academic achievement), and in his applying psychoanalytic ideas to remedial education, particularly in describing the tensions on staff members of having to hold teaching, parental and therapist roles in one setting.

John Aitkenhead took Neill's ideas back to his mentor's native Scotland, where he founded Kilquhanity School in 1940. His work emphasised the need to integrate 'problem' children into wider society and not isolate them. Kilquhanity emphasised its links with the local community in Dumfriesshire, and encouraged a controlled mix of day and residential attenders as well as of 'problem' children and 'normal' peers.

Summerhill stopped admitting 'problem children' in 1937. One idea as to why Neill made this decision involves the effects of his own therapy (with Reich) around this time, which may have 'freed Neill from needing to work with problem children' (Skidelsky 1969). Whether or not this was so, it serves as a valuable reminder for those in the field to question their own needs and motives for undertaking this sort of work (see Chapters 14 and 15).

Sharing responsibility: Planned environment therapy and David Wills

If Homer Lane can be considered the grandfather of the therapeutic community movement, then David Wills is the person who has probably had the greatest influence in therapeutic community work with children and young people. He is best known through his writing, and for his work on two particular projects, Hawkspur Camp (1936–1940) and The Barns Hostel

(1940–1944). The former was an experimental project for delinquent boys aged between 16 and 19. Wills, as Project Director, involved the whole community in constructing its own buildings from scratch ('in a muddy field in rural Essex'), with the materials available to them, while at the same time evolving the structure of self-governing management necessary to negotiate this task. The long-term success of Hawkspur Camp is difficult to judge, as the work was cut short by the war, with most of the clientele joining the army. Wills then moved to Scotland, where he was appointed warden of The Barns Hostel, a residential project for disturbed and 'un-billetable' evacuees, boys aged between 9 and 14. Again his policy of delegating decision-making to the community as a whole resulted in the Hostel passing through several stages, initially destructive chaos, then overdependence on adult authority, before a secure authority structure could be established. (It is striking how similar the process was to that described later at adult therapeutic communities such as The Northfield experiments, or at Villa 21 in Shenley Hospital, Cooper 1967). Wills developed Lane's ideas to a form that made them more applicable to work with children. He was clear that there were, and had to be, differentials in the sharing of responsibility. He recognised that in any democratic structure in which children are included adults hold the greater power, by virtue of age and experience. In this way he was more pragmatic though maybe less purist than Lane or Neill. He himself wrote that at council meetings 'if I really press a point hard, the decision never goes against me' (Wills 1960).

Equally important was his development of structures both within and outside the community to support the work. These included involving outside professionals both for consultation to the staff and for therapy to the children. He established a structure that involved discrete spheres of influence within the community. At The Barns Hostel Wills was the warden but not the headteacher; hence 'school rules' and practices could differ from 'hostel rules'. The result was to reduce the community's dependence on a single person and to create distinct spaces in which to attend to the various particular needs of each child.

Some of the professionals working alongside Wills developed what was probably the first unified model for therapeutic community work with young people. Planned environment therapy proposed that the child's social needs could be addressed through the experience of shared responsibility within the community; their emotional needs through attention to relationships with staff members and through individual psychotherapy; and their educational needs through measures designed to increase motivation for learning, such as voluntary lessons and an emphasis on creative work, as well as the provision of individual remedial work (Bridgeland 1971).

There are several qualities of Wills that make him more accessible and in a way more interesting than some of the more charismatic figures that preceded and followed him. He embarked on his work with disturbed children early in his adult life. He served his apprenticeship as a residential worker in various institutions with delinquent or maladjusted adolescents. In his writing he is open about the 'despairing terror' that he felt as an inexperienced worker. In spanning the pre- and post-war eras, and in the range of children's ages and settings with which he worked (after The Barns Hostel he worked at a school for maladjusted 8–16-year-olds, and then at an after-care hostel for ex-approved school 16–19-year-olds) he is probably unique.

He wrote well, both about others (he was Homer Lane's biographer) and about his own work. He described his aim as being 'to give the child the experience of something on which they can absolutely rely whatever they may do' so that 'however much a child wounds their own self esteem, they cannot change the esteem in which we (the staff) hold them. When that relationship is established, then therapy can begin' (Wills 1945).

The advent of child psychotherapy: The Mulberry Bush School and Barbara Dockar-Drysdale

Official recognition of the need for increasingly complex and special intervention for disturbed children in the post-war period meant that the era of the pioneers was effectively over. However, two particular individuals still stand out.

Barbara Dockar-Drysdale travelled a similar path to Leila Rendell and Mary Carpenter before her. She came from a secure upper-class background and her interest and expertise with damaged and deprived children grew out of her wartime experience of setting up a playgroup for evacuee children from poor areas of East London, and in providing support for them and for the families with whom they were billeted. Her education in this field came initially from this and then from a self-created training programme, involving a number of placements which gave her experience in relevant specialist settings. In subsequently setting up the Mulberry Bush School in Oxfordshire in 1948, she was influenced by Anna Freud, and ideas of child analysis, and especially by Dr Donald Winnicott, and the concept of the 'holding environment' (see Chapters 2 and 4). The Mulberry Bush was an institution characterised by the application of child psychotherapy with a group of severely disturbed primary-aged children in a residential school setting. Although there have been several subsequent directors and changes in emphasis, Dockar-Drysdale's core ideas remain central to the school. It not only continues to thrive, but has also developed links with a similarly functioning day unit, The Mulberry Bush/Tavistock Day Unit, in London.

A second important aspect of her work was in her links with The Cotswold Community, an institution for older disturbed delinquent adolescents, to which she was initially appointed as consultant psychotherapist. A unique feature of this community is its links with the Tavistock Institute of Human Relations, a link set up when the community was opened, whereby continual evaluation and feedback is available from an external source with expertise in institutional dynamics.

The therapeutic community comes of age: Peper Harow and Melvyn Rose

Though registered as a Special School, Peper Harow was the first institution for children that actually named itself as a therapeutic community. In many ways it set a benchmark for other institutions, through its everyday practice, its use of the large group as central in the day-to-day life of the community, and (as it developed) its concern for the detail and meaning of all that happened within, including the influence of the physical environment and its relation to the provision of compensatory primary experience (Rose 1990).

Like The Cotswold Community, Peper Harow was in part a consequence of timing, of the opportunity created by major legislative change and key individuals in the right place at the right time. The 1969 Children and Young Persons Act precipitated the abolition of the failing approved school system. Melvyn Rose was a housemaster at Park House (the approved school that was to become Peper Harow); he had previously worked at Finchden Manor, a residential school for boys of 16 and over, whose founder, George Lyward, stressed the importance of allowing, indeed encouraging, damaged older adolescents to re-experience their own childhood in their everyday experiences). Dr Nora Murrow was the consultant psychiatrist at Park House School; she had previously worked closely with Maxwell Jones at the Henderson Hospital, one of the pioneering adult therapeutic communities. Godfrey-Isaacs, the chairman of the Park House School Trustees, had an increasing interest in psychodynamic thinking and was more than receptive to the idea of a therapeutic community model which was proposed by Rose and Murrow. Together, and with the support of the trustee body as a whole, they made Peper Harow possible. Melvyn Rose was its first director.

It is perhaps as important to learn from Peper Harow's difficulties as from its successes. After 1980 it negotiated two major changes: one was the change from the single-sex community (just boys) to one that included girls, while the other involved Melvyn Rose himself leaving in 1983, following which there was a succession of changes in the leadership. At the same time all communities and residential establishments working with children were also having to cope with the consequences of major social/political changes in the balance of power and responsibility between central government and agencies dealing with this particular group of children. As these involved changes not only in wider statutory and professional frameworks, but also in the processes of funding and therefore referral, they inevitably had a greater impact on communities using a 'large group' setting as a way of working. Whilst some of the established communities for children and adolescents (e.g. Caldecott Community, Mulberry Bush School) survived by making or beginning the process of major change in their essential large group models others, like Peper Harow, did not or could not easily adapt to these changes. The extent to which this might have contributed to its eventual closure is hard to weigh up in the face of other factors and events. These included the devastating consequences of a fire which all but closed the community in 1989. The original Peper Harow establishment closed in 1993, but its 'sister unit', Thornby Hall, initially set up to run on similar lines with a younger age group (but later to adapt to take a more adolescent age group) continues as a large group community today.

In the same way that Neill's work was assimilated into schools, many of which would never consider calling themselves 'alternative' or free schools, so the role of Peper Harow will be seen as much in its effect on the wider system as in terms of how exactly it functioned or how successful or otherwise it proved. Through championing and publicising the therapeutic community approach to the treatment of disturbed children, Rose influenced work in a whole range of settings, from Children's Homes (e.g. Earthsea House in Norfolk) through Special Schools to inpatient psychiatric units for children (e.g. Brookside or Northgate). Though these would not necessarily call themselves therapeutic communities as such, they undoubtedly make use of the therapeutic community approach in their practice. Other important developments include the Peper Harow Foundation, which continues to initiate new and innovative projects for working with this group of children, and the Charterhouse Group, a group of therapeutic communities for young people of which Peper Harow was one of the founder members.

A common theme for the future

Each of the individuals and projects I have mentioned has made a particular contribution to this work with young people. However it is what connects their work that serves to define the approach, and suggests ways it might develop further. Attempts to identify the core features of the therapeutic community approach (Haigh 1999; Kennard 1983; Rapoport 1960) have all been drawn from work with adults, and though relevant to similar work with children do not take into account the differences in origins, in emphasis and in day-to-day practice.

Perhaps the most distinctive single feature of the line of work that began with Homer Lane is the unique way it attempts to provide children with a different experience of relating to adults, almost a different experience of being parented, albeit one they can not only tolerate but also reflect on and learn from. This can be seen on several levels.

Attention to seemingly minor details of everyday life was common to all projects involved. This included a particular emphasis on the actual physical or material aspects of the environment, Rendell or Rose going to endless trouble about the quality of cutlery or texture of the bed linen, even Lane or Wills concentrating on the minutiae of construction or weekly grocery bills, and all aspects of creating a home. Equally important would be the details of how a particular child would be tucked into bed, given a telling-off or hugged or tickled, again all aspects of parenting.

As significant as what parents do to and with children is how they are perceived by them. Several pioneers stressed the value to the children of seeing staff members disagreeing and negotiating with each other. As important as the staff meeting together separately, whether for consultation, supervision or coffee, is that they are seen to do so by the children. By bringing in outside professionals, and by separating tasks such as care, education and therapy inside the community Wills showed how this could be extended to the wider network of adults with whom the children would later be involved.

There is one other element present in the accounts of the work which, although also very relevant to the experience of being parented, is more difficult to define. It is perhaps most easily recognised by its absence, when attention to detail could become obsessive, an emphasis on innovation inappropriate or the pursuit of practical work irrelevant. It is the quality which validates and gives meaning to what might otherwise be idiosyncratic practices or rituals. Lane, Wills and Lyward all talked and wrote of 'love'. This is not a comfortable word, and carries a danger of over-simplifying the task (Bettelheim 1974). However it is not easy to come up with an alternative word or phrase. In addition to the elements of care, concern and positive affect, it would also need to contain acknowledgement of the transcendent in being prepared to accept a state of not knowing. (There will be several levels of meaning in any interaction, some of which will not be known, so that any single answer or explanation will be inadequate.) It would involve the development of a capacity to reflect on what is happening and what is experienced, a protective factor (Fonagy *et al*. 1992) singularly lacking in the clients at the start of treatment.

All this suggests that the future direction of this approach should not be confined to units specifically designated as therapeutic communities, but can also be applied in a range of settings and with a number of special needs. It would include any processes by which damaged children can both act and live their past in the present while at the same time being given the opportunity to experience for themselves alternative ways of being 'parented', so as to allow them first to not need to repeat the patterns of their own past, and second to accept whatever care, education and other help they might still need in the future.

Conclusion

The usual reason for including in a text book a chapter on the origins and history a particular approach is to place it in context in terms of its own past. In this particular case I would like to suggest that there is also a second reason.

The history of the therapeutic community approach is not an easy one to outline simply. It is often not a very clear or coherent one. It lacks a strong or consistent story line. This reflects the view that the approach is characterised by distinct projects working in different contexts, all separate from each other. The work developed without the umbrella of a central organisational or professional base to provide support and guidance. There is not a commonly recognised language. Different terms may be used to describe similar but not necessarily identical concepts and practices. In preparing this chapter I was also struck that many of the accounts of particular projects used a language that while clearly very actual for the authors felt stilted or dated to me as a reader. I became increasingly aware of the biases of my own personal and professional positions.

It was only near the end of the process that I realised how closely all these experiences mirrored those of working with the children I was describing, in the settings I was giving an account of. Such work involves a continuous and painful struggle to re-experience and re-name events, emotions, and memories; to borrow a phrase from T.S. Eliot's poetry, this may feel like a series of repeated attempts to raid the inarticulate (Eliot 1940). It involves holding disparate, sometimes contradictory, and often seemingly unconnected material, and learning to make sense and use of the resultant tensions. Thus, for me, the real value of looking at the origins and history of the approach is to provide a context for the actual experiences (whether intellectual, emotional or physical) of the everyday practice of therapeutic community work with this group of children.

CHAPTER 4

The Roots of Mental Health: Emotional Development and the Caring Environment

Monica Lanyado

...there's no such thing as an infant, meaning of course that whenever one finds an infant one finds maternal care, and without maternal care there would be no infant.

(Winnicott 1960)

More than any other species, the human infant is dependent for survival over many years on the care of others. Bowlby has highlighted this in his work on attachment, separation and loss, introducing the concept of the ethological dyad of infant and carer, in which the infant instinctively forms an attachment relationship with the caregiver which protects him from external dangers and keeps him safe (Bowlby 1969, 1973, 1980, 1988). The counterpart of this attachment is the caregiver's instinctive motivation to care for the young. Winnicott in his distinctive way also expressed this view when he baldly stated 'There's no such thing as an infant' (Winnicott 1960). For Winnicott it is never possible to envisage a baby without a carer. No child can grow up in a care vacuum, although some of the children discussed in this book have suffered such severe levels of deprivation or privation of care, that they seem to have at times been very close to this. At its most extreme, children die if not adequately cared for and it is these (thankfully rare) extremes that hit the headlines. Good-enough child care can be a life and death issue. However, children may somehow physically survive awful deprivation and cruelty, but be left with emotional scars which remain throughout their lives, even when the deprivation and cruelty have long stopped.

For Bowlby and Winnicott, it is axiomatic that the quality of care that a baby or child experiences as he or she grows up will fundamentally affect the type of person he or she becomes. The interconnectedness of the natural growth processes that are present in each one of us, and the environment in which this development takes place, is the central theme of this chapter. In ordinary child care, this environmental (parental) care enables the child to become his or her own unique personality and fulfil, within reasonable bounds, his or her potential in life – that is, to live life to the full. Where there has been early environmental failure, the whole structure of the child's internal world is affected because the roots of emotional health have not been established. It can take many years, some would say a lifetime, to find an equilibrium of emotional health following such a difficult start in life.

At its most severe, if there is not an adequate environmental provision for the child's emotional and physical growth, it is like a plant being starved of light, water and the necessary nutrients in the soil. The child can't put down naturally healthy emotional and physical roots. Some children have experienced such serious levels of deprivation, abuse, neglect and trauma that it is like trying to grow a tender seedling in a poisonous environment. Emotional and physical development are natural processes which need a responsive and sensitive environment if they are to unfold in the manner which is closest to the true nature of the child (Horne 1999a). Different plants need different types of physical environment – some need lots of shade, others need lots of sun; some thrive in hot climates, others would die in the heat. Each baby that is born carries his or her unique potential for individuality. The rapid expansion of research in the area of parent–infant development and interaction illustrates how incredibly finely attuned the ordinary parent is to his or her child's tiniest emotional nuances (for example, see Stern 1985). This is particularly so at the start of life before language is established, when non-verbal communication is at its most powerful. The attention to detail and degree of absorption in the child that ordinary parents show (Winnicott's 'primary maternal [and paternal] preoccupation', Winnicott 1956) are central to providing the quality of care that is required for emotional health.

The need for specialised therapeutic environments

The children that are the focus of this book have not had the benefit of such care for long enough. Therapeutic communities and other therapeutic settings which concentrate on providing carefully adapted environments to nurture severely deprived children and their families try to provide the specialised living environment that is required for some recovery to take place. It is like taking the tender seedling and replanting it in a place where it has a better chance of growing. This is an enormously difficult and demanding task, as these children and their families require an emotional and physical caring equivalent to 'intensive care' if they are to recover. Attention to detail in their everyday lives is vital in bringing about this rehabilitation and is an essential aspect of the care that is provided in all good therapeutic environments. The experiences that children such as these have suffered in life affect the manner in which they view relationships with others, and make them deeply suspicious and wary of people. These are not easy people to help.

In order to survive emotionally and physically they often become highly self-protective in a world which they perceive as being hostile and frustrating to their needs. These perceptions of a cruel, uncaring and often chaotic world are based on real experiences and relationships, which have often occurred at the most vulnerable times in their emotional development. Because much of this takes place before language has developed, they lack words with which to ground and express what they feel. This can lead to a tendency to act rather than talk when trying to express difficult emotions, hence the tremendous emotional lability of many of the children and families that are discussed in this book. Feelings very readily become overwhelming, with painful outbursts of anger, violence and distress being typical.

The distress that it is possibly most difficult to deal with is feelings associated with a deep sense of rejection together with undigested feelings of traumatic loss. Defences against experiencing these feelings are built up by the individual, quite simply as a way of surviving. The most obvious and problematic defence (for society) is anger and violence. However, the other frequently seen defence is dissociation – a form of 'cutting off' from all feelings, an effective way of leaving the individual less vulnerable to emotional pain, but resulting in severe emotional handicap which makes the richest experiences in life, particularly of loving relationships, inaccessible. This defensiveness is one of the many difficulties that foster and adoptive parents, as well as others who try to reach out to these children, struggle with.

These two main categories of psychological defences correspond to the physiological defences of 'fight or flight' and there have been recent important breakthroughs in our understanding of the brain processes that take place when, particularly, a very young child is exposed to extreme fear. Research shows that the earlier a child is exposed to extreme fear and not protected, the more likely it is that brain function becomes 'set' to experience even mildly frightening events, often only remotely associated with the original fearful situation, as highly dangerous (Perry *et al.* 1995). Tiny triggers can then set off major fear responses – in particular rage – as a biological form of self-protection of the child in the absence of a perceived caring and protecting adult. This explains the hyper-alertness and hyper-reactivity of many of the severely traumatised children who need therapeutic environments.

The experience of a therapeutic living environment can make the difference between a child who is closed off from forming relationships with adults who are desperate to love and care for him, and a child who dares to 'try again' to form a new relationship (Lanyado 2001). Psychotherapy with a child at an out-patient clinic can also bring about such changes, but there are children who have suffered such severe early environmental failure that they need to have the primary experience provided by a therapeutic environment that Dockar-Drysdale has described, if they are to recover (Dockar-Drysdale 1990).

Some years ago, social policy led to an antipathy towards residential units for these most needy children. Specialised units were closed down and policies of inclusion attempted to integrate these children into mainstream education and utilise out-patient treatment resources. For primary school children in particular the argument for this was often based on the need to preserve attachments to families. However, as the result of bitter experience, which has shown how difficult or at times impossible it can be to integrate children at the extreme end of the spectrum into the community, it is now generally recognised that for a small number of children, placement in a specialised unit may be the only wise option.

We are now aware that the *quality* of the attachment children have to their carers is crucial because severely deprived and traumatised children are often caught in unhealthy (seriously insecure) attachments to their parents or carers which can't promote emotional and physical health (Hopkins 1999). If the child is helped to form healthier new attachments whilst in a therapeutic community or similar setting, clinical experience shows us that these healthier new attachments can generalise to other relationships. Facilitating this change of quality of relationships is very arduous (Hopkins 2000). For the children being considered in this book, well-supported individual psychotherapy or placement in a therapeutic community or similar setting may be the only possibility of this happening, many other options having been tried and failed. In some therapeutic communities, residential settings or day units, individual psychotherapy is also available and this is can be a particularly potent way of helping such children as well as supporting and working with the staff who are in daily contact with the child (Cant 2002; Lanyado 1988; Maher 1999).

As an illustration of these ideas, I am going to describe 'Tim' and the difficulties that he had had in his life that led to his need for a placement in a therapeutic environment. Because of the need to protect the confidentiality of the child and his family, the example preserves the essential elements of Tim's life experience and internal world whilst also utilising some very deliberate camouflage. An incident at the therapeutic unit is described which illustrates the extent of Tim's problems and how, when they emerge in the therapeutic environment, it becomes possible to respond to them in a way which leads to a healthier development. Tim was in once-weekly therapy within the unit at the time of the events described below.

Tim's story

Tim was nine years old when he came to a residential school for children with emotional and behavioural difficulties (EBD school). He had been referred because he could not be contained in an ordinary classroom, nor in a day EBD setting. When he arrived at the school he was unpredictably violent, very restless, and easily distressed. He made it impossible for the other children in his class to relax and work and he had a powerful effect on the teachers who tried, without success, to teach him. He frequently ran out of class and out of the school. Despite this, he was liked by the staff who knew that he was a bright but very troubled child.

Shortly before he had come to the EBD school, some light had been thrown on what lay behind this difficult behaviour. A boy at his old school told his mother about a sexual game that Tim had played with him and Tim was asked about it. His response, in genuine innocence, was to say that the game he was playing (mutual masturbation) was only the same game as he played with his Uncle Phil (the brother of his birth father) whenever he visited his natural paternal grandparent's home. It emerged that during a period of time when Tim's mother was preoccupied with her own problems, Uncle Phil had given Tim 'special attention', which as well as being genuinely responsive at times to Tim's ordinary needs came with sexual strings attached. The discovery of this incestuous relationship helped to make sense of the extent of Tim's disturbance.

Tim entered the residential EBD school with the staff feeling deeply sympathetic to him. He had a tremendous need to talk about what had happened to him sexually and flooded the staff with detailed sexual material which was very hard to digest. Having kept the sexual secret of his relationship with his uncle for so long, now that all was revealed, he had a great need to talk about what had happened. It was deeply disturbing for staff to recognise the sexuality in this nine-year-old boy, particularly when he became abusive and violent. Nevertheless, the staff saw him as an innocent victim until there was an incident in which a flirtatious game of chase with Cindy, a girl at the school, suddenly escalated into him holding her down and rubbing himself against her, in a clearly sexually forceful way.

This shocking event, after much hard work in the staff group and Tim's individual psychotherapy, was eventually seen as the point from which Tim became able to start to change and develop in a more positive way. To understand how this could happen, I will first tell the story of Tim's life up to this point, and then briefly discuss the ways in which the work within the therapeutic environment was able to bring about this change. Although the story of Tim's life may sound coherent now, reaching this understanding within the staff group was a significant part of the therapeutic process itself. One of the important findings of attachment theory research is that the way in which therapeutic inputs help attachments to change is through helping the patient/client to make sense of his or her life in a way that was not possible before. This is most obviously seen in changes that take place in the quality of the person's narrative of their life. Previously when telling their 'life story' it will have been incoherent and lacking in sense with gaps, contradictions, inconsistencies and so on. Their lives will clearly have been lived without anything making much sense. Following therapeutic intervention, the telling of this same life story makes more sense. The events in the story haven't changed, but the understanding has. Where children have not had parents who could enable them to make this type of sense of their lives, and with Tim this was the case, other adults need to do this. The strength of a group of adults doing this together, as happens in therapeutic environments, is that a richer picture can emerge and gradually become a part of the child's understanding of him or herself, in response to first being understood by the adults around him or her. The struggle for understanding that is so crucial to the discussions that go on in the staff meetings, that are central to the work of the therapeutic environment, therefore have a direct influence on the child's recovery and capacity to form new, healthier attachments.

How can Tim's behaviour be understood? To do this, we have to go back to before Tim was born. Tim's mother was a troubled and rebellious teenager when she conceived Tim. In many respects she was still very much a child herself, ill-equipped to become a mother when she married Tim's father at the age of seventeen. At first the marriage may have seemed like an escape route from a conflict-ridden relationship with her own parents and it is possible that the arrival of the baby initially brought some reconciliation and closeness to her mother, neatly sidestepping the ordinary separation issues of mother and daughter during adolescence. However, we know from Tim's history, this was short-lived. Possibly, as the reality of looking after a baby sank in, and Tim's mother and father had to cope with Tim's ordinary baby needs – such as crying, seemingly endless feeding and dirty nappies, broken nights, colic and so on – the romantic notion of family bliss wore thin. Added to this, they had their own pressing adolescent needs which were in conflict with the demands and restrictions of looking after a baby. It is not surprising that the marriage broke down and mother, having tried to manage on her own, effectively handed Tim's care over to her mother and returned to the freedoms and excitements of adolescence.

It was fortunate that there was enough cohesion in the extended family for Tim's maternal grandmother to become his main carer. We cannot know how Tim coped with this transfer of care from his mother to his grandmother or what this meant to him. The change would have felt like some form of discontinuity at the very least, even though mother still lived at home and had not totally disappeared from his life. The actual physicality of the way in which Tim was handled and looked after on a day-to-day basis will naturally have felt different. Attachment theory suggests that Tim will have had to cope with some feelings of loss and separation during this change in his primary carer. The fact that he was being looked after by his grandmother, to whom he already had an attachment, together with the fact that his mother was not entirely absent, will have mitigated some of his upset. He is also likely to have been aware at an infantile level of the inevitable arguments and distress that would have surrounded the breakdown of the marriage. This might have taken the form of an awareness of erratic and inconsistent physical care, as well as the experience of not being in the centre of his parents' minds and hearts because they were preoccupied with their own needs and issues.

It is possible to see that Tim's first year of life was one in which there was serious instability in the life of his parents. Whilst this may be so for many babies for a variety of reasons, in Tim's case, this was the start of an accumulating pattern which eventually led to his need to come to the EBD school. It is important to note that many families have similar difficulties and then manage to stabilise. It is also important to note that some families in similar circumstances unfortunately go into a downward spiral, with the children becoming severely neglected or abused and going into care. Tim's situation is somewhere in the middle of these possibilities, as the extended families on both sides were able to offer help. A high proportion of the children who need the help of a therapeutic environment have, like Tim, had difficult starts in life. Quite a number will have had much more severe experiences of loss, abuse and trauma, resulting in the child going in (and out) of care for a significant period of his or her first few years of life, before becoming fostered and then possibly adopted.

Contrasts with ordinary emotional development

In order to put Tim's early experiences into perspective, I am going to make a short detour at this point, into thoughts about what is happening in ordinary, good-enough families during the first few years of a child's life. Coping with the ordinary needs of a baby demands the kind of devotion and preoccupation from parents that Winnicott has so aptly described as being so extreme that the same behaviour at another time of life would be seen as being 'an emotional illness' (Winnicott 1956). To those unschooled in the demands of parenthood, many new parents can seem so utterly obsessed with their baby that they seem almost mad, unable to think about anything else. Ordinary parents' attention to the detail of their baby's nonverbal communications at the start of life is actually a quite *extra*ordinary process. Winnicott describes the 'ordinary devoted mother' as being in a mental state of 'primary maternal preoccupation' (Winnicott 1956). Bion describes this same state of mind as being one of 'maternal reverie' (Bion 1962). Nowadays it is appropriate to add to these terms the paternal capacity to enter these states of mind in relation to the baby, that is to talk about the 'ordinary devoted father' and 'primary paternal preoccupation'. And lest it should seem that there is a state of perfection to be attained in parenthood, thankfully Winnicott also described the wisdom of parents being 'good enough' parents as opposed to striving for some impossible target of parental perfection (Winnicott 1965). Winnicott, Bion, and Bowlby, from the perspective of attachment theory (see Holmes 1993), all emphasise that what takes place within these earliest relationships forms the bedrock of mental health. A structure of the mind and emotions is laid down in these early days which has a profound influence on all that follows.

In addition to these psychoanalytically based theories, there is a rapidly growing area of research in ordinary parent–infant interaction and communication, which captures on video and from careful observation and research all the tiny attunements and mis-attunements of communication that contribute to what goes on between parents and babies during these earliest days of life (for example, see Stern 1985). These tiny communications are the building blocks of the baby becoming understood by his or her parents. They are part of what makes parenthood in the earliest days of life so intense and exhausting. There is so much nonverbal communication going on that trying to understand what the baby needs, feels, and thinks becomes all-consuming for the parents. These are the important micro-details of what is meant by Bowlby when he talks about the caregiving side of the attachment relationship in which the provision of appropriate loving care for the dependent baby is vital for the baby's physical and emotional survival.

When parents, for a variety of reasons, cannot become engaged enough in this primary parental task, the baby's needs cannot be as well attended to as they would be otherwise. At its extreme, and this is sadly the experience of many children who need the help of therapeutic communities, the child's needs will have been unmet to the extent that we would describe the child as seriously neglected. Fraiberg movingly describes work with families such as these (Fraiberg 1980). In some cases the problems extend beyond neglect to situations where immature, disturbed, frustrated and unsupported parents harm their children, either quite deliberately for sadistic pleasure (such as those children who are eventually taken into care suffering from broken limbs and cigarette burns to their bodies), or out of an inability to bear the cries of their unhappy babies any longer, for example shaking or throwing the baby to try to stop the crying. Fraiberg has eloquently described the cycle of intergenerational deprivation and neglect that these babies are the latest recipients of, as resulting from 'ghosts in the nursery' (Fraiberg 1980).

Tim's story continued

In Tim's case, it was not clear whether or not there had been real concerns about physical and emotional neglect but it does seem likely that he was considerably disadvantaged in his first year of life and that it was very fortunate that his grandmother was able and willing to take over his upbringing.

We also cannot know what the absence of his father meant to him when he was an infant. Father did keep in touch with him on a fairly regular basis. As he grew up, the lack of a consistently present father figure was to play a significant part in his life. Certainly by the time he came to the EBD school, his relationship with his father was complicated and greatly affected by his feelings of being rejected by his father.

After his parents' marriage broke up, mother had a number of other relationships and then became pregnant again. She set up home with the father, and after a few months Tim, who was now two-and-a-half years old, went to live with them. In terms of attachment relationships, Tim had had to cope with his mother leaving the family home, followed by his own departure from his grandmother, who had become like a mother to him. Again, it is possible to see a complicated mix of separations from some loved family members as well as reattachments to others. This is a lot for a little child to manage and can be contrasted with the stability of secure attachments to mother and father which form the core of an 'ordinary' child's experience of growing up. Tim never got on with his mother's new partner but had to learn to share his mother with him. Mother would have been pregnant at the time and preoccupied with her new relationship, although again there may well have been a honeymoon period during which Tim might have felt himself to be part of a good-enough new family group. However, he would soon have to share his mother further with the new baby and another pregnancy that followed soon after the birth of this baby.

There were two children from this relationship but unfortunately the relationship became very violent and this was to have a profound impact on Tim. He became a frightened little boy and was often severely beaten by the cohabitee who scapegoated him. His mother was also very frightened and therefore unable to intervene and protect him. Quite apart from the terrible male role model provided by this man, and the difficulty of not understanding why his birth father was not around anymore, the physical abuse that he now suffered seriously traumatised this already vulnerable little boy. Tim also witnessed severe marital violence and was naturally unable to protect his mother from being seriously assaulted by her cohabitee. He later talked of his great distress at the time – approximately from when he was three to four-and-a-half years old – in not being able to help her. His powerlessness in this situation was very upsetting for him and during the therapy that he had whilst at the EBD school, he often spoke about being beaten up by this man and how he longed to take revenge when he was strong enough. He had particularly hated this man when he attacked his mother, and felt terrible that he had not been able to do anything to stop this. This hatred and helplessness had fuelled his increasingly resistant and hostile behaviour towards the cohabitee, which in turn led to a spiralling of the physically abusive behaviour. Eventually, after several attempts, his mother was able to leave the cohabitee. She took Tim and his two half-sisters and went to live in a women's refuge where she stayed for a number of months. Tim was four and a half by this time.

These were very hard times for the family, but despite this, his mother had matured and learnt from these awful experiences. She became more able to stand on her own two feet and managed to get the family rehoused. During all this time, Tim had visited his father in his father's parent's home, fairly regularly. Father was not there very much, but Tim was clearly attached to his paternal grandparents and uncle. In the midst of all the troubles in mother's home and the beatings that Tim was receiving from the cohabitee, mother felt relief during the times he was with his father's side of the family. She felt he was safer with them than at home with her.

However, it was during this time that Uncle Phil was gradually making a 'special' relationship with this very deprived little boy. He spent a lot of time with Tim and made him feel wanted and 'special'. Possibly for the first time,

Tim felt he had an exclusive intimate relationship with an adult who could look after him and protect him. This 'specialness' unfortunately gradually included a sexual relationship in which Tim performed fellatio on his uncle and his uncle masturbated him. For a little boy who had very little experience of tender touching and physical contact, the slow seduction that took place, starting from very ordinary parental-type physical affection, may well initially have felt like a basic need in him being met, and therefore have been very appealing to him. Uncle Phil had learning difficulties, which suggested that this may not have been a carefully planned premeditated seduction, but more of a gradual overstepping of sexual boundaries which culminated in serious sexual abuse. This relationship with Uncle Phil probably started when Tim was three years old, and not only seeking someone who could hold him in mind in a special way, but also needing to form a more positive relationship with a man who cared for him. The secretiveness of the sexual part of the relationship became bound up in the 'specialness' and intimacy. This was apparent in the way the abuse first came to light – an innocent comment from Tim when he was eight years old and about to come to the school. The sexual secret did not seem to be the result of threats from Uncle Phil about what would happen to Tim if he told anyone about their sexual activities. Indeed this was recognised by the court's response to what had happened, which was to put Uncle Phil on probation and offer treatment. The whole situation seemed a very sad combination of two very deprived and lonely people coming together to try to comfort each other. This is obviously not to condone what happened, but to try to understand how such things can happen.

About a year after leaving the refuge and being rehoused, Tim's mother met another man and this time married him. Tim was six years old. This choice of partner showed the benefits of all the hard lessons she had learnt from her previous relationships. This man had not had an easy life, but he had also learnt a lot along the way and he was able to be a thoughtful and understanding stepfather to Tim. This marriage was stable and they had two children. However, Tim by this point was very disturbed and difficult both in school and at home. Much of this was attributed to what he had experienced while living with the violent cohabitee, for which his mother felt terribly guilty. It is not at all surprising that a child having had all the experiences that Tim had would end up extremely confused, aggressive and traumatised. Various interventions were tried with him living at home – additional help at school, treatment from the Child and Family Psychiatry Service, supportive counselling for the parents. However, these efforts did not seem sufficient, which was why a more total therapeutic living environment was sought for Tim.

The repercussions of early life events on Tim's inner world: Insecure attachments and traumatisation

If one looks at Tim's life from an attachment theory perspective, Tim might be described as being insecurely attached to his mother, whose current improved ability to care for Tim was overshadowed, for Tim, by his past experience of her as an inadequate and preoccupied mother. This meant that Tim was unable to respond to the good-enough mothering she was now trying to give him, because he was still relating to her on the assumption that she was as she had been in the past – unreliable and preoccupied with her own problems. He was unable to see or feel the changes in her.

In addition, although his current relationship with his stepfather was good enough, this relationship was also overshadowed – by his experiences of having been rejected by his birth father, severely physically abused and frightened by his mother's cohabitee, and gradually sexually seduced, and then traumatised and abused by his uncle. The attachment qualities of these relationships did not predispose him to trusting adults to be there for him when he needed them. If anything, adults were the source of much of his distress and disturbance. In self-defence, he hid himself and protected himself from close relationships by presenting a very tough and aggressive face to the world. He had discovered that this stopped many children and adults from trying to get too close to him and he preferred it this way. Relationships had become dangerous to him. (For a fuller discussion of violence in children and adolescence see Parsons and Dermen 1999.)

It is also important to bear in mind the many separations and losses that Tim had had to deal with. His birth father was only very peripherally present for him. His mother had handed him over to the care of her mother for a long period in his first few years of life, and when he had returned to live with her, he had been separated from his grandmother who had become like a mother to him in the meanwhile. His uncle, whom he had also loved and who had offered some protection and met some of his emotional needs, had sexually abused him. When the abuse was revealed in a fairly innocent way, he lost the relationship with his uncle, as he was no longer allowed to be with him. He often talked to staff about missing his uncle when he was at the school. As with many children living in therapeutic environments, a good deal of Tim's anger could be accounted for by his experience of so many traumatic separations and losses, anger being part of the normal mourning process that had not been able to run its natural course. Clinically these children can be described as suffering from 'multiple traumatic loss', which both fuels their anger and distrust of the world and makes it very hard for them to dare to make new relationships (Lanyado 2002) or allow themselves to experience closeness in relationships.

The role of trauma in the internal lives of many children in therapeutic communities is becoming more and more understood, and I believe is intertwined with the impact of neglect, separation and loss on the mind and heart of the child. Whenever a child is known to have been abused, physically, emotionally or sexually (often in all these ways), the shocking nature of what has happened to them has been traumatising and fundamentally affected their internal worlds. The child will have been totally overwhelmed by fear, horror, pain, and possibly inappropriate sexuality. As noted earlier in this chapter, we now know that the younger the child is when this happens, the more powerfully the physiological fear response becomes literally wired into the child's brain and body (Perry *et al.* 1995). Tim had become 'primed' to defend himself by fighting and violence to the extent that even the mildest of comments to him were perceived as being attacks on him which he had to defend himself from, as he had no belief that anyone else would protect him. His traumatically violent experience with his mother's cohabitee may well have made him hyper-reactive and hyper-alert physiologically, thus readily misconstruing friendly approaches as potentially dangerous (Perry *et al.* 1995). (For a more detailed discussion about the effects of traumatisation on the child see Lanyado 1999, 2004.)

During Tim's stay at the school, it became clear in his conversations with the staff and during his therapy sessions that he felt that the physical abuse he had experienced from his mother's cohabitee distressed him more at that time than the sexual abuse from his uncle. The chronic level of fear that he had become accustomed to living with whilst his mother was with the cohabitee was still very much alive in him. This is one of the difficulties with such serious traumatisation – it remains in the present and is very difficult to leave behind even when the current situation is one in which there is ample protection and security.

How can the therapeutic environment help children like Tim?

The model that I find helpful in understanding the workings of a therapeutic community is an application of Winnicottian concepts of child development to the creative emotional growth of children in a specialised therapeutic environment (Winnicott 1960). This is the model that Dockar-Drysdale used, with additional thinking drawn from Menzies-Lyth's ideas about organisational defences against anxiety, as well as an understanding of group dynamics based on Bion's work (Bion 1961; Dockar-Drysdale 1990; Menzies-Lyth 1988; 1989). This model is based on an understanding of the child–carer dyad intertwined with the impact the child has on the system around him and vice versa. In addition to Winnicott's concepts of emotional development, attachment theory and the attempt to change the quality and strength of attachment relationships, is the other major theoretical underpinning (Bowlby 1988). There are also very helpful models which start from an understanding of the way in which groups and organisations function (Byng-Hall 1995; Sprince 2002; Ward and McMahon 1998).

The manner in which a psychotherapist is used within therapeutic settings is highly individual and depends on the character of the setting and the personalities and preferred ways of working of the director and staff of the unit, as well as the skills and interests of the particular psychotherapist (Wilson 1999). Models such as these need to grow organically and develop within each setting, according to the individual need of that setting. They take a long time to develop to a mature form that can be thought of as the defining 'culture' of the particular therapeutic unit, and are therefore not readily transferable. However the principles of the model outlined here can be applied across therapeutic units to create new unique therapeutic cultures.

Having understood more about the inner world of Tim and how he came to be this way, we can now return to the incident where he was sexually aggressive with Cindy. This kind of incident in the life of a therapeutic environment for children is the life-blood of the work of the community. The staff had to think and work hard during this time to digest and integrate their personal feelings about the reality of sexual abuse and what constitutes sexually abusive behaviour in a child, as well as to understand the difference between this and ordinary healthy childhood sexual curiosity. The on-going staff meetings for discussing the children offered opportunities for working through the staff response, as did some additional meetings between those staff closest to Tim and Cindy. These therapeutic processes within the community are discussed more fully in Chapters 10, 14 and 15.

Whilst struggling to understand Tim, staff also had the responsibility to help Cindy to feel safe again and help Tim not to repeat this behaviour. In addition, both children needed adult protection from further harm in the aftermath of what had happened, because the violent feelings that were being expressed within the community were barely controlled and threatened to harm Tim, Cindy, or indeed other children or members of staff who did not tread extremely carefully. Tim threatened to run away or harm himself and others. He smouldered for days, remaining unapproachable whilst feeling terrified that he would be thrown out of the school. Cindy was deeply distressed because she had been sexually abused in the past. Tim's friends tried to protect him, and Cindy's friends were out 'to get' Tim. Immediately after the incident the staff were in conflict for a while over how best to respond to both children's needs and needed space in staff meetings to reflect carefully on what had happened before they were able to respond wisely and not purely reactively. The headteacher played an important role in holding all these conflicting experiences and feelings together so that a balanced and wise view was reached in response to Tim's actions.

The staff in the community needed to further digest and try to understand all the complexities of Tim's internal world and how it had suddenly been projected onto the wide screen of community life, before they could gain some understanding of why he had been so sexually frightening to Cindy. One of their tasks was to help Tim to recognise and own his potential to harm others in the way that he had been harmed. This psychological defence of 'identification with the aggressor' lies at the heart of the repetition across generations of abusive behaviour of all kinds. It is this unconscious defence that makes the difference between someone saying 'I was beaten as a child and it didn't do me any harm, so I can beat my child when he deserves it' (unconscious and conscious identification with the aggressor) and 'I'm never going to do that to my child because I remember how I suffered' (conscious non-identification with the aggressor). It seemed possible that as a defence at the time of being physically abused, Tim had desperately put himself in his attacker's shoes as a means of, in fantasy, gaining some control over the situation. This is not an uncommon defence and has been noted in many situations of abuse and terror – such as concentration camp victims identifying with the prison guards and becoming like them at times following their release. It is perfectly possible to have unconsciously identified with the aggressor in this way at the time of the trauma whilst still feeling terrified of the aggressor in the way that Tim was still terrified of the cohabitee.

Clinical research has suggested that the combination of the experience of a number of broken attachments and rejections, combined with the witnessing of domestic violence, are possible risk factors in children who have not been sexually abused becoming abusers. Having been abused and having directly experienced physical abuse are further risk factors towards a child becoming abusive in adolescence and adult life. (For a fuller discussion of sexually abusive behaviour in children and adolescents see Hodges, Lanyado and Andreou 1994; Horne 1999b; Lanyado *et al.* 1995 and Skuse *et al.* 1997.)

When the worst came out in Tim's sexualised behaviour, he immediately feared rejection and became violent to disguise his fear. When he was not rejected, he gradually became less fearful and was able to talk to one of the staff that he had started to trust, who built on this trust at the time of crisis. This helped Tim to feel that he could be safely held, known and protected (from himself and others) by the staff at the school. The feeling of safety is a central concept in attachment theory in promoting secure attachments. This feeling that it was possible to be known, protected and understood, even when he was at his worst, started with staff at the school and extended to his mother and step-father, whom he gradually became able to recognise as being able to care for him in this way. Prior to the incident, he could not help but respond to them as if they were the inadequate parental figures of the past because these templates were so deeply ingrained in his psyche.

The fact that Tim was able to grow and change for the better following this very difficult incident was the result of the therapeutic environment he was living in. It was as if he was unconsciously repeating and staging a deeply traumatic event, transposing it from passive to active – to a different audience. As a result, he was not met by the rejection that he most feared, he was met with a facilitating environment that was able, following a good deal of hard work on the staff's part, to help him to reach a different outcome in which he felt understood and accepted. This enabled him to start to grow again – like the seedling that has been transplanted to a place in the sun, and which is not too sheltered from the rain, where it stands a better chance of putting down roots.

One final point. It is important to remember that the parents of children like this have nearly always had very difficult childhoods themselves and thus had very little internal strength to draw on when they became parents. Tim's mother illustrates this point, as well as reminding us that parents can get better at bringing up their children particularly when help is offered to break the cycle of deprivation and abuse that they are caught in. Our interventions need to be seen in this intergenerational light in the hope that the children who receive help in therapeutic environments today will become more able parents when their turn comes in the future.

Conclusion

This chapter has presented a picture of the kind of child who needs the help of a therapeutic community. Tim's story and the incident that took place whilst he was at the therapeutic community illustrate the difficulties that children such as these are trying to overcome, but have been unable to overcome whilst living full-time at home. In such situations, less intensive interventions may offer some temporary relief. However, without the depth of intervention that can be offered within a therapeutic community destructive patterns are more likely to recur. The power of the destructive cycles of behaviour that keep repeating themselves, not only in the child, but across the generations, demands great respect. Some theoretical ideas offering a framework on how to understand what has happened to the child and how the therapeutic community can help have been suggested.

Whilst the vast majority of children with emotional and behavioural problems can be helped while remaining in their homes, there will always be some children at the extreme end of the spectrum who need a complete change of living environment. This is the equivalent of 'intensive care' in the area of child mental health, as these are the most needy children of all. The complexities and demands of this way of working are enormous, but so are the rewards. These are seen when children like Tim, who have had such unpromising starts in life, become able to form relationships, participate in learning and gradually make useful contributions to the community rather than becoming drains on its resources.

CHAPTER 5

Group Thinking

Philip Stokoe

Introduction

Although this chapter is called 'group thinking', I want to present the case for the importance of group *living*. I spent the first 18 years of my professional life working in settings in which groups of young people were living and in which staff provided a 24-hour cover. It cannot be irrelevant that my own childhood between the ages of 11 and 18 was spent in boarding schools. In fact I am convinced that it was because my own experience was so traumatic that I became so passionately involved in trying to construct environments that could be therapeutic rather than destructive. In this chapter I want to summarise some of those essential factors that can make living in a community of groups therapeutic. In order to do this, I shall try to approach the task from both the perspective of the experience of the child (in the context of working with children and young people) and that of the member of staff.

In order to begin, I need to define some terms that seem to me fundamental to my way of thinking about group living. It may be that it will help the reader if I give a brief sketch of my own theoretical development. The place where I learned most about this business was a Youth Treatment Centre in Essex. This had been set up by the government on advice from the Social Service Inspectorate (at that time dominated by social workers with a psycho-analytic background) and was designed as a place to provide treatment for the most disturbed and dangerous young people in the country within a secure setting. The staff were given the brief of trying to create a system to accomplish this task. Staff were drawn from the disciplines of nursing, social work and teaching but worked together in the units. After a couple of years as a 'groupworker', I was promoted to manage one of the treatment units. I spent the next few years dreading going to work, feeling overwhelmed by a sense of terrible responsibility and pressure to have answers. That this changed and I found it was possible to enjoy the work is entirely down to my gradual understanding of the processes that go on in such settings and it is this understanding that I want to encapsulate here.

I am not going to try to rewrite some of those really helpful books like Hinshelwood's *What Happens in Groups* (1987) or Bion's *Experiences in Groups* (1961). Instead I want to think about two things, 'why groups?' and 'what is special about children and adolescents in terms of group treatment?'

Therapy

It is a principle that therapeutic work takes place in a relationship within a setting, the assumption being that the unconscious minds of each participant attempt to distort the relationship to fit the inner world expectation of what relationships are like. If you can arrange to neutralise this process in the direction staff to child, you can create an hypothesis that any distortion of the relationship is the result of the work of the child's inner world. The business of setting up the therapeutic system is, therefore, the business of setting up structures to reduce the effect of the staff unconscious on the staff/child relationship and to maximise the chance of detecting the effect of the child's inner world on the system. In what follows I am going to try to describe both the principles of setting up the structures and the pressures on them.

In order to provide maximum chance of noticing the impact on the staff group and structures of the inner worlds of the clients, it is essential to have those structures and the methods of work set out explicitly. This is because the work of addressing the way that we have been pulled into some sort of inner world enactment often involves individual staff members confronting others about their behaviour. This is very stressful and often frightening unless it can be done with reference to a previously agreed principle.

Of course the children are also experiencing unconscious pressures from each other: transference and projective identification are ubiquitous. Outside a therapeutic community these processes go on but without anybody showing the young person involved what is happening. As a result vulnerable young people become caught up in very destructive networks. By bringing that child or adolescent into a therapeutic community, it is possible to help him or her to become aware of these processes. That is because the group is the object of study in the community. Thus we can say that what is therapeutic for the young person is:

1. he or she can observe his or her peers gaining insight and changing

2. he or she can have a direct experience of how staff help (especially in the form of interpretations, which are descriptions of what seems to be going on in the young person's unconscious) can make sense of a peer's difficulties

3. by joining in he or she can discover and then build upon his or her own ability to help and understand another human being.

All of this in addition to what he or she may receive directly from the group in the way of help to understand his or her own problems.

The Unconscious

Psychoanalysis assumes that we have an unconscious and it is this that it seeks to study. By 'unconscious' we mean a part of the mind that we (the conscious part of us) cannot know directly but which influences our beliefs, our ideas, our perceptions and our thinking. When our inner world becomes stuck or fixed, our view of the external world becomes similarly stuck. The psychoanalytical view is that we can move on only by learning about our unconscious mind, so that those beliefs and ideas that had formerly driven us can now be thought about.

Although it doesn't seem to be referred to so much in the general psychoanalytical literature, it seems to me that an absolutely fundamental concept in this theory of mind (although it is not unique to psychoanalysis – George Kelly (1955) also thought it was basic to the human mind) is what Freud (1915) and Klein (1946) called the epistemophilic instinct. This is essentially what everyone else calls curiosity, the push from within to explain to ourselves what is happening to us. It is this activity that gets called internal phantasy and which creates the 'inner world'. I don't think it is so much a drive as something like a computer programme. I think that this is what Dawkins (1976) might refer to as the particular gene that makes us human and makes us humans more successful than any other species. It is because we appear to be programmed to create explanations of our experience, which we do from images of objects (people or bits of people) relating to each other, that we create the conscious mind. In other words we appear to be animals who are driven to find *meaning* in our experience of life.

Projective identification

I don't think I shall ever forget the relief I felt when I first learned about this concept. In one afternoon I realised that I was not (necessarily) totally incompetent but that the feelings that had led me to this view were the result of a process that was going on unconsciously and in which those aspects of a young person's personal experience that he or she was unable to handle were being lodged in me. At that moment I realised something about human nature, at least in the cultures that I have encountered, that seems to be fundamental: we are extremely bad at handling our feelings. For example we seem to respond to having a feeling by grabbing it tightly (almost as if it might be stolen from us) and then rushing as quickly as we can to an explanation that is designed to prove that this really is our feeling. In this way a worker in the helping professions might feel angry at work but will rush to the belief that this is because of some row with a member of the family before coming to work. What seems to be very difficult for us is simply to note that we are having a feeling but to wonder what it might mean and wait until enough information accumulates to allow us to understand what it means.

Projective identification was a term coined by Melanie Klein (1946) for a process that she observed occurring in babies in their relationships with their mothers. As she saw it, the baby who has, as yet, no defence system is overwhelmed by raw emotions and deals with this experience by believing that what is so unpleasant doesn't arise in herself but exists in someone else (usually part of mother). The reason the word 'identification' is used is because the object into which these unmanageable feelings have been projected is now *identified* with those feelings in the baby's mind. For example, a baby finds the experience of hunger too much to bear, so she projects this into something outside herself. This allows her to believe that she is being attacked from outside herself. She must feel that she is the victim of a hunger monster.

When she first described this process, Klein believed it was an unconscious fantasy aimed at getting some distance from unpleasant sensations and, therefore, controlling them. In other words, although the baby believes that there is a bad, hunger-monster-mother, this has no effect on the real mother. It was Wilfred Bion, a psychiatrist with plenty of experience of groups and residential work, who pointed out that projective identification actually does have an impact on the 'other'. He went on to show that this provides the baby with a means of communication: by getting mother to feel what the baby can't manage, mother can discover through thinking what is upsetting her baby. This allows her to respond appropriately and, thereby, to make things better (Bion 1957, 1959, 1961, 1962).

You may wonder why I have spent so much space on this single definition – it is because I believe that projective identification is the main language of the therapeutic community. The young people are continually filling staff and other young people with those parts of themselves that they are unable to handle. A classic example is bullying: the bully is unable to handle fear, so he uses projective identification to make someone else experience fear. In this way the bully has the pleasurable experience of seeing fear *outside* himself and, therefore, controllable.

Transference

This is one of those absolutely fundamental psychoanalytic concepts that has become part of our everyday language. One way to describe this is that our earliest relationships remain powerful images in our unconscious minds. This means that we tend to superimpose these images onto anyone we meet. In fact we would say that it is very difficult to see anyone accurately because we always, albeit without knowing it, superimpose one or other of these images from the past. Of course nothing is that simple and experience shows that it tends to be aspects rather than the entire personality of early carers or siblings that are experienced as part of the personality of the other. In my view it is because of this that group work is such a powerful therapeutic tool, as I describe under 'group transference' below.

Inner world

As a consequence of the pressure from the epistemophilic 'programme', we develop, in our unconscious minds, an image of the world in which there are various versions of our self in relation to others (which we call internal objects), each of which has the merit of describing a particular sort of personal experience. For example the young baby's experience of hunger might be represented by an image of itself attacked by a hunger monster (traditionally described by Kleinians as a bad breast attacking the baby). Healthy growth throughout life depends upon our ability to tolerate the frustration of not knowing what is happening to us long enough to allow a new idea (what I would call a new model) to reveal itself. Unfortunately it is easier, and therefore a lot more attractive, to apply an already existing model to the new circumstance. You could say, then, that there is a pressure to make the external world fit the beliefs we have about life, the universe and everything rather than let the internal world adapt to the experience of the external world.

Group transference

Tom Main (1989) first described this phenomenon and I think that it is one of the chief reasons why the group method has such therapeutic potential. He demonstrated how an individual patient uses the availability of a group of staff to create particular 'roles' for each, so that you could say that each individual staff member comes to represent a particular internal object. In crude terms, Martha becomes Joe's 'good mother' while Mary is his 'bad mother' and so on.

Valency

Before I continue, I'd like to describe one more important term. In my capacity as a consultant to organisations, I am often asked to help a team plagued by 'personality clashes'. In other words the staff team has drawn the conclusion that fights between its members are the result of those individuals' personalities. The team appear to have reached the conclusion that some members of staff are incapable of maintaining a professional approach to the work. Why? Because it is always the same one who is challenging authority, and it is always the same one who is irritatingly defending the status quo and so on. Now Bion (1957, 1959, 1961, 1962) referred to a mechanism by which we tend to attract a particular sort of projective identification. In this regard he seems to have been describing something that Jung was interested in and to which he assigned the term, the 'wounded healer'. This is the idea that our own personal 'vulnerabilities' become available as openings through which unconscious communication can happen with ease. The way that I think of it is that, at an unconscious level, we tend to display neon signs that the unconscious of others pick up very easily. These signs say things like, 'all anti-authority issues through this door' and then that allows those who cannot deal with such issues in themselves to project them into the one with the appropriate sign. Bion borrowed the word 'valency' from chemistry to describe this phenomenon. Now, of course, the fact that I have a valency to pick up specific projections tells us all about my own personal vulnerability; however, it is also the means by which we can learn a great deal about the young person, if only we can have the patience to work out which young person is using this particular 'door' to get rid of a part of themselves. Where staff teams have no idea about these unconscious processes, it is not surprising that they decide the problem is entirely that of the member of staff. Where teams can think about unconscious meaning, these apparently staff-group interactions can be powerful sources of information.

Therefore, therapy in a group setting works by allowing the unconscious mind of the client to be revealed by projective identification and group transference. This enables the staff group to develop strategies to 'feed back' this information to the young people so that they can gradually accommodate knowledge about their minds in a way that allows them to choose to make changes to their fundamental beliefs about themselves and the world they live in. This is no different from the philosophy of individual therapy except that the group experience allows the various transferences and projections to be experienced at the same time rather than one at a time. In addition the business of therapy is not the sole prerogative of staff. It is vital to the enterprise that the young people have the opportunity to be involved in helping as well as being helped, that they can discover their own skills in the truly adult capacity to form reciprocal relationships in which help is not one-way and the ideal can be given up in favour of the ability truly to value another's effort.

There is, therefore, a tremendous potential in the group approach; however, there are also powerful dynamics that almost feel as if they are designed to sabotage this potential, and I hope to allude to these in what follows. In general terms I am referring to two processes, the defences against anxiety endemic to groups, and the distortion of task and principles of work that are the evidence of those unconscious processes referred to above.

The lived experience

The reader, at this point, might be thinking that I have made something of a case for group therapy but why does this require the child or young person to *live* in the group setting? I think that the answer to this question has several elements.

Probably the most important is that we are in the business of providing the best chance we can for young people, whose inner worlds are very fixed, to experience not only feedback about their own minds but also to feel supported in the attempt to face psychic reality and to feel that they have the resources to do so. The aim is to try to undo the work of several years in as short a time as possible, so the method is to be addressing various issues in parallel (at the same time).

One way of thinking about the problems presented by the disturbed adolescent is that these are problems of development. You might say that there is an unconscious view that it is dangerous to develop and, in support of this belief, attempts are made to impact upon the external world in such a way that it is made to seem like a confirmation that it would be crazy to 'develop' (whatever this seems to mean to the individual in question). In other words the disturbed child or adolescent tends to use the external world as a place to 'act out' so that his or her expectations about others seem to be confirmed.

Working with children and adolescents is different from working with adults for a number of reasons, but the one most relevant to our purposes is that the developmental task is to move the child into a position from which it can separate from its parents and look after itself. This makes the environment an important interactive element in the whole business. Those of us, like me, who have worked in residential environments and also worked providing individual psychotherapy to children or adolescents, will know that, in the latter setting, it is important to have some mechanism for working with the parents. This is why child guidance clinics developed a method in which work was done with the child in parallel to work being done with the parents. The advantage of the residential environment is that the staff are able to monitor the acting out as well as the therapy.

Alongside this is the need to do two quite different types of 'therapeutic' work with children and adolescents. In the course of 'healthy' development, the child is given opportunities to develop skills in dealing with life. Because the disturbed child or adolescent represents a developmental problem, certain resources are not developed. It is through the business of actually living with the young person that it becomes possible to see clearly where there are such deficits in 'ego-strength' and, therefore, how to encourage the development of these resources. I think that it is because of this vital need that so many residential therapeutic units have built some sort of survival skills training into their programmes.

Of course there are immediate implications for the job of staffing an enterprise in which there is something called 'therapy' going on some of the time and then the business of living (which usually involves education) the rest of the time. Those who have worked in such settings will know that I am referring to such phenomena as 'splitting'. If we think about the way that psychoanalysis tends to believe that the mind functions, we might see how these processes that often cause such problems to staff groups are simply reflections of the processes going on in the young person's inner world. I am referring to the way that we construct defence systems. This is essential because the impact of the raw emotion is too much to cope with, as we all know from those times when we have had such a direct experience of raw feelings. However it *is* important to be able to 'upgrade' our defence system in the face of changes in ourselves and possibly in our environment.

Unfortunately this requires us to be able to face both external and psychic reality, which means being able to tolerate uncertainty. We all know that this requires work, whereas the more infantile state of mind that we call the paranoid/schizoid position enables us to avoid this work by believing in certainties. Consequently there is a tendency in all of us to remain with what we know rather than having to tolerate uncertainty. And so it is with the disturbed child or adolescent, but even more so. In this way the earlier defence system, based on a very small sample (the immediate family) and a personal experience before the hormonally induced changes to body and mind so powerful in adolescence, is the one that remains. Because it is no longer based on an accurate view of the self or of the outside world, you might say that it has become crippling. Thus it is that the young people we are dealing with have a very fixed view of themselves and the world they live in that is not all that difficult for us to see and to which they cling with enormous determination. All of this is unconscious and the conscious mind of the child finds explanations to fit which he or she hangs onto with the same enormous determination. However, if you think about an analogy with continuing to wear clothes that are now much too small, the consequence is that one suffers. This suffering makes the individual want to change. This part of the child is also unconscious (although both sides are represented in conscious thought) and forces an internal conflict. Our young clients tend to try to avoid internal conflict (and often feel that they do not have the resources to manage such a thing) so they deal with this in the way that is fundamental to the paranoid/schizoid position, by splitting. I am not going to take up time defining these terms because I think they are well known. Instead I want to give a typical example of what I have in mind.

The young person was a 15-year-old girl in a therapeutic community. She had a powerful presence in the young people's group and this was often shown in her contribution to the community and other therapy groups. Here she would give the impression that it was worth being at the place and working in groups in order to confront one's problems. Staff found that they would often look to her at difficult times to support them in their work. The education staff's views of this girl couldn't have been more different: they reported that she was sullen and would rarely settle to anything unless she wanted to do it; she would delight in winding up other young people to act out, although she rarely made the mistake of doing so herself. The teachers would rather not have her there at all, whereas the therapeutic staff often looked towards her as an unofficial therapist. I think this is not an unusual example and the point is that it was possible to work with this apparently 'Jekyll and Hyde' phenomenon because it was all happening in the one environment.

It may be sensible to take this opportunity to state briefly how I think such good/bad splitting should be dealt with. The people who are usually the ones to draw attention to such events are those put in the role of 'baddy', in this case the education staff. So often this news is greeted with genuine concern by the others, who move on to try to 'help' those in the baddy role to deal with being in that position. I have often heard staff in the 'goody' role becoming really quite confrontational with the baddies, saying things like, 'You simply have to be firmer' or 'Show her who is boss', and so on. Of course it is pretty obvious what motivates this: nobody wants to be in the position of the baddy so, if someone seems to have been elected to that position, there is an unconscious pressure in the staff group to leave them there. The problem here is that nobody notices who is really being attacked. If you ask yourself the question, 'which of them (goody or baddy) is able to remain flexible and to hold onto his or her independent thinking?', it will become immediately obvious that only the baddy retains such ability – the goody needs to keep everything very much the same so as to avoid slipping into the role of baddy. This fits with the image of being put on a pedestal: what happens to you when you try to take a step? In other words the important thing to understand is that the person actually under attack in a classic split is the one in the goody position. Understanding that it was the therapy that was being attacked was an important part of the treatment of this girl but was only possible because the place where she was expressing the other side of her conflict was part of the therapeutic establishment.

Large and small groups

In order to think about the uses of small and large groups, I want to consider them from the point of view of task and shared principles of work. Not only is this the simplest system for defining and understanding groups, but the same approach can be used with any method of work. In this way, it becomes possible to compare various approaches. There are a number of ways of thinking about the importance of the establishment of an explicit primary task and the shared principles of work; in terms of our basic assumption, that it is the inner world of the child that 'causes' his or her difficulties and that we are in the business, as Freud put it, of one unconscious communicating with another unconscious: 'It is a very remarkable thing that the unconscious of one human being can react upon that of another, without passing through the conscious.' (Freud 1915)

I believe that we need to set up systems that allow us to monitor how we are being affected by the work in this unconscious way. Since we cannot know our own unconscious directly (by definition), it means that we need to set up benchmarks that enable us to think about our own practice without it all feeling terribly personal and persecutory. Thus clarity of primary task enables us to ask ourselves, 'Is this on task?' and clarity of principles of work enables us to ask, 'Is my behaviour towards this child/colleague/manager in keeping with our agreed standards?' If the answer to either question is, 'No', we are in a position to think about what is leading to us behaving in a way that is outside our agreed task or procedure. Using this method, we can predict that the effect on the work of the young person's resistance to treatment, and also of the group's tendency to create a defensive state of mind to avoid anxiety, will be to try to pull us off task or to make us behave in ways that are inconsistent with best practice. Knowing that this is inevitable and not a sign of bad work, we can monitor these anomalies so that we might understand more of the defensive world of the child. (The refusal to think about our practice in this way will be indicative of the defensive world of the staff team or individual.) As I said earlier, the young people are also affected by projective identification and transference and groups seem to me to be the method of choice to help them to recognise this and to understand it. The point I'm making is that however motivated each individual may be to learn and grow in the group, the group itself *must* be constantly pulled off task or pulled into behaviour at variance with the work principles (or ethics) of the community. Once this is taken as axiomatic, it becomes possible to transform those experiences into information from which to learn.

One of the places where it is most common to see evidence of this activity is the 'community meeting', a meeting that ought to be at the core of all therapeutic community-like approaches. This is the meeting in which staff and young people come together in order to identify the significant issues going on in the 'mind' of the community at this moment. That seems like a simple enough task to remember and yet all staff in such settings will have had the experience of not being sure what the point of the community meeting might be. They become a place in which different strategies are suggested to 'make it work better', for example by creating a particular way of chairing the group or separating something called 'business' from 'therapy'. It seems to me that holding the task in mind and then asking the question, 'Are we on task?' enables a community to monitor the relevance of that task (as well as the unconscious defensive processes). After all, circumstances change and the need to pursue a particular task may diminish (in fact we ought to expect this if we really believe what we profess, that therapy can facilitate change).

It is important that the community recognises that there will be sub-tasks that must be addressed in order that the main aim is achieved. In an environment that uses groups as the main method of work, this means that there ought to be different groups set up to address these various sub-tasks. In each the role of the facilitator is quite simply to monitor task and principles so that, when these are transgressed, it is possible to stop and think what it means.

What I am suggesting in this chapter so far can be summarised as follows:

1. that groups have the potential to be extremely powerful methods of achieving tasks;

2. that groups have a natural tendency to avoid the task (in order to reduce anxiety);

3. therefore that facilitation is the art of monitoring the defensive tendencies of the group, so as to bring them to the group's consciousness and thus enable to group to get back on task;

4. that any community will have different sub-tasks to address in the cause of maximising the potential for change and growth;

5. therefore that the community will have needs for specific groups to attend to particular needs;

and

6. that these groups will work best when they are monitored not only to understand what is going on in terms of the therapeutic agenda but also to consider whether they are still relevant.

The business of decision-making around interventions is vital but also filled with potential difficulties. There is a question as to where decisions should be made and by whom, which I shall refer to later. There is also a need to avoid making decisions that are actually 'reactions' to something. For example, I remember an occasion when I was consulting to a day centre running on therapeutic community principles. It happened that the centre had been through a rather odd period during which there were no male workers and now the first man had joined the team. After a while he began to bring to the consultation meeting his anger with his team colleagues that they didn't take seriously his suggestion that there should be a 'men's group'. After all there was a 'women's group'.

The method of thinking about the overall (primary) task and how any intervention might fit in with this allowed the staff group to consider his suggestion without falling into personality problems. It became clear that there was no particular need being expressed by the male patients that would have been best addressed in an exclusively male group; however, there was an obvious preoccupation in the mind of the community with the sexual identity of the new staff member. In other words (and not surprisingly you might say) the fact that he was the only man made this worker the subject of all sorts of projections and transferences. It was as if he was seeking a refuge from this by creating an environment in which the very feature that marked him out as different (his gender) would be the single quality that united them all. The obvious decision seemed to be to find a way to address the whole community's preoccupation with the meaning of his arrival (and the best place to do it seemed to be the community meeting).

Formal and informal

Once you set up a system that holds groups as its central method of work, you can be pretty sure that there will be attempts to set up a challenge to the system using the same means. It is, therefore, very interesting to think about how informal groups arise and what they mean. I've just been referring to the way in which formal groups can easily be established so that they are an expression of a defensive dynamic; how much more so are informal groups likely to be a way to avoid the work? There isn't time in this chapter to explore the variations on this theme but it is important for the staff in the therapeutic community to pay attention to the meaning of informal groups in both client and staff populations.

Organisational dynamics

Once again I find myself saying that I don't want to re-present the work of books like *The Unconscious at Work* (Obholtzer and Roberts 1994). Instead I should like to refer to organisational dynamics as they occur in work with children and adolescents. I want to refer to a principle that I'm sure other writers in this book will have referred to, and that is that there is a difference between children and adults. The denial of this difference is the real source of the damage of sexual abuse, so it behoves us to be sure that we protect our young people from any version of such denial.

To begin at the beginning, one of the clichés of our professional world is that the staff teams in organisations tend to present the qualities of their client groups rather as owners are supposed to look like their pets. In the chapter up to now, I have made it clear that those very powerful unconscious processes known as transference and projective identification explain how a staff team may end up behaving like their clients, because those very clients project their own conflicts into the staff. It is also pretty obvious from my reference to valency that we are likely to be drawn into a particular speciality because it fits with our own valencies, i.e. our own vulnerabilities. It follows from this that staff will be filled with thoughts and feelings that belong to adolescence because of the projections and transferences, but that they will be particularly strongly affected by these projections because they have unfinished business to do with their own adolescence. I do not think I am saying anything controversial here. The problem arises when these processes are not noticed and the staff team find themselves stuck in an adolescent state of mind.

I think a good example of this is what often happens in youth and community work. These workers are usually quite young themselves; they have a rather superficial training that is based on activities and relationships but which doesn't spend any time thinking about what it means to form a 'professional relationship' with a young person. In my experience some youth and community workers tend to argue that what a delinquent or disturbed adolescent needs is a 'friend' to relate to and who can model a different life-style. This is the logic of the hatred of difference: the claim is that we are all the same here; children and adolescents should be given responsibility; it is patronising or elitist for staff to present as if they know better than the clients. My view of this is that it is a clear example of adults being filled up with the projections of the client group and then trying to produce a philosophy, after the fact, for why they present as if they and their clients are 'the same'. I want to declare here that I think that most of the reasons why adolescents in difficulty remain so is because there are no adults around who are either prepared or willing to set boundaries and limits. I know that it sounds wonderfully 'correct' (in the sense of politically) to let your 11-year-old decide which secondary school to go to but the plain facts are that, until you've had an education, you do not have the information to make a judgement about what constitutes a good one. Our 11-year-olds are not only uninformed (by definition), they are unable to imagine what their adult selves will value in 15 years' time because they haven't developed adult capacities yet. Instead they are much more likely to make this sort of decision on the basis of who is going to which school, or something of that sort. But the true failing of the parent who says, 'It's up to you...' is that, when the poor kid decides on a school and it is the wrong one, it is *his* fault.

The reason I'm making such a fuss about this is that I think that herein lies a significant difference between therapeutic communities for adults and those for children or adolescents. In the former, there is an active philosophy of shared responsibility for the community between staff and patients. In the latter, it is vitally important that the young people know that it is the adults who make the important decisions. In other words the shape of the therapeutic community for children or adolescents is hierarchical. Now, referring to the basic paradigm for therapy that I described at the start of this chapter, we can expect that the organisational systems for decision-making will be some of the arenas in which young people's inner worlds will act to create distortion. In order to maximise the chances of noticing the effect on the structure, it is important, as I said earlier, to make explicit the principles of the structure. Group relations theory has demonstrated a particular way of thinking about decision-making structures. In brief, you make your best decisions when you have the best level of information. Good decision-making requires clarity about who is the delegated decision-maker. Bringing both these together suggests that good decision-making occurs when the one making the decision is getting good feedback from those who will be most affected by the decision. Now these principles are essentially psychoanalytic. It is, therefore, one of the strengths of the therapeutic community that it can put young people into the decision-making arena (without abusing them by giving them inappropriate responsibilities). What I mean is that a decision about some activity will be best made when the member of staff with the authority to decide is in a group meeting listening to staff and children who are going to be most affected by the decision. Of course one of the pressures that comes to bear on this process is the attempt to subvert it by making it seem elitist or unfair that one person makes the decision. Staff can become quite caught up in the idea that the decision ought to be the result of a vote or some other democratic mechanism.

I do not mean to suggest by this that there are no areas in which the young people can make their own decisions. For a start it is obvious that they decide whether or not to stay at the community. However, there are more important ways to think about this. If the primary task is to enable the development of each young person, then it follows that, as each child moves towards true individualisation, he or she ought to be able to take on more responsibility for him- or herself. In this way the community, like the good-enough parent, needs to be able to encourage each young person to take responsibility but be able to intervene if this seems to be too much. The technique is about taking calculated risks but being able to take control when that is necessary.

A final thought: pressure on the organisation can come from above as well. We are all aware of the high levels of anxiety expressed by society about looking after children. On the one hand professionals are required to keep disturbed or dangerous adolescents off the streets; on the other, we are expected to stop interfering with families. This means that any community trying to work with young people will feel under pressure from society. Some of this pressure is, it seems to me, reasonable, for instance that we ought to be able to account for what we are doing, demonstrate the effectiveness of it and be open to scrutiny. Other pressure is utterly unreasonable. For example, the (perfectly reasonable) anxiety that children are at risk from paedophiles has led to a (completely unreasonable) reaction, which is to be suspicious of anyone who chooses to work with children or adolescents. This makes the staff feel frightened of touching their charges. But children need to be touched and it seems to me that the senior management of our institutions and organisations must stand up for their staff. I have argued elsewhere that the best hiding place for a paedophile is in an environment governed by rules but the way to 'out' one is to require that he accounts for his behaviour and attitudes in the work by reference to his emotional experiences in the workplace. Where staff groups are expected to work like this, the paedophile stands out because he can't do it. So we need to be aware of the pressures from outside in order to treat them seriously but with thought.

Conclusion

I have been arguing that groups have the potential to be extremely powerful methods of achieving therapeutic aims. I pointed out that there needs to be an awareness of the tendency to avoid work/anxiety and that this has direct implications for the business of organising the group base for the work as follows:

1. that groups have a natural tendency to avoid the task (in order to reduce anxiety);

2. therefore that facilitation is the art of monitoring the defensive tendencies of the group, so as to bring them to the group's consciousness and thus enable the group to get back on task;

3. that any community will have different sub-tasks to address in the cause of maximising the potential for change and growth;

4. therefore that the community will have needs for specific groups to attend to particular needs

and

5. that these groups will work best when they are monitored not only to understand what is going on in terms of the therapeutic agenda but also to consider whether they are still relevant.

The reason why groups are so powerful is that living in a group environment allows several things to be worked on in parallel, particularly the exploration of the individual child's unconscious, on the one hand, and the building up of his or her good functioning and self-esteem, on the other. These tasks can be achieved as long as the staff group is able to maintain a 'containing' environment. This is achieved by being clear about the primary task of the therapeutic community itself, the sub-tasks of the particular groups, and the basic shared principles of how to work. These form a series of benchmarks against which decisions can be made, information can be gathered and the relevance of the task can be monitored. I have made the point that the most useful information is conveyed unconsciously (by projective identification and transference) and that this means that good workers will be caught up with the child's inner world view. Bad practice is not getting caught up in the first place but remaining caught up. As a consequence I have argued that it is the institution's responsibility to provide opportunities to 'debrief' staff; that is, it is essential to the good practice of a therapeutic community that there are formal meetings in which staff can help each other to understand how they have been caught up in the work and to understand the meaning of the material. These meetings are actually for 'testing reality' and they work by providing a space for thinking.

CHAPTER 6

The Contribution of Systemic Thinking and Practice

Colette Richardson

This chapter is about how I use systemic ideas to inform my practice in an inpatient psychiatric unit for adolescents, one that uses therapeutic community practices and ideas. My primary role in this unit is that of systemic family therapist. However, in writing this chapter my aim is to show how the theory and practice underpinning systemic family therapy can be usefully applied to the general work of a therapeutic community. In other words I want to show how systemic thinking is a useful methodology for the systemic analysis of human interaction rather than seeing it solely as a clinical tool for family therapy.

I first became interested in systemic ideas when working in a therapeutic community in the early 1980s. As a staff team we struggled with how to manage our relationship with the families of the youngsters in our care. We had a strong desire to protect them from the influence of their families but we also realised that this orientation placed us in competition with their parents, alienating them and increasing their sense of failure and in so doing increasing our view of ourselves as the 'better parent'. After one particularly difficult weekend, when we tried unsuccessfully to intervene in the relationship between a mother and son, we expressed our frustration to a visiting colleague, who suggested that we should think about training as family therapists.

This marked my introduction to the world of systems theory. I found it an exciting and intellectually stimulating experience and one that eventually opened up new possibilities. At the level of the organisation the exposure to systems theory resulted in the development of family therapy as one of the core therapies available in that therapeutic community. It also, I believe, helped us to begin to see ourselves as 'a part' of a system rather than 'the system'. Therefore, we became more alert to the 'knock-on' effects of our behaviour on the family, the referrer, and other institutions involved with our residents.

We became less competitive and instead tried to build more co-operative relationships with the wider system. It also heralded a shift in our thinking away from locating the explanation for behaviour within individuals to locating the explanation for behaviour in the relationship between people. This of course led to us questioning the meaning of accepting one member of a family into our community. By doing so were we not cementing the view that the young person for whom the placement was being sought was 'the problem'? Questions like this led to much soul searching, and eventually led to us reconceptualising the function of the residential setting.

A caution

A central concept in systems theory is that everything is situated in a context. The ideas that I am about to share have been shaped by my experiences and position in specific settings and are therefore context dependent. I do not believe that they can or should be transported directly into all settings. The ideas are offered and the reader is invited to consider whether and how they might be of value for their particular setting. I am also writing from my perspective as a systemic therapist, whereas in fact systemic thinking can be applied throughout therapeutic community work by any and all members of the staff team, whether they are residential workers, managers, teachers or whatever: what is important is the way of thinking and intervening, rather than the particular disciplinary 'hat' being worn at the time!

Systems theory, what is it?

For readers unfamiliar with systems theory, it may be helpful at this point to say something about what systems theory is, explain briefly some of its core concepts and comment on how systems theory and psychotherapy became connected.

Systems theory embraces both general systems theory and cybernetics. It is a theory that offers a framework for understanding complex phenomena, i.e. phenomena that have the characteristic of being a whole with parts, while the whole is itself is a part of an even greater whole.

This body of ideas emerged in the years following the Second World War. Ludwig von Bertalanffy is considered the originator of general systems theory and Norbert Wiener that of cybernetics. Systems theory was adopted by a number of disciplines, e.g. engineering, biology, anthropology and organisational psychology. It provided these disciplines with a paradigm for dealing with complex problems. Prior to this, science had tended to evade the study of complex systems (Ashby 1956), and used reductionist methods of scientific enquiry. These methods fitted disciplines such as chemistry and physics very well but not the natural and social sciences. 'The programme of the systems movement might be described as the testing of the conjecture that these ideas will enable us to tackle the problem which the method of science finds so difficult, namely the problem of organised complexity' (Checkland 1981).

The impetus that pushed the different disciplines towards systems theory arose out of problem situations in which usual ways of thinking were proving inadequate. This was true also in the discipline of psychiatry. Several practitioners in the fields of psychiatry and psychotherapy in the UK and the US were frustrated with the outcome of some of their work with individuals. (Broderick and Schrader 1991). They began to look for other ways of approaching the problems they were encountering. They found it useful to involve other members of the family in the session, thereby engaging with the complexity of the patient's situation. However, they needed a theory that would underpin this and give direction for practice. It was at this point that they made contact with the world of systems ideas and drew on these ideas as a resource.

The shift from working with individual family members to working with the whole family system heralded a shift in conceptualising and explaining human problems and pathology. Essentially a systemic perspective posits that problems are best understood as being located between people, i.e. in the relationship rather than in the individual. Dallos and Draper express this shift as:

> The spotlight of problem explanation moved from the narrow beam that had focused on the individual to a broader one which illuminated the rest of the cast…this shift was a profound one and shook the psychiatric establishment to its roots, as well as much of psychology and other person-centred sciences. Problems and pathology which had hitherto been regarded as individual phenomena came to be viewed as resulting from interpersonal processes. (Dallos and Draper 2000)

The interaction between the therapeutic disciplines, general systems theory and cybernetics helped family therapists conceive of the family as a system. By this they meant that were seeing the family as a phenomenon which was a whole with parts, and with the parts connected to each other in such a way that a change in one element has a knock-on effect on the other parts or elements, (von Bertalanffy 1968) thereby highlighting interdependent and mutual influencing processes. Cybernetics introduced the idea of the family as a self-governing entity, meaning it could alter its own behaviour through feedback processes whereby the results of past performance are reinserted back into the system (Wiener 1950).

The above ideas, which include the concept of interdependence, mutual influence and feedback, constitute in my view some of the most central concepts underpinning all models of systemic therapy. There have of course been important developments since these original concepts were employed. These core concepts have been added to and extended in various ways, some of which I will be introducing later in this chapter as I describe the particular ideas that underpin my own way of working and which I refer to as a set of biases.

Systems theory and psychotherapy

Out of the cross-fertilisation of systems theory and psychotherapy emerged different schools of family therapy. Each school found different aspects of systems theory useful, e.g. The Structural School (Minuchin 1974) was attracted by systems theorists' ideas about the hierarchical structures of systems. The MRI Strategic School (Watzlawick, Weakland and Fisch 1974) was attracted by insights into communication patterns.

An important characteristic of these schools was that they were first-order cybernetic based, meaning that they viewed the family system as being external to the observer/therapist. Their approach was one of assessment of dysfunction, diagnosis and intervention. These models focused on observing how family members interacted with each other through their verbal and nonverbal behaviours, and then intervening in the patterns of interaction deemed dysfunctional or unhealthy.

The thoughts, feelings and ideas that the therapist brought with him or her to the encounter with the client and those that surfaced during the encounter were not considered relevant. These aspects only became seen as relevant when the field (under the influence of the Milan Associates) shifted to a second-order cybernetic position. When it first emerged the Milan model was first-order cybernetic in its approach and was very influenced by the Strategic model of Watzlawick. Later however, the Milan school developed a model of therapy based on second-order cybernetic principles (Boscolo *et al.* 1987), in which the therapist was seen to be part of the system (von Foerster 1981), i.e. a sub-system within the therapeutic system, and the family another sub-system. Both of these sub-systems, the family and the therapist, were now regarded as co-constructors of the therapeutic reality. The Milan Associates also introduced the important idea that it was how people perceived their problems that led to difficulties. The aim of therapy became helping family members to develop new meanings that allowed for new ways of behaving.

The contribution of the Milan Associates was complemented by the work of Anderson and Goolishian (1988; also Anderson, Goolishian and Winderman 1986) who switched the focus away from social systems and on to language and meaning systems. They coined the phrase, 'the problem has a system' rather than viewing the system as having a problem. Another important contribution was made by Tom Andersen who introduced the idea of reflecting teams (Andersen 1987; 1991).

It is obvious from the above that different family therapists use different concepts from systems theory. While I have been influenced by all the ideas my particular position is that of a second-order cybernetic approach. My particular orientation has been shaped by the Milan/Post Milan school (Andersen 1990; Boscolo *et al.* 1987; Selvini Palazzoli *et al.* 1978) with influences from the narrative school (Anderson 1997; Freedman and Combs 1996).

In the world of therapy the term 'systemic thinking' is often distinguished from the term 'systemic therapy'. The phrase 'systemic thinking' was introduced into the domain of family therapy by the Milan Associates. When the Associates taught their first formal course in family therapy many of their students who worked in public health settings returned to tell them that while they could not transport the model as learnt during their training they had been greatly influenced by the way of thinking which they had developed through attending the course (Cecchin and Pirotta 1988). Particularly they had learned how to disrupt their own 'stuck' ways of thinking which had enormous benefit in their work situations. One member of that early group went on to develop the model in relation to wider systems (Fruggeri *et al.* 1991). Similar important contributions were made in the UK by Campbell and Draper (1985).

A congruent style of writing

A comment on the style in which I have written this chapter may at this point be useful. I have tried to write in a style congruent with systemic thinking. Systemic thinking does not offer a body of ideas about how any system should be. The systemic practitioner tries therefore not to be prescriptive. He or she offers ideas that may trigger new thinking and acting for those in 'stuck' positions. What follows is not a prescription for working in a therapeutic community, but a story which the reader might find new, challenging of his or her assumptions, and one that might trigger the reader to new ideas and new practices of his or her own.

I am imagining the reader as an observer, and an enquirer about the ideas that underpin my practice. My intention is to present the systemic concepts that inform me as a set of stances or biases and to suggest practice guidelines that may help the reader interested in practising systemic thinking take the first steps.

I have deliberately chosen to use the word 'bias' in what follows. I am aware that in using this word I run the risk of being misconstrued. Being biased is normally understood as something very negative and certainly not something to be promoted. Traditionally knowledge has been seen to require the characteristics of objectivity and impartiality. Many today, particularly in the social sciences, challenge this view of knowledge (Cecchin, Lane and Ray 1994; Gergen 1999). These theorists believe that all theories have in-built biases, and claim that true impartiality and objectivity is not possible. They claim that all knowledge is 'perspectival'. For these reasons I use the term 'bias', meaning a preconceived preference. I want to convey the idea that the theories and models we use are not incontrovertible facts or truths but sets of ideas that we have agreed to call 'truths', and privilege over other 'truths'.

First bias: When people act they are normally trying to do something good

The origin of this bias lies in the early work of the Milan team. It is often referred to as 'positive' or 'logical' connotation (Jones 1993; Selvini Palazzoli *et al.* 1978). When working with families the Milan team would positively connote the symptomatic behaviour of the identified patient as being in the service of family survival. Their intention in designing this intervention was to make the 'crazy or difficult' behaviour meaningful and to take blame out of the situation. The Milan associates believed that an important part of the therapeutic process was the liberation of the identified patient from the negative frames within which they had been placed by family members and indeed by helping professionals. They also believed that when a person's behaviour was positively connoted, it was easier for that person to abandon such behaviour.

A related but slightly different concept is the idea of reframing (Watzlawick *et al.* 1974) whereby the meaning of behaviour is changed, e.g. a youngster who does not talk in group discussions could be re-framed as being a good listener.

In a recent community meeting one adolescent said that he was in a bad mood because another adolescent had been asking him questions about his past in one of the therapy groups and that she did this to upset him. The girl in question at the time was viewed quite negatively within the community. I asked the upset adolescent how he understood the behaviour of the other adolescent. In response he said that she was being insensitive and uncaring. I then asked the other adolescent whether that was her understanding of what she was doing or did she see it differently? She replied that she had asked the questions 'because things needed to come out'.

In listening to these two different accounts it would be easy to take sides and perhaps join one or other account if not ostensibly then perhaps privately. In the very effort to liberate one person from the negative frame it is easy to cast the other person into a negative frame. But if you take the position that both parties were trying to 'do something good' then the 'complaining' adolescent's behaviour needs also to be positively connoted. Both could be seen as trying to be good community members ('good' in the sense of being loyal to the traditions of the community), one by trying to help the other to talk about difficult things, the other by trying to teach a younger member that the way to do this was to ask questions in a more sensitive way.

This intervention had the effect of allowing the female adolescent to be construed more positively and to feel less blamed, and the male adolescent to feel that his point had been appreciated. The difficulty was shifted from the domain of personal culpability to the interaction of meanings.

Suggestions for practice

Remembering that there is a difference between intention and effect can be helpful because the effect of an action which has been experienced as negative does not mean that the original intention was negative. It is often worth asking people about what they hoped to achieve by their actions, and asking them questions that get them thinking about how they understand their own and each other's behaviour. Asking questions about difference or comparisons generates new information.

Second bias: The observer is in the observed

This is an idea influenced by the second-order cybernetic phase in the development of systemic therapy. Second-order cybernetics introduced into systemic therapy the idea that the therapist is part of the system observed and therefore that holding an objective view of the system is not possible.

The statement 'the observer is in the observed' refers to the fact that what we observe in each other is observed through the lens of our individual family, professional, religious and cultural beliefs (von Foerster 1981). In other words we perceive each other through the lens of our own stories. One of the effects of holding this bias is that it helps us not to assume that we can fully know another and to treat our perspectives on situations as partial truths or stories which in turn leaves space for other truths or perspectives to emerge. It should also help in examining the assumptions we make about each other and in holding ourselves accountable for our assumptions particularly in situations that we deem problematic.

A colleague asked me to help him think about a problem he was experiencing with the mother of one of the adolescents. He was particularly concerned because he was about to attend a meeting with the family and professional network. He stated the problem as one of feeling very angry and negative towards this woman and that, given how he was feeling, perhaps he should not attend the meeting.

I started the conversation by asking what had changed because I knew that this was not how he had always felt. The immediate context for understanding this change was the events of the previous weekend when the adolescent had been returned early to the unit by his mother saying that she could not cope with him and 'handing him over to the staff, dirty washing and all'. My colleague viewed this behaviour as very rejecting of the adolescent and disregarding of the boundaries of the unit, treating it as a 'baby-sitting service'. (The unit operates on the basis that adolescents will live with their families at weekends unless there is a psychiatric emergency.) After some discussion I suggested that an alternative view might be that this woman being a single parent was feeling very overwhelmed and was looking to the unit staff to be the other parent. In response my colleague said that he was also angry with her because she just arrived at the unit, presenting us with a 'fait accompli' and giving us no choice in the situation. I then suggested that given what we knew about her history, she was perhaps someone whose experience particularly with men was one of being given no choice and of experiencing herself as unable to exert any influence, hence her presenting us with a fait accompli.

The effect of this conversation on my colleague was that he was able to alter his view of this mother, seeing her as more vulnerable and in turn feeling less angry and negative towards her and more able to attend the meeting. In conversations such as this I normally try to offer ideas or interventions that help the person with 'the problem' see the issues in a new light which will then, I hope, open up alternative ways of acting.

Suggestions for practice

Getting another member of staff to brainstorm with you and generating alternative ways of viewing a situation can be helpful. In this sort of conversation your partner's job is to help introduce a different perspective, not to back you up.

When trying to generate alternative ways of viewing a situation, it is often useful to consider how the person's behaviour might be logical given their history.

Third bias: The only person you can change is yourself

This might seem like a strange bias to hold given that we spend most of our lives trying to help others to change. It is based on the principal of neutrality. Neutrality was one of the therapeutic stances introduced by the Milan team as part of their interviewing strategy with families. Their view was that we create resistance in others when we try too hard to change them and that paradoxically if you want to create change you have to sometimes stop being on the side of change.

It often happens that when working with the adolescents we can become over-zealous in our efforts to change them. This can result in a situation where the more you try to change them the more 'resistant' they become, and in turn the harder one tries, and so on. The example that comes to mind is of a 15-year-old girl whose treatment goals included the development of skills in sharing her thoughts. At a meeting she was encouraged by a staff member to give her own account of a conversation in which they had both participated and in which some new information about her difficulty in attending school had come to light. The girl hesitated and the staff member pressed her again and again to share her thoughts. I remember feeling a growing sense of frustration as I watched the escalation of tension between the adolescent and the staff member. Another staff member intervened and asked the adolescent to clarify whether her silence indicated that she did not want the community to know the new information or whether it was that she felt unable to speak on her own behalf. In response the adolescent said that it was because she felt unable to speak on her own behalf. She was then asked if she would like the staff member to share the new information with the community on her behalf and she agreed to this.

Systemic thinking involves watching the communication between people as it is happening and seeking to create meaning in relation to what is going on. The staff member who intervened was, in systemic language, an 'observer to an event'; she construed the situation as a 'stuck' situation and intervened to create change. With practice it should be possible to become an observer to one's own behaviour in an interaction and to step back and watch how one's own actions contribute to a situation and then alter or change behaviour as appropriate.

Suggestions for practice

It can be helpful to try to observe the feedback to your own actions, i.e. to watch what others do with what you do, and to note when what you do elicits more of the same in the other.

Fourth bias: When working with one part of a system hold the other parts in mind

Systemic theory teaches that a system is a set of interconnecting parts and that a change in one part will have an effect on the other parts. In clinical work with families this principle is easier to hold in mind because you can see it operating in the room. It is a much harder principle to keep hold of when working in settings where the intensity of the work with the adolescent group can result in a strong 'boundary' being created around the institution and connections with the group's wider systems are not kept in mind.

One evening a colleague invited me into a conversation she was having with an adolescent who was very upset and crying. When I asked what the upset was about my colleague said that the adolescent was crying because her mother had been nasty to her. My impression from the conversation was that my colleague was in agreement with the adolescent. I felt uncomfortable with the situation because I was concerned that taking sides with the adolescent was going to make the relationship between the unit and the family very difficult, and while at that moment our concern was rightly with the adolescent we also had to act in a way that did not place blame on the parent. Further, from a systemic perspective I would have understood the adolescent's description of events as just one among various possible tellings of the story or 'punctuations of events'.

To say that the adolescent was crying because her mother was nasty to her is to infer that her mother caused her to cry and thus to invite blame into the situation. In systemic theory this would be called a linear description.

Systemic theory prefers a circular description of events because individual acts then become both cause and effect. The task then is not to search for the cause of the problem but to become curious about why each person acted as he or she did and to trigger curiosity about their own and each other's behaviour.

To return to the story, I asked some questions structured in a particular way which had the effect of opening up new thinking. When the mother's actions towards her daughter were seen in a new context, both the adolescent and the staff member were able to have a different view, one that accepted the feelings of upset of the daughter as still real but re-contextualised in a way that did not alienate the mother.

Suggestions for practice

When listening to a description of an event, e.g. 'my mother was nasty to me', it can be helpful to become curious about the meaning of this, rather than simply assuming that you 'know' what it means. The answers to your curious questions may lead to new information which may in turn open up new meanings and new options for action.

It is also helpful to widen the frame when trying to make sense of behaviour, and to think about the connections which there may be with other events.

It can also be effective to ask questions which invite circular description as distinct from linear description, e.g. a linear question would be, 'why was your mother nasty to you?', whereas a question that invited circular description would be, 'at what stage in the conversation with your Mum did you begin to think that she was being nasty to you?'

This fourth bias also has relevance for the therapeutic community or residential unit as a whole, particularly as change is constantly occurring and decisions are being made in different parts of the system. Despite the best of intentions, decisions will often be made in one part of the system without attention to the knock-on effects for the other parts. Organisations therefore need mechanisms for keeping the systemic view, e.g. regular meetings where people can share the effects of the different activities and decisions with each other. At times of very significant changes this is probably best done by the use of an external facilitator who can enable that kind of conversation. For these mechanisms to work they need to be conducted according to systemic principles whether by the community or by the external facilitator.

Fifth bias: Be irreverent

By the time that most of the adolescents reach residential services they and their families have had a long career in acting out of 'problem-saturated' stories. In other words their difficulties are fairly entrenched. Consequently one has to be on the alert for the smallest steps towards change.

At a recent community meeting a 16-year-old boy was giving an account of his weekend, in the midst of which he mentioned in a low-key way that he had made contact with one of his friends on the Internet. In the context of his history of depression and social withdrawal this was a really important development. It was the first time since his admission three months previously that he had made any efforts to re-connect with his friends. In fact just a week prior to this he had stated that he was not yet ready to make any contact with his friends. During the meeting I commented on how well he had done and asked him how this change had come about and what was the next step. In his reply he said that the next step would be to phone his friend. Shortly after this the same adolescent was asked to put away something he was fiddling with. He refused, was given several opportunities to comply and eventually was asked to leave the meeting.

What was striking for me was the two different images of this young person. On the one hand a story of change and new behaviours, and on the other hand a return to old behaviours.

In reflecting on these events one task from a systemic perspective is to think about how these two pictures fit together, and also to notice one's own part in the process.

Starting with my own behaviour, I noticed that I took opportunity to comment and build on something new that had happened. In this way I defined the behaviour as one of change and development. I did not check with the adolescent his understanding of his own behaviour but imposed my own definition of the situation. This was followed by the adolescent refusing to comply with the rules of the meeting. One way of understanding this is that the adolescent might have chosen to disagree with my imposition of meaning by becoming noncompliant and breaking the rules of the meeting and eventually having himself excluded.

What is interesting is that I was acting out of a strong theoretical position, that change should be noticed, encouraged and amplified, but in this case it might either be that the theory did not hold good, or that I interpreted it wrongly at that particular moment. It is important for the systemic practitioner to be irreverent and ask questions in respect of all theories – especially of his or her own most cherished systemic theories! (Cecchin, Lane and Ray 1992).

Suggestions for practice

A curious enquiry as to the meaning which an event or action has for the person involved often produces new and helpful information. On the broader point about irreverence and theory, it can be helpful to make a list of your favourite assumptions about what helps to create therapeutic change – and then to consider how willing you would be to drop or change this assumption if it did not seem to be producing helpful results.

Sixth bias: Every perspective has a value

An important development in the world of family therapy has been the use of teams in working with families. The use of teams in the Milan school initially began as a research tool and later was developed as therapeutic technique. The team consists of the therapist who works directly with the family and two or three colleagues who observe from behind a screen. Part of the observing team's task is to contribute different perspectives on the situation. While valuing and promoting different perspectives it is also important not to allow the situation to become like a 'tower of Babel'. Each member of the team is encouraged to be influenced by the views of the other, thus recognising that their observations and understandings are only partial 'truths'. Family therapists working in this way take as their starting position the idea that everyone's perspective has a value. This helps to eliminate competition and rivalry for whose idea is the better one, and creates a setting for the development of a 'team mind'/collaborative conversation.

On one occasion one of the adolescents' parents requested time out from the programme for their daughter. In discussion with the family the staff on duty came to the opinion that this was not the best course of action. The following week a second request was made by the same adolescent's parents but for a different reason and this time the staff involved agreed to the request.

In working situations, particularly residential situations, this type of scenario leads to expressions of anger, feelings of being undermined, appeals to those in a leadership role to take sides and often an escalation of frustration and annoyance.

Using the systemic principle that every perspective has a value I intervened at a staff meeting to help elicit the 'logic' of the two positions. In the conversation that ensued those who had refused the first request for time out explained that they had done so because they believed that the parents of the adolescent in managing their daughter's behaviour needed to provide clearer and firmer boundaries, and perceived the parents as being 'too soft'. The other group said that what underpinned their actions was the idea that the adolescent was worried about spending time at home with just her father and brothers and felt safer with her mother (the second request for time out had been to allow the adolescent to accompany her mother on a week's visit to her grandmother's house, and if the team had refused the request for time out, the adolescent would have had to spend the weekend at home with her father and brothers in order to be able to return to the unit on Sunday evening).

As this exploration was pursued, it was noticeable that there was a decrease in annoyance and frustration as people became curious about each other's positions and began to appreciate that both groups had got in touch with and triggered valuable information about the family and each group's view was more 'nuanced' than previously.

Suggestions for practice

Rather than asking questions which might be experienced as veiled challenges, it can be helpful to ask questions from a position of genuine curiosity, seeking to understand the others' beliefs and perspective.

It is also worth aiming to speak from a position of uncertainty rather than authoritative knowing, e.g. by beginning a comment with words such as, 'I am not sure' or 'maybe' or 'another view is'. The aim here is to try not to rule out other views but to develop a 'both/and' orientation.

Another way of helping teams develop the skill of 'collaborative conversation' is the use of reflecting teams (Andersen 1987). In this way of working those attending the meeting would be divided into two groups. Group A begins the discussion about a problem event while group B listens. Then group B reflects on the discussion they have been listening to. The only rules are that the order of speaking is sequential; this is often referred to as a sequential conversation. (Campbell, Draper and Huffington 1988). Each person in turn builds on what the previous speaker has said, while adding ideas of their own.

This is a useful way to interrupt unhelpful group processes where one or two people always do the talking or where there is a lot of competition for 'air time'. It ensures that everyone's voice is heard.

Seventh bias: Language is not neutral

I take the view that when we talk we are trying 'to do' something. I think of language as active, as creating a reality, not just mirroring it (Gergen 1999). When we talk we choose to describe things or people in certain ways, e.g. 'she was disruptive'. These descriptions are not the only way to describe a situation, there are others. An important question for me therefore is why talk in this way, what reality is being fashioned, what kind of identity is being created, who benefits from each description? Once the worker moves away from the belief that she/he is reporting on how things are, she/he is involved in taking responsibility for how the situation is being constructed and the implications of the construction for those involved in the story.

I think these ideas are particularly relevant for the ritual of 'handovers' in residential settings. When information about the group, or a family or an individual is handed over it is not an act of handing over impartial facts, but a story which defines all those involved in particular ways. How the story is constructed can have considerable implications for the staff coming on duty, for those going off, and for the 'characters' in the story.

An interesting contribution from a systemic perspective on the subject of handing over has been made by Barry Mason (Mason 1989). Mason introduces a way of doing handovers which allows staff to see the process from a wider perspective and gather information in a new way. The focus is on the meaning of behaviour rather than on factual information and also on how staff may be contributing to the issues needing to be addressed. He also proposes that it is more helpful if the staff coming on duty take charge of the handover rather than the staff going off duty, which is the more usual format.

Final words

The seven biases above constitute some important ideas that underpin the work of a systemic practitioner. They do not represent a complete account of systemic ideas, but are representative of those that I have found most productive in my work.

As I stated in the introduction, systemic thinking is not prescriptive in orientation. It does not provide a body of ideas about how any system should be, rather it provides a frame for thinking about how to create change. It assumes that everyone has this ability, but that from time to time people become 'stuck'. A central task for the systemic practitioner is to help people (both self and others) to reposition themselves so that they can perceive things from a different perspective and consequently choose to act differently. It is also worth reiterating the point which I made earlier in the chapter, that when I refer to a 'systemic practitioner' I mean not just someone with that official title, but any member of the team working from within a system perspective – this could be a residential worker, a manager, a teacher or a support worker.

In conclusion, my view is that systemic thinking is of value within therapeutic communities because it makes available a frame for analysing the interactions of the members of the community and provides a set of powerful tools for creating change. It is non-pathologising. It encourages self-reflexivity, facilitating staff members to be aware of their biases. It assists staff to place themselves in the picture and consider how their actions are contributing to the situation or reality being created. It also pays attention to the power differentials between the members.

Finally I would suggest that a work environment underpinned by systems thinking and practice creates a respectful, collaborative environment, which reduces unnecessary stress on staff and adolescents and promotes change.

Part II

Practice

Introduction

'Where's the therapy?'

The director of a therapeutic community for young people reported that, towards the end of an inspection visit, the inspector said that she was very impressed with the work of the place. She felt that she had seen all that she needed to see, having observed young people and staff together in the school rooms and the living areas, as well as in the outside play areas, but that what she still wanted to know was 'Where's the therapy?'

This part of the book is intended to answer that question, by showing how everyday living situations and the network of relationships between young people and staff can be converted into experiences which will have profound and lasting therapeutic value for children. Chapter 7 focuses on the opportunities for helpful communication which arise out of everyday incidents and exchanges, while Chapter 8 concentrates on the symbolic importance of the most basic human experiences such as food, bedtimes, play and so on. These two chapters, then, will argue that it is the way in which the everyday is thought about, understood, organised and mediated by the staff that can make it of therapeutic value to young people.

Having said this, however, there still remains the question of the focus and individual detail of the work. It is not enough to just provide a 'therapeutic environment': there has to be something much more focused and engaged about the work with any individual young person. Chapter 9 describes in detail the ways in which the individual relationship between a young person and an adult can contribute to the young person's growth, healing and development.

Chapter 10 shows how this work is planned and provided, looking at the ways in which individual and group sessions for young people complement the more general experience of the therapeutic environment. There is considerable variety in the ways in which such planned work is provided, as will be seen from the examples offered. Chapter 11 concentrates on the role of education, which is of central importance to the development and progress of children and young people; this chapter shows how one long-established community reviewed and improved its educational provision over a number of years.

However, no amount of therapeutic input for the child can change his or her circumstances unless a parallel effort is invested in working with the child's family, towards either the child's eventual reunion with them or in some cases their longer-term separation from them. Chapter 12 concentrates on the work with the families of the young people. This is an area in which the work of many therapeutic communities has developed considerably in recent years, and this chapter demonstrates the range of possibilities here, including work with substitute families as well as with children's families of origin.

All of this therapeutic input, whether planned and structured or more en-vironmental and 'opportunity-led', needs to be organised and managed, otherwise it may not all pull in the same direction. Part III of the book will pick up this theme in its focus on 'management and development'.

CHAPTER 7

Using Everyday Life: Opportunity Led Work

Adrian Ward

Introduction

A central theme in this book is that the therapeutic community approach is one which is holistic or systemic, in that it entails working at many different but interconnected levels towards achieving an overall therapeutic task. This means, among other things, that the therapeutic work with young people is not confined just to the 'therapeutic hour' of planned individual sessions, nor to the equivalent in groupwork, family work or community meetings, or in classroom work. The therapeutic work is also potentially ongoing in all the other times and contexts in which the young person is involved, and especially in the course of everyday life and the social and other interactions which this entails. Thus there may be incidents or moments in everyday interactions which affect the young person in unexpected ways, or which open up the possibility of communication and insight, perhaps triggering memories of earlier events and feelings, or maybe giving some hint of underlying anxieties or fears about current or future events in their lives. It is in these moments, and with the sometimes fleeting feelings which they may engender, that some of the most useful work can be done. This is the work which I have called Opportunity Led Work (Ward 1995; 1996), partly to distinguish it from the more planned or scheduled activities, but partly also to draw attention to the opportunities for communication which this mode of working may offer.

What is critical in this work is that the staff are able to spot and use the opportunities for communication which arise out of daily interactions. The approach outlined below aims to analyse this moment-by-moment decision-making and responsiveness on the part of the worker, to try to identify what it is that they are having to do here. The very business of analysing such fleeting and subtle interactions, of course, may seem quite paradoxical to the reader, since it involves us in putting into slow motion or even 'freeze-framing' a process which, when it works well, needs to appear seamless and natural. My hope, however, is that by looking very carefully at how the handling of such moments unfolds, we can identify and understand some of the thinking processes involved, without at the same time suggesting a mechanistic or 'programmed' approach.

As a way into thinking about the skills required, let us consider the following incidents, which all occurred in residential treatment settings:

> An adolescent boy, Paul, comes out of an office where he has been talking with his mother and social worker, saying 'Right, that's it, I'm finished with the lot of them!' He goes and sits in the TV room and begins tearing pages out of a notebook which has his name on the front.

> Two 12-year-old boys, Mick and Jai, are listening to each other's music collections, when suddenly one accuses the other of breaking the cover of one of his CDs, and hurls a racist insult at him, then turns to the worker for back-up.

> A 14-year-old girl, Becky, returns much later than expected from an evening out with her friends, and slumps down on the kitchen floor swearing about one of the other girls she has been out with.

In each of these situations the residential worker has a number of possible courses of action, depending (among other factors) on what she or he thinks will work, and on what she or he judges will fit with the needs of the young person. In each instance she or he might wish to open up communication with the young person, or to promote communication between them and others, or equally want to avoid opening up communication if the time is not right. He or she might decide to take some other course of action such as contacting a key colleague, or sitting quietly next to the young person in question, or even just ostensibly 'doing nothing' and waiting for the young person to make the next move. The aim of this chapter is to draw specific attention to the ways in which he or she might arrive at these decisions. For an experienced worker, the range of options is almost infinite, and we cannot spell out here what they all may be, but what we can do is to focus on what he or she may need to be thinking about in making this sort of decision.

The emphasis in the approach outlined here is based on a primary distinction between reacting and responding. By 'reacting' I mean a hasty and un-thought-out way of dealing with situations, whereas by 'responding' I mean dealing with situations on the basis of a well thought through judgement. In what follows I will describe a 'process' model of thinking about how to plan an appropriate response to the sorts of situation outlined above. This model has been written up in more detail elsewhere, and it is based on earlier models described by Redl (1966), Keenan (1991) and others. I am not arguing that it will always be possible in the heat of everyday practice consciously to work through the whole range of items listed here – that would be tedious and impractical; what I am saying is that these are the sorts of issue which need to be thought about if the best outcomes are to be achieved.

Opportunity led work: The process

I have divided up the process of opportunity led work into four main stages: observation and assessment, decision-making, taking action and closure. This terminology may appear rather too formal for this sort of work, and it might seem preferable to talk about 'weighing up the situation', for example, rather than 'observation and assessment'. My intention, however, is to show that the skills involved do relate to the skills used in other forms of practice (the skills of assessment, for instance), except that in this context things happen rapidly and often without much notice. In the heat of handling an actual incident, of course, these four stages may also appear to merge into each other, and in some situations there may be a whole string of decisions which lead from one to the next, with each decision or action either closing down or opening up further options.

Observation and assessment

The first stage of the process I have called 'observation and assessment'. While it may be hard in practice to separate observation from assessment, it is very important to start from an emphasis on observation – first of the detail of the incident and second of its context.

OBSERVING THE DETAIL

What will strike the worker first is the immediate detail of the incident. He or she will be asking him- or herself straightforward questions such as:

- What is happening?
- Who is involved?
- What is likely to happen next and how should I respond?

These simple questions may open up many areas. Some of the observation may need to be of events which appear so minor as to be almost imperceptible, and their detection as significant details may depend largely on the workers' sensitivity and intuition.

Meanwhile, he or she will soon need to expand his or her horizons to think about other factors which may be contributing to the incident, for example:

- Is this an isolated incident or does it connect with other events?

- What are the current concerns and needs of the individual(s) involved, and how may these be influencing events?

In weighing up this information the worker will be drawing upon his or her professional knowledge about children's emotional needs, about their levels of intellectual understanding, and about other developmental issues. He or she will, I hope, be in a position to draw upon an extensive knowledge of the child and his or her circumstances, as well as on his or her own knowledge of the other children. The worker needs to know what may have happened in the past and what may be about to happen – especially in terms of significant developments outside. Thus he or she will be wondering:

- Why this person or group? Does the incident really 'belong' with this individual or group, or are others involved in the background?

- Why now? Has this sort of thing happened before at this time of day/week/month/year?

The worker is already starting to move well beyond the immediate detail into reflecting on the context of the incident, and even in this preliminary assessment he or she is also likely to be weighing up a possible response, by asking him- or herself:

- What is my instinctive response and is there a good reason to override this?

- In what sense does this event represent a challenge, and in what sense an opportunity?

ASSESSING THE CONTEXT

It is not enough just to think about the detail, however. To make a proper assessment of the situation, the worker also has to think about its context, including the atmosphere of the unit, the network of relationships, and key issues such as those of power, prejudice and dependency.

Atmosphere refers to the emotional climate of the place, and to the 'micro-climates' which develop in different parts of the building with different groups. In order to 'read' the atmosphere, the worker will need to be aware of the concerns and emotions of individuals and groups, the quality of communication between them, and so on. In most cases, the atmosphere does not happen suddenly, it evolves and develops continually as people come and go, and as time and events bring changing concerns and feelings. A simple incident occurring when the atmosphere is calm and relaxed may feel quite different from a similar incident occurring in an emotionally charged atmosphere, so the worker needs to know how to distinguish between the meaning of the incident itself and the effects of the atmosphere in which it has arisen.

The network of relationships: In assessing any incident, a worker must always be aware of its implications for the whole group; this matters even if the incident itself only involves two people, because they are each part of a much wider network of people, first within the unit itself, and second beyond the walls of the unit. Some of these connections will operate at a clear and conscious level, while others may operate much more indirectly, and may be much harder to detect.

Power, prejudice and dependency: Finally, assessing the situation will also involve taking account of the issues of power, prejudice and dependency which permeate every group care setting. For example, there may have been undercurrents of bullying or racism in the events being assessed, either within the group of children or within the staff, or perhaps involving outsiders such as parents, friends or neighbours – who may be influential even though not physically present at the time of the incident itself. Thus the 'simple' incident of a racist taunt in the case of Mick and Jai may turn out to be connected with a broader pattern of racist abuse among the young people or even of latent racism in the staff team.

As well as weighing up these specific elements in the context, however, the worker must also take into account the broader implications of his or her assessment, and the extent to which his or her chosen response will fit within the accepted practice within the unit. The ethos of the therapeutic community will sometimes give more scope for individualised responses than other types of setting, which may have more tightly prescribed policies and procedures for 'dealing with incidents'.

So, for example, the response that the staff member gives to Becky when she comes in late and angry might be handled very differently in a therapeutic community as compared to a less therapeutically oriented place. In the latter, the predictable response from the staff might be to impose a penalty on Becky for the 'offence' of breaking the curfew, and this might be justified on the grounds that 'they've got to learn to obey the rules'. A therapeutic community approach might allow for a more flexible response, in which the worker might decide to use the opportunity for communication first, and deal with the transgression at a later stage. This is not about permissiveness (though the worker would have to be aware of the risk of collusion), but about promoting every opportunity for young people to learn from experience as the experience itself unfolds. Both responses aim to promote learning, but the therapeutic community one is based on what might be seen as a more dynamic awareness of the emotional and psychological processes involved in such learning. The greater use of an 'opportunity led' approach should not therefore be seen as somehow 'looser' or less disciplined, since the worker's decision must certainly take into account the risk of being seen to collude with unacceptable behaviour or with the infringement of important boundaries.

Decision-making

Observing and assessing are not the same thing as making a decision about what to do, but they do provide the evidence on which that decision will be made. Making the decision itself is complicated, even though it may have to be made in an instant. The emphasis in what follows will be on how the decision will be made, and I will focus especially on the priorities and aims involved.

PRIORITIES

Being clear about priorities may involve three main considerations: urgency, feasibility, and ethics.

- First what is most *urgent*: the worker's overriding priority must clearly be the safety and well-being of all those present; in this respect he or she may need to operate on the basis of a 'hierarchy of needs', putting safety and survival needs first, followed by other sorts of needs. This also involves judging what must/can be done now and what can wait or would be better done later, elsewhere or by someone else.

- Second, the worker must decide what is *feasible* – in terms of the available resources of time, space and personnel, but also in terms of his or her own abilities, confidence and energy-level, and in terms of the quality of his or her relationship with the individual and with the others involved. This decision will lead him or her into the detailed consideration of tactics and methods, some of which are outlined below.

- Third, he or she must consider the *ethics* of the situation, including the legal requirements and constraints upon him or her. This will involve being aware of the rights and needs both of the young people (and their families) and of the staff, as well as considering issues such as privacy and confidentiality.

AIMS

It may be useful for the worker to think in terms of what *sort* of results he or she wants her intervention to achieve (e.g. calming a troubled individual in the case of 'Paul' above, or achieving contact with a depressed and isolated group member in the case of 'Becky'), and second, to think about *how* he or she proposes to achieve that result (e.g. by making a direct verbal appeal to the individual, or by seeking to influence another group member to reach out to the person in question). The worker will therefore need to think in terms of task, timescales, and tactics:

- *Task*: How will his or her proposed action connect with the agreed task with this particular young person or group, and with the task of the unit as a whole? Is he or she clear that his or her own perception of the current task accords with others' understanding, and as to how the short-term tasks of the day connect with the longer-term task of the unit as a whole?

- *Timescales*: What does he or she want to have achieved in the next two minutes, what by the end of the day and what by the end of that person's stay in the unit? For each of these, the intervention should be based upon his or her judgement about what is happening and why, and on a hypothesis as to what difference these actions will make.

- *Tactics*: In relation to each combination of task, timescale and priority, there will be a range of possible tactics open to the worker in planning a response, and it is this range which we will be considering in the next section. One of my assumptions in mapping out this framework has been that the worker should always assume that he or she has a *choice* as to what to do or say, even though it may not always feel like this. Indeed, the mark of an experienced practitioner is that, rather than being driven to react unthinkingly to situations, he or she is able, upon reflection, to select an appropriate response from his or her repertoire to any given situation. This does not mean, of course that the worker will not sometimes take calculated risks or trust to intuition where he or she is uncertain, but that even in these scenarios he or she will be making a conscious choice as to how to respond – and of course, the decision-making may not stop at this point, as the practitioner may have to make many subsequent decisions as the situation unfolds.

Lest the impression be created that this is all just a matter of picking out a suitable rational response from a bag of ready-made interventions, I want to emphasise again here that we all learn as we go along, and especially as we review our actions and discover our mistakes along the way. Our first action very often involves a strong element of 'reaction' – and in some situations this may indeed be appropriate. Thus, in dealing with the sudden conflict between Mick and Jai, we might simply and rightly give Mick a 'telling-off' for his racist insult. It might only be later that we discover the history and meaning of the conflict between the boys, and learn that there has perhaps been a continuing pattern of mutual provocation and attack (and even that this pattern may be 'fed' by quite external factors elsewhere within or even beyond the unit). In due course, we might then find that we need to return to the incident with them and seek to promote some recognition and understanding of their recurring conflict, to help them prevent its further recurrence. This does not mean that our first response was wrong, but that it was not sufficient in itself to remedy the situation.

Another important area to acknowledge here is that, as we have seen elsewhere in the book, the therapeutic community working method seeks to take account of unconscious as well as conscious elements in communication and behaviour. This involves the development of a way of thinking about and understanding the feelings which may be underlying a situation. In the case of 'Becky', swearing about her friends, her anger may of course relate directly to an immediate incident, but it might also stem from other, perhaps less conscious, feelings from the past which turn out to have been triggered by some aspect of the current conflict. Equally, as we saw in the discussion on systems thinking in Chapter 6, Becky's expression of anger might relate to an unconscious need to draw an adult into her own way of relating to the world, to join her in what might be a quite unhealthy and 'persecuted' frame of mind – in which case it might be more helpful for the adult to maintain some separateness until things become clearer. 'Cheering up the poor victim' is a favourite trap for new therapeutic community workers, who may then find themselves stuck in a collusive relationship with the young person. This aspect of opportunity led work suggests the need for individuals and teams to reflect together on the ways they have handled certain situations, so that they can learn from and support each other in developing more productive ways of handling dilemmas such as these.

Action

We come now to the 'action' phase of this process, in which we shall consider some of the specific types of response from which the worker may select. As we have already seen, the range of potential responses is almost infinite, so for the sake of mapping out this framework I shall concentrate on types of intervention rather than listing each possible action or formulation of words. One broad distinction to be made is between those interventions with a short-term or 'behavioural' aim and those with a longer-term focus on the child's or group's needs.

SHORT-TERM/BEHAVIOURAL/'FIRST AID' INTERVENTIONS

I shall deal with these first, because it is safer to assume that most everyday incidents require an everyday response, rather than always leading into deep and meaningful communication. In many situations, what is appropriate is to 'keep the show on the road' by means of a brief response which acknowledges the situation but which also allows people to continue with their plans. The goals of this kind of intervention are likely to include maintaining or restoring a sense of order and calm, achieving control, establishing and maintaining communication, etc. The worker will aim to stay positive as far as possible, perhaps offering validation and support for even minimal co-operation at first; and praise/thanks for sustained co-operation.

Some of these short-term interventions will focus on an individual and some on the group, while other options may include ignoring the incident and focusing energy elsewhere, or indicating an intention to deal with the matter later. These short-term responses might be summarised as variations on the theme of 'managing the situation', rather than seeking to open up communication (although communication will still be the means towards the end). Examples will include:

- Managing individuals through a one-to-one focus, e.g. acknowledging the situation, and either requesting conformity to a rule, or offering brief support to an individual.

- Managing the group through focusing on a key individual, e.g. drawing explicit attention to the way in which an individual may have been discriminated against by other group members.

- Other tactics for managing conflict: where the situation to be managed is one of conflict, there may be other tactics to bear in mind, including: offering people alternatives where possible; defusing the tension in the situation; and allowing people to climb down from conflict, e.g. making a brief tactical retreat or taking a pause for reflection.

The above ideas are only a small selection from the possible range, and for other suggestions see Fahlberg (1990), Redl (1966), Redl and Wineman (1957), Trieschman (1969) and Ward (1996).

LONGER-TERM/THERAPEUTIC INTERVENTIONS

While many incidents just need the sort of short-term handling outlined above, there are many others in which something more is required. Here the appropriate response may be to take up the opportunities for communication which the situation offers, and to use the ensuing communication with the young people to promote insight, learning or other positive change for individuals and/or for the group. This is skilled and intricate work, which we can only summarise here. One main distinction to be made within the possible responses is in terms of whether to concentrate on an individual or group focus, and whichever focus is selected certain key questions will arise.

An individual approach may be preferable where there is only one child apparently involved, or where it is primarily an individual concern for this child which has been raised. Even where several individuals are involved, it may still be preferable tactically to focus initially on one key individual, or to deal with each individual's concerns first, before progressing to group discussion or bringing in outsiders or external issues. If the individual mode does seem preferable, the questions which will arise will include: should the discussion be held right now, immediately afterwards, or perhaps at a later time? Should the discussion be held right here on the spot, close by, or somewhere well away from the group? In the case of Paul tearing up his notebook, for example, it may be urgent to get beside him and enable him to reflect on his conflict with his mother, but this may be best achieved away from the public arena of the TV room. The worker will also need to ask him- or herself whether he or she is the right person to be pursuing this discussion with the child, or whether he should be passed on to his keyworker – or in the case of

Paul, whether he should be encouraged to return to the meeting which he has just left.

The actual techniques which may be used in such a discussion with a child would require a chapter in their own right. For the sake of an example, two of the main techniques are:

- *Reflecting back*: helping the child to piece together the sequence of events in an incident (e.g. identifying and recalling significant details), and thereby promoting the child's ability to explain and predict his or her own and others' behaviour and feelings, and the child's understanding of consequences;

- *Making links*: helping the child to explore the possible connections between this incident and other events, such as issues from his or her own family life/earlier problems/current concerns.

Similar questions will arise in relation to decisions about a group-based response to an incident, and the main question will be whether it will be better to talk with the whole group or a sub-group rather than 'picking off' key individuals from a group incident. If there is to be a group-based response, should this be in the shape of an immediate informal group discussion among those involved; should the matter be brought to the next planned meeting, e.g. house/community meeting; or should an 'extra meeting' of the large group be called at once? The timing and location of a group meeting may depend on the degree of seriousness of the incident and on the judgement as to whether it is better to interrupt daily life for an extra meeting or to contain the feelings and issues until the next scheduled meeting. There will also be a question of feasibility, in terms of the availability of other group members and of suitable space. The worker will need to remember the 'systems' principle that in a group care unit, everyone is a member of a large group, and they will be affected whether we plan for this or not, so it is often better to involve the whole group even if only a sub-group appears to have been involved in the original incident (Ward 1993). There will nevertheless also be an ethical question: in what sense does the communication really 'belong' with the rest of the group, or in what sense may it be confidential?

Again the range of groupwork techniques is large and readers should turn to other sources for the full range. Here I will simply highlight some key functions of therapeutic groupwork in this context.

These include the following:

- providing 'containment' for troubled individuals and groups, by helping them to recognise and think about their anxieties, fears or other difficult feelings

- providing a forum in which issues of personal and social power within the group may be safely raised and learned from, rather than being re-enacted in destructive ways, e.g. racist comments, bullying

- enabling young people to understand themselves and each other by talking about their family situations and thinking about how such factors may be affecting their state of mind and their current behaviour.

Sustaining the intervention

The discussion so far might appear to imply that opportunity led work involves a single decision or set of decisions, after which the situation either closes quickly or evolves along a predictable path of interactions. In reality, of course, nothing could be further from the truth: while some events do require only the simplest of responses, many others require a much more complex and evolving sequence of interactions, with the worker needing to re-assess and re-evaluate at regular intervals. For example, an initial short-term response may have to give way rapidly to something quite different as the situation unfolds – and vice versa; opportunities for communication occasionally have to be cut short prematurely in order to prevent further difficulties.

In one sense the daily life of a busy residential unit consists of a virtually seamless flow of such events, one merging into or overlapping with another, one situation influencing the handling of the next, and so on. To have separated out one hypothetical 'opportunity' from this mêlé might be seen as wholly artificial, were it not for the fact that for the child and the worker involved, each incident does have its own significance and does require the same attention to detail: this is one reason why the work is so challenging but also so potentially rewarding. The task of 'sustaining the intervention' therefore begins almost as soon as the 'action' phase has begun, and may continue for some considerable time. We should also note that, if the intervention is to be sustained, then the worker, too, may need to be sustained: he or she will certainly need to stay in touch with other staff or managers as the situation unfolds and may need the availability of ongoing support in the form of 'live supervision'.

Closing an incident

There are three main things to consider in the 'closure' phase of an intervention, whether it has been a brief exchange of words, a sustained dialogue between worker and child, or a more substantial group meeting.

First, it is obviously important to bring the situation to an agreed and clear ending so that those involved can resume their other activities and responsibilities, but also to minimise any risk of the situation being misunderstood or misrepresented at a later stage. This can be thought of in terms of closing down the communication – making sure that no 'loose ends' have been left, in the sense of people who are not sure what has been said to them or not clear about or satisfied with the response which they have had. It may be important for the worker actually to say something like 'Well, that's finished with now', or 'Let's leave it there for the moment'. It will not always be clear when this can be said, and the worker may need to check with the child or group, e.g. 'Are you ready to leave it there?' or 'How do you think we should finish this off?' Clearly this process will be more delicate where a situation has developed into some deeper or more painful communication.

Second, decisions may need to be made as to what else has to be done in connection with the facts and feelings of the situation. For example, information may need to be conveyed to other people inside or outside the unit, or strong feelings may need to be allowed for during the ensuing period and may need to be raised again later elsewhere – perhaps at a handover or community meeting or at a family meeting, or with the child's social worker. Sometimes the worker may need to close the incident by giving a firm undertaking as to how it will be followed up, either with this individual or group, or with other people. The worker will also need to think about how an individual's or group's learning from an incident can be incorporated into the mainstream of their development or treatment.

The written recording of significant incidents is essential, so questions will arise as to who records what and why? There will also be questions about how far the private concerns of an individual are to be made public, either through discussion or recording, or in what way it will be appropriate and productive to convey the learning from an incident to others who may be affected.

Third, after the situation has been resolved there is the need for team review and evaluation – for people to evaluate their ways of working and to improve their understanding, incorporating any changes into their policies and procedures. Individuals (both workers and children) may need supervision, catharsis, free time, relief, etc. If the situation has been an especially difficult one to handle, other people may not realise how strong the worker's feelings were, and he or she may need to seek out an appropriate team member and ask for immediate support. Moreover, if the worker has strong feelings, it is likely that the child and others involved will also have equivalent feelings, and somebody (not necessarily this same worker) may need to offer them some further support. The period immediately following a sustained piece of opportunity led communication may be an especially sensitive time for some of those involved – including those only apparently involved at the fringes of the communication.

The above discussion also brings us back to 'context': not only, as we saw under 'assessment', do the workers have to be aware of organisational context, but the context has to be aware of them. In other words, staff can only provide opportunities for children if they, too, have opportunities for communication and reflection. This way of working therefore requires regular and supportive supervision, and a programme of staff meetings and consultancy as detailed elsewhere in this book. An atmosphere of trust and respect within a staff team working under these pressures is essential but not easy to sustain: staff need to be able to reflect on their uncertainties and acknowledge their mistakes so that they can learn from them.

Conclusion

This chapter has outlined the main elements of an approach to handling everyday situations in therapeutic child care settings. Although the range of possible situations and responses is infinite, the model itself is a simple one, involving observation and assessment, decision-making, action and review, and the emphasis is mainly on identifying and using those opportunities for deeper communication with children which will sometimes arise out of such situations. The skill is first in spotting the opportunities, and second in making the best use of them. It is an approach which requires attentiveness, responsiveness and creativity, but for the approach to be used well in a team, it also requires support and encouragement within the team itself. As we have seen many times in this book, in this sort of work all interactions need to be seen within the broader contexts of the group, the staff team, and the place as a whole, and whatever response is offered to the young person needs to be planned bearing in mind their treatment process as a whole, including their connections with their family and network.

CHAPTER 8

The Meaning of Good Experience

Jenny Carter

Introduction

This chapter focuses on the thought given to how children are physically cared for, how this links with emotional health, and what this means for disturbed children. The ways groups of children are kept alive, safe, well and clean, and are fed, stimulated, comforted and helped to learn to play and relax within a network of relationships are central to the 'therapy' offered in therapeutic communities. The containment embedded in the environment and daily structure as well as the quality of discussion about primary care are intrinsic to the treatment process. The recognition that these basic tasks have complex meanings which require thoughtful discussion in order that opportunities for development can be properly understood and used has been a significant contribution from therapeutic communities to the general field of substitute care for children. Daily primary experiences offer an 'opportunity for restorative experiences' (Woodhead 1999), a powerful medium of communication between children and carers and an arena in which to come to enjoy life with others.

The main focus of this chapter is on the experience of food, mealtimes and what happens between the children and their carers. However, I also make briefer reference to other areas of primary care and the meaning of good experience. Throughout, I draw particularly on my experience of working with the Peper Harow Foundation, first at Thornby Hall, a large group provision for very troubled adolescents, and more latterly in establishing a smaller therapeutic centre, Abington House, for younger children with similar emotional difficulties. Here, a feature of creating an integrated and containing experience for the children has been the way in which a small group of staff, with little experience of working and thinking psychodynamically, has come together as a group to think about the meaning of good experiences.

Primary experience

Most babies have generally good experiences of being lovingly fed, cleaned, kept warm, safe, well and stimulated by their mothers and primary caregivers. Within a framework of broadly sufficient response, which reliably alleviates distress and is responsive to the infant's needs, babies learn what it feels like to be understood and thought about. Bion's notion of 'reverie' describes how mothers attend to the detail of their infants' communications, interpret them, and respond accordingly, providing the critical experience of maternal containment (Bion 1962). The repeated experience of this process eventually enables babies to develop a concept of, and trust in, a reliable and hopeful world where they can bear to be alone, know how to relate to others and become people who can feel that they deserve love and are able to love others.

The process helps infants to learn how to think, to hold a concept of something good in their minds even when it is not there physically. The capacity to meet basic needs and to process emotional experiences, originally a function of the carer, can be gradually introjected by the child.

It follows, however, that those children who have not had this helpful kind of early experience will not have learnt how to process emotional experiences and may become easily overwhelmed by their feelings, holding a concept of relationships and the world which will not be conducive to healthy development. Such children can feel deprived and hurt; they often feel themselves unlovable and they continue to have difficulties processing emotion. A baby who has suffered repeated and/or long periods of hunger, cold, pain, fear, messiness and loneliness will often find later attempts to provide care difficult to accept and may even attack the offer of help (Waddell 1998). Understanding the process whereby children defend themselves against the pain of deprivation by attacking sources of potential good provision may help residential workers and foster carers to cope with such attacks. Children who are referred to therapeutic communities may well have not enjoyed the repetition of good experiences enabling them to learn how to think, and may also have been unable to accept alternative interventions, and attacked later attempts to care for them.

> It is not enough to give emotionally deprived children good experience, we must also help them to keep the good things inside them, or they will lose them once more. (Dockar-Drysdale 1990)

Helping very deprived children with the process of internalising good experience is a complex, painstaking, emotionally and intellectually draining task. How do we begin? Dockar-Drysdale's application of Winnicottian principles to residential work is central in this area. She considers not only how to provide good experiences (warm, nutritious, bright, fun, thoughtful and complete experiences) but also how to do this in a way that recognises their meaning for particular children and enables them to use and accept these experiences so that they can progress. In addition to this thinking about individuals, the structure, environment and culture within which care is provided are essential parts of the treatment process providing the opportunity to learn from a repeated experience of needs being understood and met.

Understanding a child's early primary care experiences helps the thinking about current needs and also helps to anticipate how primary care might be received. Conversely, observing how primary experiences are received now sheds light on what has gone before. Learning to deduce the emotional content of a child's early experiences provides an understanding of each child essential in the therapeutic task.

In the first year of life, a primary caregiver spends time physically holding the baby and also more figuratively holds the understanding for a baby and so integrates the primary tasks. Both these functions are vital to combat the fear of falling apart, physically and mentally, which infants experience when their needs are not met. Holding, or containment, provides a safe world with boundaries within which to negotiate relationships with others. The 'good-enough' mother, as described by Winnicott is able gradually to allow the child to come to think for himself (Winnicott 1960). Children who have not had these experiences early in their lives often demonstrate vividly (with chaotic and disruptive behaviour) their panic that such a world can never exist for them, that they do not deserve it and they cannot make use of it. A major part of the task of helping these children is to demonstrate, despite steadfast resistance, that it can, and to provide for them clear boundaries and a safe world.

Compensating for early deprivation in residential care

For children looked after by the state, especially in a group home, this holding happens in several ways. It happens physically, perhaps by being hugged or restrained or contained by a strong and safe environment. It is represented by the structure: how the children's daily lives are organised and thought about. Most importantly it is signified by the 'culture' in which the thinking is embedded, which determines how the physical and structural holding mechanisms are to be understood and which is founded on staff thinking together. All this becomes essential to the children's feeling of being 'held in mind' and they come to know and accept that they are thought about in this way. Only when children begin to trust in this knowledge will they be able to learn to think for themselves and develop a mind that is less vulnerable to becoming overwhelmed. As we have experienced at Abington House, after time the children's group itself becomes a carrier for this culture and established children can tell others about 'the way we do things here'.

Essentially, integrated care and thinking needs to be underpinned by what Winnicott calls 'primary maternal preoccupation' (Winnicott 1958). That is, in order to develop mentally one must not be forgotten. One can successfully learn to think only by having the experience of being thought about. Often it will become apparent that the children who come to therapeutic communities will have missed being the object of this preoccupation in their first year of life. Part of the thinking together for residential workers is to remind each other of the need of all children, but especially muddled ones, to be understood. One of the tasks is to help the children come to know that their needs will be met within a consistent, containing and predictable time frame in a tolerant and loving way. The statutory frameworks for child care offer only a minimum of guidance in this complex area and are not designed to address the difficulties inherent in providing this thoughtful containment to a group of children or the possibilities of using the group rather than focusing on individual needs and rights.

Food and mealtimes

Food and feeding of course are essential and basic physical requirements and without them a baby will die. For the infant, the experience of being fed is even richer than this. As Lisa Millar puts it, 'the baby takes in far more than milk at every feed' (Hindle and Vaciago Smith 1999). As well as the potential to be a mutually pleasurable and satisfying experience the infant can come to experience that there is a world (represented by a mother) which understands the anxiety and neediness of hunger and knows how to comfort and take away distress. So the feeding experience can come to represent psychological sustenance and is part of the infants' developing picture of themselves and the world, and the relation between the two.

Deprived children will often have missed these physically satisfying experiences, and the accompanying emotional sustenance. Hunger is then accompanied by acute anxiety and the panic that it will not be responded to. It is not surprising that food remains an area that elicits powerful emotions given the potential difficulties in the feeding relationship. For example, children have been left hungry, been forced to eat by an anxious or angry parent, while for another the experience of feeding is not a pleasurable one for the mother, and so it becomes a confusing and unpleasant one for the child. It is an emotive area for the mother or provider – she conveys her needs through how and what she gives, and in turn is affected deeply by whether the infant either accepts it hungrily, lovingly and with pleasure, or rejects it, perhaps because he is in physical pain or because the experience is not pleasurable in some other way. This is upsetting and causes anxiety, a sense of failure or even anger if the child, for whatever reason, rejects what she offers and may have spent time preparing for him or her.

For most children, and adults, the experience later on of enjoying eating, or eating together as a family, reflects this early experience. With children for whom early experience has been complicated, unpleasant, a battleground, it becomes evident very quickly just how emotive this area of food, eating and coming together to eat really is. It is through food that children communicate a powerful range of emotions (linked with their earliest experiences) as well as evoke emotions in those who provide for them: of rejection, punishment, failure, disgust, of being unloved, unappreciated, not valued. In the care situation, whether in the foster home or in the residential setting, it is important that the adults have time to think about what is being communicated, to understand it, and to manage the impact that this has on them, both individually and together, because it is not only a difficult and sensitive area but also one that divides them around how best to respond. We have found that discussions often involve the notion of how to provide children with a healthy diet and how possible it is to understand the child who prefers to fill up on a less nutritious option.

Understanding the emotional content of feeding can aid in the task of helping children to accept food from adults. The ability to convey understanding and empathy for the difficulties children may be communicating rather than purely reacting with disgust, anger, rejection or a sense of hurt, is likely in itself to have a positive effect and to help children eventually move towards more healthy and acceptable habits. Our experience has been that setting boundaries from this starting position (i.e. one of empathy rather than antipathy) is itself more likely to change the child's own feelings (and therefore behaviours) than to exacerbate them.

Fundamentally, for children who have never had enough food, love or attention from adults, a plentiful amount of good food on the table in the same place, at the same time and with the same care each day begins to offer the experience of a world which will sustain them. Well prepared, well presented food adds layers to this experience of being truly considered, as does a calm group of adults who are able and prepared to enjoy the food and the eating experience, at the same time as containing and processing the children's anxieties. This includes the worry that there will not be enough food or that the conflicts when people come together will become unmanageable. Of course, with children whose starting point is one of turmoil, ambivalence and conflict about food and about being 'mothered', it is very difficult for carers to repeatedly convey a sense of pleasure and love in preparing, presenting and partaking in a meal, if they anticipate a lack of appreciation, rejection or a tense and unpleasant experience. Carers therefore also need to feel understood especially in coming back mealtime after mealtime to an experience that may be filled with a sense of panic, rejection and failure and that they will not always be able to turn into an experience of reassurance, acceptance, satisfaction and, most importantly, pleasure and fun.

Melvyn Rose conveys this in describing the thinking that went into the provision of a new dining room at Peper Harow:

> Many of the youngsters referred to any meal, however well presented, as 'Shit! Poison!' Food was regarded with considerable suspicion. We wondered how these problems, which stemmed from very early childhood, could be tackled. But it was difficult to confront these youngsters with the disparity between their infantile responses and the present reality that food was now actually good enough, at the same time as we recognised that the only cooking and dining facilities available to them were actually terrible. (Rose 1990)

> We thought of the fortunate baby's experiences during the feeding process and imagined the specific ways in which all the senses are engaged, not simply his mouth, and we tried by design and furnishing to fill the area with similar, pleasure-giving, sensual experiences. (Rose 1990)

Of course, children who find it impossible to sit down to a meal, or accept the food that has been prepared for them, and demand food at all other times, arouse all sorts of feelings in their carers. Coping with children who need 'feeds on demand' conflicts with straightforward notions about snacking between meals. This needs discussion – it is frustrating to prepare a meal for children who have filled up five minutes before on something less healthy. At

Peper Harow and at Thornby Hall, one attempt to deal with this dilemma was the provision of a buttery where food and milk were available at all times; in the much smaller provision at Abington House, the solution has been to allow access to fruit and milk, with limited access to the fridge. With only four children and two or three adults at any mealtime, it is noticeable that the cooking and eating experience at Abington House is a much more deeply personal one than in a large group setting. It can be difficult for the person who has cooked a meal, maybe with a particular child in mind, to have that rejected in favour of other food. In the first year at Abington House, a great deal of staff meeting time was spent thinking through and coming to some collective understanding about how we could and should manage not just the children's difficulties, but also our own emotions, expectations and responses in a way that contained the children's experience rather than exacerbated their sense of confusion and conflict. One instance of such a discussion involved the timing of the last meal of the day. On the one hand it was thought to be unhealthy to eat just before sleep, and to evolve the habit in childhood of doing so; on the other it was appreciated that the emotional void of going to bed with little or nothing inside is difficult to bear for emotionally deprived children and eventually it was decided that a comforting supper might help them get through the night.

In the therapeutic setting, the whole process of food – its preparation; its presentation; how it is given; how it is received; the wider experience of the meal; and the relationship between those who share it, is an integral part of how children are helped to address the consequences of their earliest deprivation. So the question of who cooks becomes a very important one. Every setting has to balance a range of institutional needs and will come to different solutions about who does the cooking; whether the care staff themselves cook all or some of the food, or designated cooking professionals do so. The task and those engaged in it will need individual and group forums in which the psychological implications and symbolic significance can be thought about. Any decisions or changes regarding the kitchen or dining areas need similar attention.

The symbolic significance of food can be more consciously utilised to convey emotional nurturing to the children. Barbara Dockar-Drysdale (1993) provides examples of creative adaptations made to suit individual children and there will be many more in different settings. Simply, adults consciously demonstrate that they keep children in mind even when they are not there, by remembering to buy favourite foods and cook them in particular ways. Additionally, food can be a useful way of providing transitional experience when children separate from carers. For example, if a keyworker is about to go on holiday, they may leave a favourite food with a child or interim keyworker to symbolise a continuing good experience. They may even provide a jar to store them in.

Dockar-Drysdale (1993) explains how, as in other aspects of thinking about children, working with the symptom rather than against it, seeing children and their behaviour as one thing and accepting them together can help them to grow and separate from the symptom. For example, when 'Mark' arrived at Abington House he was unable to accept food from the staff group and found it intimidating to eat with others. We knew Mark had spent his first three years strapped into a car seat, had been fed *Calpol* to subdue him, and had watched his mother feeding the other siblings. We began by simply setting his place at the table but he forcefully rejected, ignored and spat at offers to eat with the group, continuing to binge on chocolates and jam, raid the fridge at night, and sometimes accuse staff members of plotting to poison him. The issue became a battle as adults tried to coax Mark in and help him accept a healthier diet. Mark's rejection seemed pointed in such a small setting and it became frustrating as he became less and less healthy and more withdrawn. After months of discussion, observation and beginning to under-stand some of his difficulties – how food had been used to punish him in the past, how attacked he felt by our offers of care – the strategy we needed became clearer. For several weeks we provided him with his own cupboard with Pot Noodles, which he could prepare himself and eat where he liked. His place was still laid at the table and he was always quietly invited to join everyone. He chose however to prepare his noodles and eat alone. Gradually, as he sidled past, he occasionally took up the invitation and chose to half sit on a chair with the group and perhaps share a bought cake for pudding. This progressed and he eventually became able to add food from the serving dishes to his noodles and by the end of his stay would join the group mealtimes. This was a significant development for someone who had found this area so difficult.

The task of feeding such children is emotionally taxing, but it is a part of daily living where all sorts of emotional difficulties can be addressed. It is an area rich with symbolic communication. In order to communicate usefully in this arena, it is necessary to come to understand where each child stands emotionally in relation to the adults who feed them. Tolerating the difficul-ties, understanding the process and containing anxiety about the nutritional aspect of food can allow children to progress physically and psychologically. In this aspect of children's care – as in all others – there are no short cuts, no right answers, no handbooks, no substitute to devoting time and energy to thinking about the children involved, on a level which takes into account their early history and their individual complexities as well as the complexity of the group.

Bath-times and toileting

Managing bath-times and toileting can be difficult with any group of children or adolescents. This arena is an important place to explore notions of care, privacy and boundaries, inside and outside, and is fraught with difficulty, especially those who have had premature sexual experience.

For most babies the bath-time and nappy changing time is where they experience being kept safe and have their dirtiness accepted and cleaned. Normally, it is an intimate and pleasurable experience that provides a basis for children's feelings about themselves, about their bodies, and about what is inside them. The adults are able to accept their messiness and the children can hold in mind an adult who can tolerate their messy and unacceptable feelings too until they can do this for themselves. Similarly, as Erikson so usefully describes, toilet training is an aspect of a child's development that normally arises out of the small child's mutually loving relationship with his or her parents and the child's willingness or wish to please (Erikson 1965).

However, for many children, these intimate primary care experiences may have become areas of conflict associated with punishment, sexual abuse, a parent's revulsion and disgust, or a battle of wills. They may consequently have distorted views of their body and what it means to others and this may well affect their entire notion of themselves. Depending on their experiences such children may be muddled about faeces or about sex, they may be encopretic, smear, hide their excrement, relieve themselves in unusual places or keep used sanitary wear. They may withhold their faeces for days or weeks. They may offer their body for adult gratification, feeling rejected when the offer is not accepted – all ways of expressing their anger, confusion, uncertainty. These are not just difficulties for the child, however. They raise acute feelings of confusion, helplessness, repulsion and anger in carers, which, if not contained in a way that is helpful to the child and empathetic to its link with earlier, disturbed experience can simply exacerbate the anxiety or the dynamic that drives it. But just as food represents the taking in of good experiences, so being kept clean can come to represent being accepted and can go a long way towards helping children negotiate those aspects of themselves they are most ashamed of.

The recent 'climate of fear' adds to anxieties inherent in this area of adult–child interaction, around the intimate tasks of bathing, cleaning and toileting. This can provoke a defensive response which may in some ways make it easier for adults to abdicate responsibility for engaging and thinking about this aspect of children's care. Careful thought is needed to provide for children who need to learn to make sense of their own personal boundaries, sexual boundaries, and about where and when they should have privacy. It is around bath and bedtimes that it is hardest to negotiate looking after the 14-year-old as well as the infant inside. The most difficult matter sometimes is to ensure that there is more than enough time planned for the task of washing, bath-times and cleaning up after them. At Abington House, we have found that morning and evening times spent with the children, bathing, and helping them look after bodies and by extension bathrooms, bedrooms and clothes is invaluable. Again, staff meetings are essential to think about what these spaces come to mean for children in the context of early experience, and how best to adapt these opportunities to convey their understanding to the children. Brushing teeth for instance, offers all sorts of opportunities to understand how children may feel about their insides, and we have found acknowledgement of this is eventually more effective in the long run than only stressing the health consequences of not brushing or overbrushing.

As with food, and as written about by Melvyn Rose (Rose 1990), one of the important starting points in this area of primary care is a bathroom that will give the child every chance to feel that it is a nice place to be and that it has been thought about with love and care by the adults. This is one way to symbolise 'being with' the children (especially as they enter adolescence) and to offer children whose early primary experiences may not have been pleasurable a chance for them to be so. Similarly the degree of adult involvement in the bathing experience will vary according to setting and child, and different solutions will be found to convey a feeling of care and of safety. Appreciation of what dirtiness means to an individual child, perhaps distress or protection, as well as understanding current hygiene needs, can help in devising routines which can help a child move forward, and knowing how to respond to unusual behaviours. One boy at Abington House, whose early experiences had been of neglect, and who at 12 still found it difficult to get out of a soiled bed or clothes, found a way to talk about the issue with his linkworker by using a toy turtle. Eventually, after 'confessing' that he only pretended to wash the turtle, both he and the turtle would emerge having really been washed and he began to enjoy the pleasure the staff took in his appearance.

Bedtimes and night-times

Bedtimes can be terrifying for children, and this raises a number of anxieties. The key question for staff is: how can we make this a time that feels and is safe for each child and the group? For some it is a time of unbearable loneliness, nightmares or fear of abandonment, while for others it raises memories of traumatic separations or sexual intrusions. The management of night-times has preoccupied all of the staff teams I have worked with in residential care and will always remain an area needing thorough discussion. The task of balancing the issues that are raised about children feeling and being safe, feeling supported without also feeling intruded upon, and (for some) actually being supervised, is a delicate one.

Just as with bathrooms, and the environment in general, a policy of providing bedroom spaces that will feel warm, safe, cosy and represent appropriate adult relationships with the children, in a way which takes account of the children's needs and anxieties, seems to be the most important starting point in providing night-time experiences that are not just bearable, but are an integrated part of the wider, therapeutic experience. Nightlights, televisions, mobiles and music are some of the many areas which will need careful thought and discussion about their meaning for each child and for the group. The danger that night-times become split off from the day, raising the children's anxiety, can be avoided by properly using the structure in which staff meet regularly together to think about the integrated experience and the whole therapeutic programme that is split off from the day in a way that the whole ceases to exist as an integrated experience and simply raises the children's anxieties.

It is important that everyone is clear about who is allowed in children's bedrooms and who looks after them. Again, individual settings will have their own discussions and as long as it is borne in mind that the bedroom can come to symbolise a child's internal world, solutions will be different and individual. These discussions will involve who cleans the bedroom; that is, who is allowed inside to touch and move private things; how locks or alarms operate; how and where the discussions about the 'mess' that children may make take place; how to understand the child who demands a change of bedroom; whether children are permitted to invite other children into their rooms and many other topics. Time to think like this about a bedroom offers opportunities gradually to help a child move from a world of uncontrollable dirt and chaos to more order, or for a meticulous and obsessive child to progress to leaving an unmade bed. It is bedrooms which are most often 'trashed'. The way they are repaired and put back together, speedily, thoughtfully and where possible with the child, offers further therapeutic opportunity.

Recently, at one of the Paper Harow Foundation centres for younger children (aged 7 to 11), a potentially unsettling move of premises was being planned. At the earliest possible time after this had been raised with the children, they were taken to see the new premises and the Director discussed with each of them which bedroom they might like to have, how it should be decorated, and what 'special thing' would be added as a welcoming gift. One of the children had the idea that before the move they should each put something of their own into the room. Two days before the move, each child was taken to the house and each left a soft toy in his or her bed 'to look after it', to help them make the transition, and to be there for when they arrived.

To cope with and to contain children's anxiety, it is important to have reliable and predictable boundaries. By sticking to the routine, particularly at bedtime, children come to experience that adults will not become muddled about boundaries, and everyone will understand clearly where they are all supposed to be even in the face of disruption. So it is important that everyone is clear about what time is bedtime, and that every effort is made to help children upstairs to begin settling. Some children may try to keep carers present at bedtime by any means possible, and strategies which start from the child's expressed need and see their 'attention-seeking' as rational behaviour rather than misbehaviour may have the greatest chance of effecting long-term change. The task of helping a child to be in the right place at the right time at night-time takes on a significance for the whole group. This process may take a long time for young or anxious children. It is the most major transition of the day, and needs extremely careful management. Our experience has been that setting a rather early time works (8.30 p.m. as a starting time for our 11–13 -year-olds). This allows a slow and careful transition and gives time to get to know the child's fears and to learn about them and how to reassure him or her. It hardly needs saying that children should be put to bed and woken up only by those whom they know well, and where the person waking them is different from the person who settled them, a reassuring sense of continuity will be provided by knowing that these two people talk to each other.

Bedtime offers the opportunity to work with separation, and demonstrate that adults will return when they say they will, and can be predictable. Adaptations can be devised at both ends of the day to address particular issues and common difficulties of being left alone, and then of facing the day. Each setting develops its own strategies and rules for particular children, or particular groups of children. Time for staff to think together about the meaning of these, for individuals and for the group, will ensure best use is made of tools such as stories, hot water bottles, leaving something with the child, looking after something belonging to the child, use of nightlights, story tapes and so on.

Knowing who will be in the building at night-time and that the building is safe and secure can come to represent much more than the safety of one particular night. Repeated safe, predictable experiences will help children relinquish some anxiety and the need for control which often accompanies it.

When, over the last ten years, the issue of 'waking night staff' became a requirement for particular residential settings, other questions to do with who should stay awake for the children was an item of intense debate. Should children have relative 'strangers' looking after them at times when they are feeling at their most vulnerable? Can staff really be expected to work days and nights? A number of very important issues have needed, in each setting, to be thought about and decided upon. Our experience has been that there is no one practical solution that does not raise incompatibilities, but a solution that is reached via a process of careful thinking and talking through has the least risks, especially in a culture where these things can be and are talked through with the children. At Thornby Hall, when after long debate, waking night staff were introduced, the most important, single, reassuring factor for the children was the reassurance that the staff had thought about this thoroughly.

Environment

I have underlined the relationship between children's experience and the environment, particularly with reference to kitchens, dining rooms, bed and bathrooms. Of course the relationship is broader, and starts at the boundaries of the building or garden. It is important to insecure children that the house is secure and safe and that people cannot just walk in unnoticed. Children should be told about any visitors who are due, and unannounced visits kept to a minimum. Entrances and exits in the house need to be firmly shut and managed by the adults.

I will only briefly comment further on the importance of the quality of environment and its maintenance and refer people back to Rose's seminal lecture on this matter (Rose 1977). Much of this early thinking has now become assimilated into the rules and regulations about basic good childcare. When in 1972 Rose undertook the considerable task of converting an Approved School into Peper Harow, a therapeutic community, he drew not only from his own professional experiences but also from the growing body of thinking about the care, education and treatment of children. Bruno Bettelheim, for example, had been exploring and writing about the relationship between environment and personality, and drew from his experience of incarceration in a concentration camp during the war in Europe. He had noticed that every aspect of life in the concentration camp seemed designed to break the human spirit and had contrasted this with his life of freedom in

America, explaining that this contrast 'led to the conviction that as much as environment can destroy, it can heal' (Bettelheim 1961).

Rose advocated that every physical element of the house, from the cutlery on the tables to the décor in the toilets, is an opportunity to communicate to the children that they are worth caring for and deserve good things. This thinking means ensuring that the environment is well cared for, and comes to symbolise that the children are valued and important. It means buying good quality furnishings, which have a chance of staying whole. For the children this will represent the idea that their future care is guaranteed and ongoing. For the same reasons, repairs should be made as quickly as possible, even when damage has been done deliberately. The adults' ability and willingness to fix material things, clean up mess, will come to symbolise for the children the adults' ability to heal their hurts, cope with their emotional mess, and not punish them for being unable as yet to look after things themselves. Children will gradually internalise this and take care of their own things and eventually themselves. Adults who fold the washing with care, clean shoes and sew up holes in clothes come to represent adults who want to make things better and will take the trouble to do so. Just as in the case of food, thinking carefully about who looks after the environment, and how, will be important. The best therapeutic workers are those who participate fully in this aspect of caring for children. It will be important for the children that their mess can be coped with by people they know.

Conclusion

There is so much to say about this area that the only conclusion to draw is that time provided to say it (i.e. plenty of group supervision) in individual settings makes the difference between a setting which can be therapeutic and one that cannot. All areas of life together can be usefully thought about in these ways. A culture and structure which repeatedly demonstrate themselves to be thoughtful and safe, take time and thought to develop and to maintain. Attacks come not only from the children but also from the staff, and sometimes even from the statutory frameworks in which we operate. The ability collectively to notice and hold boundaries around primary care experiences, collectively to notice and acknowledge behaviours and feelings, and collectively to ensure that the environment, structure and culture continue to provide opportunities for communication and development will all be eroded without continual maintenance. Central to this maintenance will be the provision of space for the staff to think about the impact on them of providing for these children. A group of adults who can continue to enjoy good experiences themselves, and make them fun and reassuring for the children while understanding the difficulties, is clearly critical to the endeavour of helping the children to accept and enjoy good primary experiences. The complexity of understanding which takes into account past experiences and current dynamics is most often of best use held in the adults' minds rather than delivered unprocessed to the children. It can be conveyed using the range of personal, group, structural and environmental opportunities touched on in this chapter to provide the good experiences which can help heal a deprived or damaged child.

CHAPTER 9

Relationships and the Therapeutic Setting

Alan Worthington

Introduction

The children and young people who are referred to therapeutic communities have histories and circumstances that are varied and complex, but they have two things in common. One is that they are all victims in some way of the failures of their relationships with the key adults in their lives: relationships that have failed to meet their emotional and developing needs either at key points in their lives or throughout. The second is that they continue in some way to cope with the consequences of their earlier deprivation, loss, separations, trauma or abuse. These pervade all aspects of their lives and affect their abilities to engage adequately in relationships of all kinds, with adults and other children, be they parents, siblings, carers, teachers, casual or close friends, and even strangers. They affect the young persons' capacities to learn or be taught, to be looked after, to join in normal social activities, make friends, or to be hopeful about the future. The young people find it impossible to make consistent sense of what they experience and most usually express this confusion through what they do, through how they make those closest to them feel, and how they feel about or what they do to themselves. They are unable to invest in new relationships without ambivalence, the fear or expectation of disappointment or rejection, and the hope and fear that they will again have what they have lost. These children are susceptible to engaging in quite inappropriate relationships and are vulnerable to recreating the abusive relationships that they have had in the past. Without the foundation of, in Bowlby's term, 'a secure base' (Holmes 1993) founded in sound relationships with parents or carers, many will recreate in their own partnerships and marriages and for their own children the circumstances that they themselves have endured.

How then does one provide a base that will compensate for what has gone wrong? The therapeutic community view goes along these lines: first of all, one must begin with an awareness of how complex it is for such children to make new relationships, and therefore how complex it is for the adults who make themselves available for such relationships. The impact on both can be immense. Second, that in whatever setting, a crucial part of the care task will be to provide young people with opportunities to form relationships that are positive: successful futures will be dependent upon this. Moreover, these relationships will need to impact on them in a way that will challenge their pessimistic and incongruous assumptions about themselves and others, and to be experienced as lovable, creative and worthwhile. This will be a critical platform for making and sustaining good relationships in the future. Within or alongside this, they will also need to have the opportunity to reflect on and make sense of both their current experience and their histories, and each in relation to the other.

One of the key tasks in the therapeutic community setting is, therefore, to establish for each child a network of relationships that will contain, hold, protect and provide opportunities for personal development. In this chapter, and based on my experience of work with young people in residential therapeutic settings, first as a member of staff at Peper Harow, and later as Director of Thornby Hall, I try to identify and discuss some of the key issues relating to these networks of relationships. In this chapter I focus particularly on the relationships that children form with adults. However, it is also important to put these into the context of the wider networks of relationships: the children's relationships with their peers and their relationships beyond the care setting; the adult's relationships with each other and the impact of these relationships on the children. Moreover, in moving away from the therapeutic community setting, it seems important to consider the implications of what can be drawn from this and applied to the wider field of child-care, particularly foster placements.

The broader context

When considering the significance of relationships in residential therapeutic work, it is perhaps important to begin by placing this in a wider context. All therapeutic communities for children and adolescents in England are registered and inspected as either schools, mental health institutions or care homes (children's homes). Some have dual registration between care and education, but care and mental health operate under quite separate statutory frameworks and are seen as separate tasks with distinct sets of responsibilities.

This has significant implications for the models of care that apply to the broad range of children's homes, on the one hand, and therapeutic communities on the other. The former – children's homes – are embraced by a *social care* model, in which the task of children's psychological and emotional development, and more particularly the consequences that arise from earlier deprivation, trauma and damage, are outside the boundary and remit of the care institution. Therapeutic communities, on the other hand, operate within the framework of a *psychosocial care* model, in which the tasks of care and emotional/psychological development are seen as but two parts of a single, integrated task.

This difference between the social care model and the psychosocial care model (or models – there is not a single model) is of significance in a number of ways, and in the context of this particular chapter is reflected in the place, priority and meaning given to the relationships that are formed and the roles and responsibilities that are designated to care for therapeutic care staff. If one takes the social care frameworks as they are represented in the main statutory guidelines and regulations relating to children's residential care (Department of Health (DOH) 1991; 2002), the implication is that 'sound' relationships between adults and children emerge naturally, so long as they are 'based on honesty and mutual respect' and contained within 'safe, consistent and understandable boundaries' (DOH 2002). Overall, the view taken here of the place of relationships in the residential setting is a relatively simple one. It is perhaps also indicative of a wider ambivalence and defensiveness arising from deep concerns about the consequences of inappropriate adult–child relationships, not just for children, but also for social workers and social work managers. This in turn has also been both an influence and outcome (at the same time) of the discernible shift over recent years towards a broader social work profession in which welfare, psychology and an understanding of relationships have been replaced by a preoccupation with rules, guidelines, procedures and the law (Howe 1998).

The psychosocial care model embraced by therapeutic communities, on the other hand, takes the view that the relationships that are formed between the adults and the children (as well as the children and each other) provide a foundation for the work. They are inevitably complex and these complexities need to be engaged with, thought about, understood, worked with and contained in a framework that looks after the individuals involved, both children and adults.

Adult–child relationships in the therapeutic setting

Frameworks for containment

Throughout this book, the point is made again and again that therapeutic work is as much about the framework for thinking and understanding as it is about doing. This also applies to the notion of how different relationships are held, contained and utilised as part of the wider therapeutic endeavour. Therapeutic community practice is based in many ways on psychodynamic principles which (in part) means that what happens between the adult and child comprises both conscious and unconscious dimensions, not just for the child but also for the adult. In other words, each brings to the space between them different assumptions, anxieties, expectations and agendas.

These individual relationships in turn form part of, and are contained by, a wider network of relationships, within the framework of the broader therapeutic environment. Together, these provide a setting that not only ensures a space for experience, reflection and understanding, but also ensures, as much as is possible, that relationships of different kinds (pairs or sub-groups) do not become isolated in a way that is split off from the wider whole.

The focal adult–child relationship

Children in residential care usually have opportunities for different adult relationships that are a mixture of the informal and formal, and arise out of the different professional and social interactions. In most of these institutional settings, children are designated one particular adult whose job it is to take a special interest in and responsibility for particular needs and tasks. Within the wider context of children's homes, this role is usually assigned the title of keyworker, although in therapeutic communities there has been a conscious effort by most to move away from the use of this term, partly due (I think) to an endeavour to underline the differences in the roles and the institutional settings, not just of children's homes but others (approved schools, for example) (Rose 1990).

At Peper Harow in the 1970s, the term 'guru' was used, initially a joke invented by one of the boys, but one which stuck and which, in the context of the particular decade, did not sound quite as corny as it does today. In turn, the boys (and later girls) were called, in relation to their gurus, 'guruees'. At Thornby Hall the term keyworker was (and is) used. This emerged as a result of indecision about what to call staff, and so in a different way, the young people filled the gap. In this context, I am going to use the term keyworker, partly for simplicity's sake, but also because it was the term that became established at Thornby Hall in the time of my directorship. I also think that the issues that are raised are relevant across the span of different models.

Selection and allocation

In examining what happens and is expected of the adult–child relationship in the therapeutic setting, one starting point might be to look at the ways this is thought about prior to the allocation of staff to children (or vice versa). At Peper Harow and at Thornby Hall, for example, this began prior to the point of interview of the child, but perhaps one should really begin with the appointment of staff.

As outlined earlier, the children bring with them their previous experiences of being parented, of adults and of relationships and experiences of different kinds. In many ways, the same may be said of what we as adults bring to our relationships, personal or professional. One of the aspects about 'growing up' is to do with how well we come to know ourselves and to manage and contain the unconscious influences that may confuse the present and the past. In all professional settings, organisations endeavour to contain personal agendas by rules, codes of conduct and deterrents that rigorously define professional and personal boundaries. This applies as much, and now even more, to residential child care. However, these boundaries are then challenged at the point that we ask workers to engage with the children's internal, emotional worlds (see Chapter 5). In this context, professional and personal again begin to merge, and the boundary between the two comes under attack in all sorts of ways, potentially for the good (it provides the possibility for relationship in which both child and adult engage) but it also has the potential for disaster if not held within a wider framework of understanding (Dockar-Drysdale 1990).

With this in mind, one of the essential tasks in appointing new staff is to assess what this will mean for each individual. For example, will any person's own experience (and ability to sustain and understand this experience) of being parented, of growing up, of making personal relationships, of loss and trauma, of coping and resolving, be one that can be accessed and contribute creatively to the children's development, or will it be one that is fragile to the extent that the adult's own unresolved experiences are resurrected in a way that is traumatic and distressing?

So, what we might call a 'second phase' is where thought is given as to who will be the most suitable adult for a particular child. At Peper Harow and Thornby Hall this was addressed in the latter stages of the referral process as the Director and staff built up a picture of the child and of his/her history, personality, interests and needs. Which of the adults might be most likely to 'gel', work with that background, and form a compatible and empathetic bond? Of course there were other factors that came into this consideration of selection. One obvious factor was the existing staff caseloads. Another important consideration was to do with the anticipation of how long a member of staff intended to stay beyond the arrival of a particular child, and what the implications of a keyworker change might be at a particular time. When staff were appointed, it was made very clear that – extenuating circumstances aside – an expectation was that once committed to working with a particular child, they would be there to work with them through their stay, if that was possible. This was not always possible, and where a member of staff left earlier, the implications for the young person were thought about carefully and he or she was supported and helped to work this through.

Another factor given careful consideration was whether the keyworker should be a man or a woman, and whether there were background factors that indicated a need for one or the other. So, for example, a child or adolescent who had had a particularly bad and unresolved experience of mother (or father), or of adult males or females, might not be in any way ready to engage with a male or female keyworker, and might need to be given time to begin to establish relationships with men (or women) in a less intimidating way. Therefore, it may be recognised at the outset that his or her special adult would in the first instance preferably or even specifically be a male or female worker. Early experiences form a basis for the assumptions and expectations that children bring with them about men and women, and about adults who will step into this 'pseudo-parental' role. It is here that issues of transference and countertransference, referred to earlier (see Chapter 5) arise for both child and adult. These need to be understood and contained, initially by the adult but, in a gradual way, also by the young person. As such, the experience of and later understanding of engaging in a relationship with an adult, indeed relationships with different adults, become a central part of the therapeutic milieu and are used as a therapeutic tool. Any particular adult–child relationship, however special or designated, must therefore be seen and understood in the context of the wider network of child–adult relationships, not just within the residential unit itself, but also beyond.

Making the link and 'being with'

When I first became a keyworker after joining Peper Harow, I was very inexperienced in therapeutic work. My previous professional experience had been of three years' teaching in a high school in Australia. Jim, the first boy to whom I was guru, was 14 and in the care of one of the London Borough Social Services departments. He was referred as a response to his being 'out of control', refusing to attend school, and his accumulation of a growing list of delinquent and criminal offences, mainly involving burglaries of shops and criminal damage. He had been taken into care a year previously and placed in a local authority children's home, a situation that had become not only untenable for him, but also for the others with whom he was living, principally as a result of the delinquent sub-culture of which he was a central part.

In the course of my initial weeks and months as Jim's guru, I learned a great deal about Charlton Athletic, East London street life, warehouses that were broken into, bunking off school, 'crap teachers', 'shit social workers', 'pigs', 'judges' and 'shrinks'. My main activity, apart from intervening in daily conflicts that started with Jim's resistance to getting out of bed at all ("What's the point?"), was to listen, although at that time that was not a strategy based in any particular wisdom, but more one of not knowing what to say. As it so happens, however, I came to appreciate that listening is not a bad starting point. Moreover, some of the stories, whether true or otherwise, were actually very creative and sometimes quite funny. Some of it was no doubt for my amusement (and collusion), and so the creation of a relationship is not just about the adults finding a way to the young people, but also about them finding a way to the adults.

The other 'skill' that I needed to have, also quite unconscious, was in being able to make myself available at times and in ways that were unthreatening, over a cup of tea in the dining room, over meals as part of a wider group, and (especially in Jim's case) playing table tennis. At Peper Harow, staff and young people cooked meals together and washed dishes and cleaned the house, and this was a way of putting staff and young people together around opportunities to play and do things together so that the focus was taken away from the potentially awkward space between them. The greatest mistake for a member of staff to make is to try prematurely (either in terms of their own development or the child's) to 'become a therapist'. The same applied to mutual interests: fishing, model making, football, playing music, painting, drawing, photography, making things or shopping.

From these starting points, a different type of conversation gradually emerged as the space between us became less filled with our respective anxieties. One day, Jim began to tell me about what it had been like for him at home: his mother's and father's arguments; of the day when he was six when his father went to work and simply never returned; of his mother's frequent suicide attempts and what he had done when, on his own, he had found her unconscious on the bathroom floor. Over time, the impacts of these and other events became possible to talk about, and were thought through with links and connections made and opinions given, as were the various sorts of issues that came up on a day-to-day basis.

One of the key elements of the therapeutic community – in fact in any child care setting – is for there to be time just to 'be with' in a supportive and healthy way, at least for a part of each day even if it is small. It is important that it is available and valued (by the institution, even if the child rejects it at first). Within this, there is a gradual shift from 'being there' to 'being with', which can be as painful and difficult for the adult as it can for the child. This is why staff need the support that is provided by good supervision and consultation (see Chapter 14) and which will help them to be with the child in a way that is supportive and nurturing, rather than in a way that is not good for either of them or even not to be with the child at all. One of the concerns that is created by the degrees of procedure and accountability that has grown so much in recent years is that paperwork becomes an excuse or reason to spend less time with the children. The balance must be managed.

Holding the child in mind

One of the central tasks for the keyworker is that they become, both within the overall responsibility of the institution, but just as importantly for the child, someone who holds everything about the child and his needs and concerns in mind, much as a parent would. The details of the child may be held in different places, but it is in the keyworker's head that they all come together. In his or her mind, the keyworker holds some sense of the child's whole life, and sorts that on a day-to-day level into some kind of order that is manageable, or if not manageable at first, then bearable. This may not involve very much actual 'doing' as such. This holding in mind is also about the child having some sense that the adult always has him or her in mind, and that what happens to him or her matters. One of the skills that really effective keyworkers develop is an ability to check in with a child when they know that a meeting or an event will have had particular meaning, or when it's an anniversary, to be able to send a card when the child is on holiday, phone if he or she is at home and so on, not leaving the child on his or her own when under threat in some way.

This link that is formed initially between a child and keyworker provides an important base from which other dialogues and conversations for the child can begin to happen. These can be about family, early memories and experiences, daily events, relationships and conflicts, anxieties about education or joining a group, how to contribute to the community meeting, home visits and how they will go, or went. Helping children to find a way of talking about things that matter is akin to holding someone's hand through a new experience such as a small child's first day of school, and taking the parent's role in helping the child make this transition. In this, the depth of the keyworker's own expertise in any of these areas of a child's life is not as important as the trust, mutual respect and reliability that is built up, and the child's sense that you will be alongside. In some ways, it is a journey made together.

Part of the wider 'whole'

It is in this area where the importance of the keyworker–child relationships and their connection to the wider whole become most important, and this notion of 'triangles' in the residential setting is a useful one in a number of ways. For all staff it is important to remember that the principal purpose of their relationships with the child is to be a starting point to address issues and conflicts that belong elsewhere in the child's life. It is neither a refuge in itself nor, with very difficult children who are very hard to work with or live with, a dumping ground that allows others not to have to think about the child. That would be destructive not only for the child, but also for the member of staff (and for foster carers who are so often put in that situation).

When I look back on my experience of the keyworking task and relation-ships, I have two different perspectives: one as member of staff/ keyworker, and one as Director. In many ways this director–child–keyworker relation-ship is a very powerful triangle, and certainly in the large group at least, issues to do with transference are more powerfully evoked by the director and people (men and women) in senior roles than the keyworker. The relationship with the keyworker, however, plays an absolutely crucial role in helping the child begin to negotiate a range of issues with which he or she is confronted in the residential setting. There are of course, many other sets of triangles that are created in the various working partnerships that are formed around each child, and each presents opportunities for the resolution of differing issues. One of these triangular relationships is that which is formed between the con-sultant, staff member and child or consultant staff team and children's group.

Adult relationships and their impact on the child

A crucial part of the network of relationships, therefore, is not just the rela-tionships that the children have (with either adults or other children) but also the relationships that the adults have with each other and how these impact on the children. The partnerships that adults form in the course of working with children, the ways that they complement each other's strengths and weaknesses, the ways that men and women work together, junior staff and senior staff, care staff and teachers, all have a meaning and impact. Splits and divisions, in the same way as particular couples becoming in some way 'over-involved', inevitably raise various degrees of feeling, anxiety and fantasy. These need managing, containing and understanding because unless these are contained in some way, their impact on the child or children's group can be quite profound, and invariably result in acting out: ('...this is how you make us feel...'). So, for example, if the adults behave in a way that heightens the children's anxiety – by arguing, or by demonstrating conflict – that the adults may be 'breaking up', it is inevitable that the children will act out this anxiety by doing whatever it is that will heighten the adults' anxiety (climbing on the roof, doing dangerous things, threatening) until the adults contain it in some way. If the adults don't rein this in, then the situation can spiral out of control quite rapidly.

Peer relationships

Finally, there is a whole area that I have not yet touched upon, but which is crucial to the wider consideration of the relationship network. This is to do with the children's relationships with each other. Within the therapeutic setting, the task is of how to establish these within a creative space that is contained in a way that enables them to contribute creatively to the wider therapeutic task and not become either a zone of acting out, or straight-jacketed by rigid sets of rules and regulations that leave no room for the exploration of what happens between them. The starting point is, I think (but it depends on the nature of the group, their ages, their stages of development and their histories), to think about the ways in which one can involve the children in becoming responsible (with the adults) for what goes on between them.

For now, the notion of peer relationships needs to be considered in three ways, and particularly in the context of thinking about what it is that holds and contains these relationships.

One is to do with the children's relationships with his or her wider group of peers and a crucial part of this is to do with group culture. By this I mean the sets of conscious and unconscious rules, assumptions and expectations that underpin group behaviour and process that is developed and assumed by the group as a whole. This is to do with what is sanctioned, encouraged and expected by the children's group, and may or may not correspond with the 'adults' rules' or indeed what is stated openly. It is about the attitudes and be-haviours that are encouraged and sanctioned, or challenged or forbidden by the children themselves. It is about the ways in which they develop collec-tively a sense of shared responsibility for the home, for what happens in it, what happens for or to each other, what secret activities (delinquent or sexual, for example) they do with each other. One of the tasks for a staff team is to nurture a culture that will be in the best interests of each child, and one that underpins healthy (enough) peer relationships.

A second factor is to do with the quality of the children's relationships with the adults and how these provide a container for the children's relation-ships with each other. If they are able to turn to adults to have their emotional needs met, they are less likely to turn to each other inappropriately or destruc-tively. When our children turn to each other to have their emotional needs met in a way that is split off from the wider whole, or from their relationships with the adults, it is potentially disastrous. Without containment this is, in the first instance, exciting and quickly becomes sexualised and they become over-whelmed by each other's needs and feelings of loneliness or anger, and by the complex feelings of guilt and humiliation that are associated with previous experiences of abuse. They become lost in feelings of hopelessness or help-lessness which result in either depression or a need for a 'buzz' (Redl and Wineman 1951).

A third factor is to do with how each institution ensures, as it admits new residents, that the impact that they will have on the wide group or any indi-vidual within it is kept in mind. All the children who come to us are very vul-nerable and susceptible to inappropriate or exciting relationships of various kinds. It is unfair on individuals and destructive for the group if careful con-sideration is not given to how able the group itself is to contain the impact that any new child may have. The existing group needs to know whether a child who may be offered a place is at a point where (potentially at least) they can join with the group, rather than overwhelm or be overwhelmed by it.

Finally, it is important to note that in the therapeutic community setting, the significance and meaning of the relationships that children or young people have with each other is not just about ensuring their rights to make friends and form relationships as part of any normal adolescence. What makes friendships special is the opportunity that they give for each young person to learn from the other's experience, so long as there is an investment in providing the space to reflect on this and to understand it.

Conclusions: Wider implications

Most of the children who are referred and placed in therapeutic communities have been placed in other care settings, children's homes and foster placements, prior to their placements in therapeutic communities. Today, many of the children who need a psychosocial care facility will be placed with families or foster carers because of the cost implications for local authorities, or because of negative views about residential care or therapeutic community provision, or often because of the rather simplified notion that children must be better off in a family.

It is of course important to say that there are many children in the UK who, for whatever reason, cannot live at home with their parents and are looked after in other families very successfully. Perhaps 80 per cent of children in foster care placements are provided for successfully, lovingly and with great skill and commitment. This, however, still leaves a significant proportion of children who move from one placement to another, mainly because of the impacts that they have on carers, on homes, on families and on other children.

The implications of the constant breakdown of children's placements for the children themselves are well documented and, over recent years, the aim to reduce the number of placement moves for children in care has become a key aim of the government's 'Quality Protects' programme. The impact of failed placements, however, is not just about the effect that it has on the children, but also about the impact that children have on carers and their families, in relation both to what happens while they are placed, and also to the sense of failure that is left afterwards.

There is no simple solution to the problems that very damaged children throw up for carers in different settings, whether these are therapeutic communities, children's homes or foster placements. Therapeutic communities also have many children with whom they cannot work. Nevertheless, there are conclusions that one can draw from experiences in each of these settings. One is that there are issues for those responsible for placing children in different settings, and especially where families are considered as the first option. To begin with there is an issue about assessment and selection, and second there is an issue about support, and the kind of support that is offered.

It could be argued that the social care model that is applied to looking after children within the broad care sector is adequate in perhaps 80 per cent of cases, if one bases success on the number of places that remain 'stable', although many of those, and particularly those with foster carers, are maintained at great cost, commitment, bewilderment and often with little help or support.

The notion of therapeutic placement is not one that is applicable only within the therapeutic community or smaller therapeutic unit setting which utilises a psychodynamic framework. A psychosocial care model starts with the notion of a framework that will help carers make sense of what happens between them and the children they look after, and deal with the impact that each has on the other. That makes positive relationships much more possible, so long as they are placed in a wider framework that supports and nurtures, and does not abandon.

CHAPTER 10

Structured Work:
The Space to Think

Alan Worthington

Introduction

Not long ago, at a conference that was addressing issues behind foster placement breakdowns, I was asked to summarise 'in two minutes' what I thought was meant by 'therapeutic' in relation to children's placements. The request seemed to sum up so much about the pressure that is currently placed on practitioners and managers to over-simplify what is essentially complex about the needs of very troubled young people. In two minutes? I thought the one point I would emphasise was the importance of maintaining a space to think and to understand. This applies to those who look after troubled children (residential workers, teachers, foster carers, parents), those who make decisions about them, as well as to the children themselves.

Perhaps the task of all therapeutic work is to provide for the young people with whom we work an experience that will compensate and challenge all that has gone before, and help them develop a capacity to think and to understand (Dockar-Drysdale 1990). However, when we are talking about developing the capacity to think, to understand and contain in therapeutic work for children, we are referring not only to what is provided for the children and young people, but also for the workers: the two are inseparable in that one cannot go without the other. In this chapter I would like to reflect on the use of formal, structured space in the therapeutic community, and how this is used to complement the wider experience of the residential setting and what happens and has happened beyond for each child.

The material that I provide here is primarily based on my experience as the first Director at Thornby Hall from 1985–1995. This was the first new establishment set up after 1983 under the Peper Harow Foundation, which had emerged from the work of its founding therapeutic community, Peper Harow.

It may seem confusing to the reader that when I talk about Thornby Hall, I move between the past and present tenses. In my current role within the Peper Harow Foundation, I maintain regular contact with the Director, and gain great pleasure from its continuing development. My perspective on this, however, is very much an external and supportive one, and so when I talk of my personal involvement and its internal world, it is strictly in relation to my time as Director and in the past tense. I am not in a position to speak about Thornby Hall's internal world in more recent years: that will be for its current Director and staff, and those involved more intimately. Nevertheless, there are points to be made about the broader model and its relevance today; this is where I speak in the present tense.

The large group therapeutic community model

When speaking about the use of formal, structured spaces in the therapeutic community, I mean those spaces that are provided specifically for particular dialogues, activities, groups which have specific therapeutic aims, occur regularly (e.g. daily, weekly), have fixed boundaries and membership in relation to when they start and finish, where they occur and who attends.

I think that it is also important, when thinking about the use of formal, structured space in the therapeutic community setting, to place this in the context of the therapeutic community model and the age and needs of the children for whom it caters. So what I say about the group structures that were developed at Thornby Hall must not be assumed to be either indicative of therapeutic communities everywhere, or necessarily applicable in the same way. For now, perhaps, five key aspects of the Thornby Hall model need to be highlighted.

The first is that it is a large group community that caters for up to approximately 25 young people, boys and girls, aged between 13 and 18 (and in its earlier days it catered for up to 32 children aged 9 and upwards). By large group, I mean that the client group lives essentially as a single group within a large house. The living area is divided between a boys' and a girls' area, and although boys and girls are not permitted to go into each other's areas, there are no locked doors between the two (in other words, a crucial part of the responsibility for the management of this boundary is with the children themselves, underlined by the lack of any system of locks). Within their respective areas, both boys and girls live in bedrooms that are either single or shared.

The second aspect of the Thornby Hall model is that it provides care, treatment and education in a single setting. One of the characteristics of all therapeutic communities is the integration of all aspects of each child's life, which at the very least are thought about and worked with as a whole. Education is a major element in this integrated task, and therapeutic communities are divided between those that include education as something that is provided on-site, and those that link closely with educational institutions outside. Some, Goldwell and Caldecott Community, for example, have their care and educational provision on different sites. At Thornby Hall, the education is provided in a separate block/education area on-site, although most of the older children undertake courses (GCSEs, A levels and vocational programmes) at local colleges. The education within Thornby Hall is provided by a group of specialist teachers with support from the residential therapeutic staff, some of whom have backgrounds in teaching. Teaching and therapeutic link together within particular supervision, dynamic and casework forums, so that there is a very strong investment in thinking together.

The third aspect is to do with the place of therapy and the respective roles of the staff and of the psychotherapist or consultant psychotherapist. This issue is an important one for therapeutic communities and the ways in which formal spaces and roles are thought about and deployed. This is discussed in more detail in the next section.

The fourth aspect of the therapeutic community model that is relevant here is to do with the way parents or families are included and worked with. This is a complex and difficult issue, particularly for children in care, who may not be allowed contact with parents, or whose parents are not accessible to being worked with within an integrated, therapeutic framework. This is made more complex for children who are placed geographically a long way from their parent, parents or families. Nevertheless, most children have some contact with one or both parents, or sometimes long-term foster carers.

Finally, there is something that needs to be said about the client group, relative to the therapeutic model and the use of individual therapies. All children express themselves, what they feel and how they struggle with particular sets of experiences, through what they do. One of the tasks of the therapeutic community is to help children articulate that experience in a way that can, over time, be worked with. Different mediums for therapeutic endeavour enable children and their therapists to access and articulate their respective experience in different ways: for example, through play, art, drama, storytelling or talking, and through cognitive as well as psychodynamic therapies. Play and the creative arts have always been central to Thornby Hall. Indeed, in our earlier years when working with younger, preadolescent children, the use of structured play was something that was quite central to our work with the children (Wright-Watson 1990). For the most part, however, and particularly as the group evolved to becoming a wholly adolescent one, structured group (therapy) work has focused very much more on the use of verbal dialogue. For other communities working with different client groups, that may be a second phase or longer-term aim, but each will have its own starting point according to the needs and abilities of the children with whom they work and for whom they exist. That is also relevant to the question regarding the location of therapy.

The location of therapy

Within the traditional therapeutic community model for adults, one of the essential characteristics is that the task of therapy is contained within the wider group function and through the integration of the various aspects of the therapeutic experience: the interplay between the experience of the social, physical and creative environment and the spaces that are provided for reflection, and coming to understand the meaning of what happens in the living, social group and what each child has brought to it. Therapeutic communities for children and adolescents vary around the location of the therapy and therapist in two ways. The first is fairly much in line with the traditional therapeutic community model, to have the role of therapist located within the function of the staff team and wider therapeutic structure, overseen and supported by the inputs of specialist consultants. In this model, the psychotherapist operates in a consultative, supportive capacity, meeting directly only with the staff, but never with the children, at least not in a formal way. This was the model established at Thornby Hall.

An alternative model, less common but used in some therapeutic settings, and especially with younger and extremely damaged children, is for the child to have regular sessions with the psychotherapist. Where children receive individual psychotherapy from someone external to the therapeutic institution, the 'split' between institution and therapy is considered by some to be in conflict with the therapeutic community model and method (based on the classic therapeutic community model established in adult work) and the distinction is thus occasionally made between, on the one hand, therapeutic communities and, on the other, 'children's homes that offer psychotherapy'. This is a relevant distinction. However, there are important reasons why some children might need regular, individual psychotherapy (see Chapter 4) and also be placed in a therapeutic community setting. It is not therefore a simple

distinction, and one of the key issues is the way the work of the psychotherapist is integrated with the work of the therapeutic staff team, how it is used to
help inform the broader therapeutic task, and how what happens in the
day-to-day work and relationships of the residential social group is made
available to the therapist and is alive within the therapist's work (Cant 2002).

That appropriate boundaries between the work of the therapist and staff
are maintained is clearly very important, but how they are thought through
and negotiated seems crucial (Maher 1999). It seems to me that it is sometimes
the failure to deal effectively and thoughtfully with the notion of 'confidentiality' that results in the total split between individual psychotherapy and the
wider therapeutic task or, rather, between the therapeutic task and the child's
care and/or education.

The therapeutic community: A network of interrelating groups

Melvyn Rose described Peper Harow as 'a network of interrelating groups'
(Rose 1990). This is a description applicable to all therapeutic communities
and, in this context, Thornby Hall. Such a conceptual model provides a
framework for thinking about the life and function of a therapeutic
community in terms of the different groups of people in the social, experiential context (staff, children and respective sub-groups), in the organisational,
clinical context (roles and groups) and in the interplay between the two.

The large group

At Thornby Hall, as at Peper Harow earlier, the large and small groups
together formed an inextricably linked 'whole', at the centre of which was the
community meeting or large group, which brought together all of the aspects
of the wider community into a single forum. I still remember vividly the first
community meeting I attended at Peper Harow, which went something like
this:

> At 9 o'clock the community, which at that time consisted of around 45 boys,
> and all the staff (about 20) came together with the Director in the large 'gold
> room'. Once the hum of informal conversation died (with the arrival of the
> Director) there was a short silence that left room for anyone to speak or start
> the meeting. Then one of the boys said (a little tentatively) that 'someone
> had smashed two of the windows in the gym last night'. Then there was a
> silence followed by a somewhat disjointed and speculative discussion

within a sub-section of the meeting, but which others listened to and thought about. Some of the boys looked intently at the floor, others shared glances and others listened. Undoubtedly, there were those who had their fingers on the pulse. A couple of boys were sharing a private, whispered joke that was ignored. One or two boys (who I guessed were associated in some people's minds with acts of vandalism) were challenged about the window incident: did they know about this? No, they certainly did not (so they said).

Then, one of the staff turned to one of the boys, who was (I assumed) not generally associated with this sort of activity: 'Oliver, I was wondering whether you might have had something to do with this?' Oliver, who went red with either anger or embarrassment (as I got to know him I realised he did this whenever spoken to at all) angrily dismissed the question, or accusation (as it felt to him), adding a 'why me then?' 'Well, I thought you were quite distressed after your social worker's visit yesterday and you looked…well…I wasn't sure what you would do with the conversation you'd had with him… It had obviously been very difficult… (Oliver had been told by his social worker that his parents didn't want to have him for the week's holiday coming up, as had been discussed and planned with them)…and later when you went off on your own for a bit…I was worried you might do something destructive. I came looking for you, but couldn't find you until I saw you in the dining room later'. 'Well…you're wrong', said Oliver, and withdrew from the discussion, while others added thoughts and views. Someone asked Oliver about the conversation Dave had referred to, but he didn't want to reply, and, after a while, this subsided into another, longer silence, and someone raised another issue.

Eventually, a small voice came from the corner of the room: '…yes, it was me', said Oliver, and with a great deal of help, managed to tell everyone about his conversation and how it had upset him. How far removed this kind of discussion was from the school I had worked in earlier, and the culture that it had created, I thought.

When we set up Thornby Hall, it was unthinkable (to me) that a large group community could be created without the nucleus of a regular, daily large group meeting that would in some way hold the complexities of the large, living group. Perhaps it is useful to point out that when the first community meetings happened at Thornby Hall (in 1986), they began with the first four children and the small staff team (six of us to begin with). As the children's group and staff team grew, so the daily community meeting grew too, quite rapidly in relation to the resources needed to nurture it, and in some ways possibly too rapidly for it to absorb at a digestible rate, not only the various degrees of disturbing experience every child – boys and girls – brought with them, but also the lack of cohesion and different sorts of experience and inexperience that the staff brought. Over the period of (approximately) the next 18 months, this group grew to one of around 15 children and 12 staff, and over 3 years to 30 children and 20 staff (about half of whom attended on any one day, according to the shape of the staff timetable). Numerically, at least, that's how the group grew. From a point of view of the group process and the development of the group as a place to reflect, think and contain, the story is a much more complex one. Elsewhere, I have written about the community meeting at Thornby Hall in its earlier days (Worthington 1990).

A large group meeting of this kind in the therapeutic community setting is complex and works at a number of levels, serving different functions. In general, it is a place where everything that impacts on the life of the group is acknowledged and discussed. One of its functions, therefore, is to do with the management of the wider social group. It may be used to communicate basic information, provide a space for planning, or discussing rules and establishing boundaries. It is a place where the meanings and impacts of leavings and arrivals can be acknowledged, shared and understood. It is a place where incidents and conflicts that impact on the wider group can be raised, looked at, discussed and perhaps resolved, but at least contained, for the individuals involved and for the wider group. Where they cannot be, it would be agreed as to where such resolution would need to go. It is a space in which time is given to making sense of relationships that exist within the groups, particularly where they have an impact on the wider whole. In a broader sense, it is also about providing a sense of containment and the holding of individual and collective anxieties, as well as a place in which unconscious processes can begin to be explored and understood. Sometimes, that understanding is for the staff to hold on behalf of the residents. The essential element of this seemed always to me to be that the staff could reassure the children's group, in whatever way, that they were mindful of and quite able to contain their anxieties and manage the issues that were driving it.

One question that might be asked is whether there was any subject or issue that would not be discussed in the community meeting? The short answer is no, and it was always our policy that anything that had an impact on the group or community in any way could be acknowledged and discussed. This, however, did not mean that the Director or staff did not need to remain mindful of their responsibility to manage certain discussions very carefully and sensitively, or point out that particular discussions would need to happen elsewhere – where they might, for example, raise sensitive, personal, private issues that touch areas of confidentiality (e.g. about one of the children and his or her family). How issues that are personal and private but which may have such an impact on others at the same time are negotiated with individuals is an important and complex issue in the therapeutic community (see Chapter 2 on values in therapeutic community practice). What mattered, however, was that if the adults could not discuss something with them absolutely openly, the children understood why, could ask why, and were reassured that it was being thought about properly and being managed.

One of the tasks for the large group in the therapeutic community is managing to develop a capacity to contain those things 'about which we dare not speak'. One of the areas of community and personal life that raises great anxiety for both staff and children is the experiences of sexual abuse and premature sexual experience that children bring with them, how these relate to their emerging adolescent sexuality, how they gain expression in the residential setting, in the relationships that the children form with each other (or even as we know, within the relationships that the children form with the adults) and impact on the wider group and on individuals in their different ways. These experiences need to be engaged with by the adults in a way that addresses their complexity, contains both adult and child anxiety, makes the development of dialogue possible and establishes appropriate boundaries. All of these tasks in some way begin with what is established in the large group, but perhaps in no other area can the importance of the links between community meeting, small groups, individual work and the work that is done with the staff be illustrated so clearly (Sprince 2002).

Small groups

At Thornby Hall once we had established a large group meeting it met every weekday morning for 40 minutes from 9.00. Then, at a point when the children's group had grown to about 15 in number, we introduced some small groups of 4–6 children and 2 staff on a Thursday morning in place of the large group. Some time later, in the course of discussing bedroom changes (who would like to share with whom, etc.), the children asked if these could be discussed in separate boys' and girls' groups. This 'temporary' split in the large group facilitated other discussions, the children asked if we could keep the small groups going and they remained as a permanent part of the group structure.

One of the reasons for setting up the small groups was to give each child a chance to be included more directly in a group discussion, and to be helped to do this in a more personal forum, where aspects of their own early experiences could be thought about, talked about and considered as to their impact on the present. It did not follow, therefore, that the small groups were necessarily easier. And for some, the small groups became more intimidating because at least in the large group they could sit silently, nestled in beside a keyworker or 'special' member of staff, whereas in the small group, conversation was more direct and more personal, and the pressure to contribute felt more immediate.

As with the large group, any item for conversation could be raised by anyone in the group, adult or child, although the adult groups' leaders needed to be very mindful of how issues raised (by them or by the group members) would affect levels of anxiety. The task to begin with was one of creating a space that felt containing and reassuring – not easy with younger children especially. Initially it was about helping children learn to value and engage in dialogue; in some ways, the subject matter was secondary, which is not to ignore the ways in which the things that needed to be talked about could be avoided by talking about something else. That could become a topic for discussion in itself, even with the younger children, and could be done in a fun way.

There would never in reality be any shortage of issues that could be thought about, whether these were to do with relationships in the community, day to day events that resulted in a conflict with a member of staff or a peer, what happened in groups itself, or things that children brought with them. So, for example, one item for discussion might arise from a child having come back from a home visit or a telephone call. This would of course raise issues about earlier experiences of families, loss and trauma for each child, but finding a way of first of all acknowledging this or coming to talk about it together was a step-by-step process in the development of the small group. Gradually, the groups generally got to know each other and in a particular way, very much dependant upon the skills of the staff (with weekly supervision from the consultant), to nurture this process and work together. Much thought was given as well to when children were ready to join in these groups, and the judgement on such readiness was a crucial part of the nurturing process.

The groups could focus on how relationships between the members affected each other and children drawn towards understanding what they felt and why they did what they did. A new child might be initially relieved to know that he or she was not alone in his or her particular experience and that others were equally intimidated by the nature of the discussion. From within the group itself an issue might arise, for example, from someone being late (boundaries around groups were made an issue) and being challenged about this. Maybe all of the members of a group might be late (or even boycott the group altogether) and in these cases there was a potential staff-child split: "How come you're all late?" "Because this is all shit, that's why!" Such a starting point did not usually augur well for an enlightened conversation, but it related to the understandable levels of anxiety and staff needed help in responding in a way that was not just about their own feelings of diminished authority, rejection or anger. This is where the supervision and consultancy is so important as responding only on a behavioural level is almost bound to exacerbate the potential split between the adults and the children

With the instigation of small groups we introduced, with the consultant psychotherapist, a system of supervision for the staff running the groups. These met once per week for an hour, with each pair of group leaders presenting their most recent group, and this would be discussed with the other group leaders and the consultant. As the staff skills in running the groups developed, so the instances of children boycotting them or being late reduced too. As the culture in the wider community developed to becoming one in which the groups, like the community meeting, became valued, then attacks on these were focused on or thought about more in terms of an individual's struggle about something else.

Individual work

Earlier in this chapter I outlined some of the issues surrounding the location of therapy in the therapeutic community. This is closely linked to the role of the psychotherapist or consultant psychotherapist, as it is to the employment of other therapy specialists in residential settings: play therapists, drama therapists and art therapists. A key issue to do with the therapeutic model is whether what they provide is integrated as part of the wider therapeutic whole, or whether it is something that is provided as a parallel service, bounded by confidentiality or by the absence of an integrating framework.

For now, however, my discussion of individual work is limited to the provision at Thornby Hall, in which individual work was focused particularly on the relationship and partnership established between child and keyworker (or special adult).

In therapeutic communities, this role of the child's special adult is a complex and multilayered one. At its core is the notion of 'forming a relationship' with the child, to listen, to be there and provide a continuity, to provide advice, to be an advocate, to hold the child in mind, to maintain links with the family (where this is possible) and the external environment, with the referring agencies, the social worker; and to ensure that specific administrative and statutory requirements are met and overseen (see Chapter 9).

Both at Peper Harow and at Thornby Hall this relationship was established, as is much else is in the therapeutic community setting, through the interplay between the formal and the informal. These include the experiences of engaging in various activities and having time to be together and to 'play', as well as, over time, developing a regular and more formal space that is reserved for looking more seriously and in a focused way at specific issues that preoccupy the child and the various aspects of his or her life. These include the things that affect him in the residential setting as well as events and relationships beyond, especially events in the past and family. From this point of view, keyworker time is divided in two ways: keeping the child in mind (as a parent might) and 'being there' when needed, as well as ensuring regular, formal times. Three things seem to affect the balance of informal and formal time. One is the stage of the child's emotional development: it is much more noticeable with the younger, less integrated or more fragile children just how much they need the adults to be close by and to hold them together in moments of crisis. As development progresses, so too does the capacity to withstand upset and contain it until the time allotted with their keyworker (or whoever has the role of providing this individual space). The second is the development of the relationship and trust that the child has in the adult's support. The third is to do with the adult's own development and his or her capacity to hold the child in a way that makes him feel understood and supported.

Spaces for staff

At the outset of this chapter, the point was made that the need for space to think and understand is not just about what is provided for the children, but as much or more to do with the space that is provided for the staff.

All therapeutic communities place a high priority on having a framework that helps them to think through and to understand the requirements and needs of the children, but also the meanings and the impact of the work on them as workers. This is essential if they are to engage with the children in a way that holds them emotionally, but ensures that staff are able at the same time to maintain their own personal and professional boundaries and also to work with the children in a way that engages with their internal worlds from a position of empathy and understanding.

At Thornby Hall, the framework that was developed for supporting and developing staff was one that built upon the principles and practice established at Peper Harow before it. Within this there were different focuses for staff understanding and this has continued to be developed within the framework of an accredited staff training programme (run in partnership with Middlesex University and developed with the help of the Tavistock & Portman NHS Trust). These are evident more widely in therapeutic community work and other trainings. The first area for focus is about understanding children and the meaning of the personal histories that they bring with them, and how this is expressed in their day-to-day interactions and relationships. This is the focus of (things like) the Case Discussion meetings. These focus almost entirely on the child's history and needs, care, education and treatment plans, and implications for practice.

The second area is to do with the spaces that are created for staff to reflect on what they bring to the working forum, the ways that the work and the institutional setting impacts on them, how they impact on it and on each other. At Thornby Hall, this was gradually established (with our consultant psychotherapist) within a framework of staff dynamics and experiential groups.

A third area of focus is the space that exists between the adults and the children and what happens within it in relation to how they meet particular aims and objectives. It is about how staff bring together their understanding of the children and their needs, their understanding of themselves and their engagement in the work, and apply this to the task of 'working with' the children – individually, through their day-to-day interactions, but in a way that maintains their capacity to engage, to keep a clear and separate sense of child and self, and to think. This was addressed through the establishment of work discussion groups and individual supervision.

Integrating the whole and implications for wider practice

Throughout this chapter, the point about the 'integration of the whole' is made constantly. This is central to the ways in which the groups and individual structures and spaces complement each other in a single, broader task which is both about the maintenance of the wider therapeutic environment and about each person within it. All of these groups and individual spaces in their different ways link to each other in a way that is akin to the operation of a zoom lens, moving between the wider picture of the whole and the more minute details and meanings for the individual.

The management of boundaries of confidentiality is a crucial element in this: how they are established; what is or isn't regarded as confidential and where, on what basis, and how sensitive issues are taken from one context and placed in another are important. A great deal of thought, sensitivity, skill and clarity is needed in this area.

For all the children at Thornby Hall, it was made quite clear that whatever had been provided through documentation and related reports was shared and discussed with all of the adults, and would be thought about, 'looked after' and contained by them. Similarly, the understanding with children was that anything that they themselves shared with a particular member of staff would also be shared (at the staff member's discretion) with other staff in the course of their work and in supervision forums. This ensured two things: first, that all staff were included in a joint sharing and understanding of each child, and second, that staff could not be split off from the wider staff team through, for example, the sharing of 'secrets'. This may seem axiomatic, but I am aware of how easily this happens, especially in the absence of good supervision for (especially) inexperienced staff, and when staff and children get caught up in collusions, or the disturbed child's own personal 'scripts': the unconscious re-enactments of earlier relationships and experiences into which the adults, without a holding framework of their own, are drawn (see Chapter 5). This shared knowledge and understanding of the wider staff team has a number of important aspects, one of which is that the child is able to feel held and under-stood by the staff as a whole. It also ensures that the staff too are held within an integrated and wider whole, in which the various elements of the organisa-tional and professional framework are linked together. For each child and adult, these come together in particular roles and forums: the director and community meeting, in relation to the individual's relationship to the wider whole; and within the relationship with the keyworker (or therapist) and one-to-one sessions, with respect to the bringing together of all the different aspects and details of the child's own life.

This notion of integration is an important one for how very damaged and deprived children are looked after, taught and helped in the wider fields of social care, health and education. Perhaps the implications are best illustrated by the extent of the impact of children's emotional states and behaviours on their teachers, foster carers and the wider public. This is bewildering and, in many instances, traumatising and they are left feeling like the children who have impacted upon them. There are no simple answers. Nevertheless, a crucial starting point is to preserve the space to think and to understand.

CHAPTER 11

Developing the Quality of Teaching and Learning in a Therapeutic School

Andy Lole

Introduction

Therapeutic schools and communities in Great Britain have for many years provided an educational component to the overall treatment plan for children and adolescents experiencing severe emotional and behavioural difficulties. Traditionally this education provision would have been strongly influenced by the therapeutic task of the organisation, rather than by a set curriculum. Education areas may have provided an environment within which young people had a choice of what they wanted to learn, and how they wanted to learn, with a significant emphasis being placed on access to regressed learning experiences, aimed at building solid foundations for learning, and meeting infantile emotional needs. Opportunities to communicate symbolically through play and creative activities would also have been widely promoted. Literacy and numeracy skills teaching would have been the main curriculum focus. It was not seen as a high priority for these young people to reach their academic potential whilst in these placements, or leave with any externally re-cognised qualifications.

As part of the nationwide reforms of the education system in the late 1980s/early 1990s it became clear that much improvement was required to the educational provision of many schools for children with emotional and behavioural difficulties. The challenge for therapeutic schools and communi-ties was to improve the quality of their educational provision, whilst maintain-ing and developing their psychodynamic approach. In this chapter I will outline the work in which I have been involved, of developing the educational provision at a therapeutic school to fully meet the requirements of today's schools, and the particular learning needs of children who require residential therapeutic placements. The principles behind many of these developments would be relevant and transferable to all schools, although it is clear that the resources available to the school I describe are well beyond those of many other schools.

Educational profile of pupils

Jenny

By the time Jenny reached nursery school at the age of three and a half she was already well known to social services, having been taken into care one year earlier, following an early life highlighted by terrible abuse and neglect in her natural family. She was a wild thing, tearing around the room, knocking everything over, shouting and swearing, throwing toys and sand everywhere, in a constant heightened state of excitability and anxiety. Any unsupervised contact with other children led very quickly to Jenny attacking them, or touching them inappropriately, so consequently the other children were very fearful of her and did not want to play with her. Anything that was breakable from a pencil to a book, would become the focus of attack from her without any obvious reason. When staff intervened physically she would kick, punch, scratch and bite, and often fall into a huge rage where she would need to be restrained for up to 45 minutes at a time. She constantly disrupted any group activity by shouting and screaming, or prodding and poking other children. She was unable to engage in any activity for more than a few minutes, and then only with one-to-one assistance from a very patient adult. She had no idea how to play with toys or how to play with others.

Despite all of its efforts the nursery struggled with Jenny from day one. Every day saw a large number of incidents where both children and staff were being hurt by her. Her foster parents were regularly called to the school to try to help, which usually resulted in them having to take her home. A year and a half on she had made very little progress in her learning, and her behaviour difficulties were becoming worse as she got bigger physically.

The transition from nursery to infant school was very hard for Jenny. She found sitting at a table for more than a couple of minutes impossible, her basic skills were very underdeveloped, and her physical skills were very immature. She demanded individual attention from an adult almost continuously through her disruptive and aggressive behaviour, which often meant that the teacher had to leave the other children to their own devices, or ask for Jenny to be with the head teacher. She was unable to be out on the playground during break times as she would attack her peers as soon as she became distressed or upset.

Douglas

Douglas' mother had become pregnant with him by accident. She suffered badly from postnatal depression, and did not feel attached to him in the way that she felt she should. At 18 months she could not cope with him any more and asked social services to help. Douglas ended up with his maternal grandmother. His mother disappeared for the next three years. When she came back on the scene she wanted to have him living with her again, which happened virtually overnight.

Douglas had done fairly well at nursery school, although he could be quite withdrawn and only really liked playing with one or two children at a time. He had formed quite close attachments to the staff, and seemed fairly contented most of the time. His basic skills were developing reasonably well, as was his general knowledge. However, he found the move to infant school very difficult, becoming very clingy to his mother before school, not wanting to go or to be left by her. He also found all transitions at school very problematic, and also any changes to the normal routines. At these times he would become incredibly violent, saying that he wanted to kill the person who was having to deal with him, and then seeming to try to do this. Staff became very fearful of him and tended to back away from him when they saw he was becoming unsettled, which tended to increase the likelihood of him becoming aggressive. His mother's response was either to blame the school for upsetting him, or not dealing with him effectively, or feeling that he was a monster who could not be helped.

With both children the local education authority provided additional support in their classes, and a wide range of different strategies was tried following assessments from an educational psychologist. Both then received statements of special educational needs and were transferred to day special schools for pupils with emotional and behaviour difficulties. In these settings they were taught in smaller groups, by teaching staff that were experienced in supporting pupils with similar behaviour problems. The focus of their new schools was to provide additional help with accessing the curriculum. Both children clearly required extra help with their academic learning, but this alone was not the answer. The behaviour difficulties they had exhibited in their last schools continued to be the dominant features of how they presented in their special schools, and fairly quickly it became clear that their new schools were going to struggle to contain these extreme difficulties. This seemed to be due to the fact that they stemmed from significant very early life experiences, which had had a profound impact on each child's ability to develop emotionally, socially and academically.

To help children such as Jenny and Douglas learn, careful attention must be given to all aspects of their developmental needs, in an environment where they can be contained safely, and their overall difficulties can be understood enough to be able to address them. In this context it then becomes possible to help them make academic progress.

Background information

I arrived as Headteacher at the Mulberry Bush School in Oxfordshire in April 1994. The school had been founded by Barbara Dockar-Drysdale in 1948 and was well known for its therapeutic work with primary-aged pupils, placed mainly from London Boroughs, the Home Counties and the West Midlands. When I arrived at the school it was just beginning to transform itself from a large group model, where, in the residential area of the school, all 36 children were looked after and managed mainly as a whole group, into a small group living model, where children would live in groups of up to 10 in separate, mainly autonomous households.

Being aware that its educational provision was not up to the required standards needed to satisfy the new OFSTED criteria, the school commissioned a local educational authority quality assurance team to carry out a full inspection early in 1994. It was on the basis of this report that we put together our first development plan, to create a therapeutic education area that fully met the needs of the children referred to the school.

Curriculum and classroom structures

The first stage of our development plan was to create a clear educational structure for the school that defined what we were aiming to achieve and how we were going to achieve this. To do this we decided that the basic foundations onto which the education provision would be based should be the National Curriculum. This would mean that the children at the school would have access to the same learning opportunities as all other children in the country, and that our teachers would need to have the same curriculum knowledge base as all other teachers. This was an important step that would help the school become less isolated from the world around it, and open up a wider range of opportunities for the children and teaching staff to be included in learning experiences outside the school. It would make the possibility of children transferring back into a mainstream school much more feasible. In their national examination of special schools providing for pupils with emotional and behaviour difficulties Cole, Visser and Upton (1998) identified several key characteristics in identifying proficient schools. These included well-organised programmes that interested and challenged pupils, including 'normal goals' which helped to build pupils' self-esteem.

One of the first education policies we wrote was our Policy for Teaching and Learning. In this policy the teachers identified the conditions by which our children were most likely to learn, and most effective ways to teach the children. As recommended in the Elton Report (1989) we agreed common rules and expectations that all children and staff members should know about and conform to. This policy played an important part in raising our expectations of the children and of ourselves as teachers by sharing good practice across class teams and challenging staff to look at the way they thought about and organised the learning environment.

Curriculum training was a very high priority at this time, and we allowed it to take precedence over any other training needs. Alongside developing the teachers' knowledge of the content of the curriculum we provided training for all teachers on a common approach to plan lessons effectively. This required teachers to be very clear about the exact learning outcome for each lesson, in order to sharpen the focus of teaching and to be able to measure whether or not the children had successfully achieved the intended outcome. The children at the school tended to express high levels of anxiety about learning new things and being challenged, and low levels of self-esteem by displaying very disruptive and aggressive behaviour, focused directly on the adult who was placing a demand on them. This placed extreme pressure on the adult whether to continue with these demands or back down to avoid the power of the child's attack. A more clearly defined learning task helped the teacher stick to the plan, whilst still having to deal with the very difficult feelings being projected by the child.

We paid close attention to the difficulties many children had during and just after the transitions to the classrooms. To help with the transition from households to class after breakfast and lunch we decided to have the same structure in all classes, so that children would learn exactly what to expect when arriving in class, which would be an activity that they could do fairly independently. In the morning this was called early work, which would be handwriting, spelling and simple maths activities, and the first half-hour of the afternoon would be devoted to reading activities. We also asked care staff to accompany the children into the classrooms and help them engage in these activities for the first part of the session.

The children tended to damage their own and others' possessions when they were feeling frustrated or angry, which were emotions regularly expressed. This led to a deprived physical environment, where things of personal or group value could not be left out for fear of attack. Alongside this there had been inadequate investment in resources and equipment for teaching and learning at the school over preceding years, and in the actual fabric of the classrooms. The Board of Trustees agreed a substantial increase to the education budget to enable planned improvements to happen, and we began the process of raising our expectations of the children, to make sure that all classrooms became properly equipped with a wide range of good quality resources, and that these would be looked after and valued. This was a long and slow and at times very painful process. It required determination from staff that even when we went through times of severe damage we could find a way forward, and that we would continue to invest in, repair and replace things to establish and maintain a warm, homely and cared-for environment. What we learnt was the importance of continuing to think deeply about the most effective ways of working with these difficulties, and being prepared to approach each problem with as open a mind as possible, which allowed us to look at the individual circumstances in each case.

Providing supply cover to a class of children at the Mulberry Bush School was not easy, as the children tended to become very unsettled by a teacher's absence. As Salzberger-Wittenberg pointed out:

> Part of the anxiety experienced by the individual relates to phantasies about the reason for the loss. They may be of a persecutory nature, e.g. fearing the teacher is punishing them, or that he dislikes and rejects the group, just as the child feels unwanted and unloved by the parent who goes away. They may be of a more depressive nature, concerned with having exhausted the teacher's strength and/or tolerance, evoking earlier feelings of having emptied or damaged the breast, or tired out his parents. In addition there will be all sorts of ideas about what the teacher may be doing when he is absenting himself from the group. (Salzberger-Wittenberg 1999, p.142)

It was important that teachers could be absent from their classes, and that the person covering the class would have some understanding of the difficulties the children might be experiencing. We were able to create a new senior teacher role at this time, so that an experienced teacher within the school could cover classes when needed. This continued to be very challenging work for this teacher.

Support structures

The establishment of this new role enabled us to address another area of difficulty in the school. When a child was being so disruptive in the class that s/he was stopping all the others from learning, as they had been able to do in their previous schools, or a child was out of the classroom without permission, there was no clear procedure for managing these situations, or for taking responsibility for dealing with them. Children would ensure that their own disruption and chaos would control the environment around them in and out of the classrooms, which the teachers seemed powerless to interrupt. What we decided was needed was a small team of people based outside the classrooms, who were constantly available to support the running of the classes, in order that the curriculum could not so easily be hijacked by the behaviour of the minority. This team would help to ensure the safe containment of the children and support the administrative, support and planning work of the care teams that also took place whilst the children were in class. We decided to call this team the Learning Support Team, and it began its existence based in a small corridor, with the senior teacher leading it in the mornings, and me leading it in the afternoons. Care staff were then timetabled to work in the team for half a day per week. The brief of this team was either to support a child within the classroom to help him or her focus on the classwork, or to support a child outside the class, to prepare him or her to return to the class as soon as they were ready. What this initiative also did was to help provide conditions within which teachers could feel safer, allowing them to work more creatively with the difficulties they faced.

We were very fortunate to have some flexibility of staffing to be able to deploy people into this role, which other schools would not be able to do. The Learning Support Team immediately provided greater stability to the school day and enabled difficulties to be addressed more directly with the children. This work was very difficult, continually focusing on the children who were presenting the most difficult behaviours. Some children would be extremely intimidating and violent, requiring frequent restraint, and high levels of attention and support. Staff working in this setting needed to be constantly aware of managing their own feelings, being exposed to such raw and uncontained feelings from the children. The benefit of this work was that teachers could establish clearer boundaries around acceptable behaviours in the classrooms, knowing that children who pushed these boundaries could be helped to conform to them by the Learning Support Team.

At this time we changed the way in which we organised our class groups, putting a group of children who had previously been very uncontained in their classes together into a class, with a single, clear objective of increasing their attendance in class. These children had been having a huge negative impact on the school as a whole, and on the individual members of staff who had been working with them. We needed to replace the amount of time and energy that had been spent either managing their behaviour or worrying about them or the staff who were regularly being abused by them, with a more positive approach. In their new class they would be rewarded if they were able to remain in class all day. Once this objective had been achieved expectations were raised, whilst maintaining simple, clear objectives for the class. The main development for the school here was recognising the benefit of creating a class with a specific brief to address extreme difficulties that were presented by a minority of the children. The aim of this type of class would be to provide the right conditions for the children to have access to the curriculum, and to help them mature sufficiently to integrate with the other children in the school. This could be compared to the function of a pupil referral unit in the mainstream school sector, working with children to enable them to be able to cope back in their own schools.

For the children to change, to be able to form trusting relationships, feel safe and secure, build their self-esteem and self-confidence, and develop social skills that allowed them to live comfortably with others, they required regular and repeated experiences that helped them reframe their view of themselves and the world around them. Staff teams needed to be prepared to deal with the same issues, same extreme levels of resistance and insecurity, and fight/flight reactions from the children on a daily basis. What was achieved the day before would need to be faced again and again, maybe over several years, before any real change would be effected. To support the staff in coping with such challenging work regular supervision sessions were provided with line managers, and meetings with the therapeutic adviser. These meetings allowed space to focus on how staff members were feeling, how these feelings might be connected to the children and other staff members' feelings, alongside thinking together about more effective ways of working with the children. We also made sure that our internal training programmes for all staff paid equal attention to the content of what people needed to know, the process of providing and accepting support, and sharing the load of such difficult work.

Meeting individual needs

The completion of the first stage of the development of the educational area, with clear curriculum structures in place, run by teachers and learning support assistants who had a good knowledge of the curriculum, well-resourced and equipped classrooms, and a more contained working environment for both children and adults, took about four years. The second stage of development was to build onto these foundations learning experiences that were increasingly adapted and differentiated to meet children's particular needs, and that fitted more clearly into an integrated whole school approach to provide therapeutic treatment plans for each child as an individual. Fundamental to this was the creation of an individual target-setting procedure that provided more structure to our long-established system for assessing children's social and emotional needs. At regular intervals throughout a child's stay at the school the teacher, keyworker and family team worker would report the outcomes of assessments carried out in their respective teams to an Internal Case Conference, which was chaired by a senior member of staff, and at which the school's therapeutic adviser was in attendance. Out of this meeting a number of targets were agreed, which identified the key areas of work to help the child progress over the following six months. These targets were then presented to the child's external network for their input at the child's next statutory review. This process further developed a holistic, therapeutic overview of the child's development, providing clear guidance and direction to all the different staff teams and individuals working with the child.

For Douglas the targets initially focused on helping him deal with anticipated failure, and for him to feel less intruded upon, which would reduce the need for him to defend himself. Both seemed to relate to his violent attacks on others. The next group of targets was aimed at helping him learn that he could have some things unconditionally, without having to be either over-sweet or aggressive, and at helping him interact more comfortably with other children. We then worked on building his self-confidence to explore his own interests, to help him develop his self-identity and self-esteem, and to learn to use self-reflective spaces, which he could use when feeling stressed. The final part of our work with Douglas focused on helping him work through his violent feelings symbolically, particularly through his art therapy sessions, and his newly found interest in *War Hammer* toys, and for him to begin to use his, by then developed, relationships with adults to talk about, work on and deal with his anxieties.

In Jenny's case her first set of targets looked at providing her with focused, reliable primary care and nurture, opportunities to develop her ability to play with an adult and other children, and the introduction of a flexible system of sanctions that she could understand and would provide some structure around her behaviour. To raise her self-esteem we helped her develop her own respect for her body and its cleanliness, and helped her not to feel so worthless or a victim. Next we decided it was important to minimise the physical contact she was having with staff, as this appeared to be taking the place of her develop-ing broader relationships with others; for example she demanded physical contact by being violent, which led to her needing restraint. We continued to boost her self-esteem, partly by valuing the things she made, and helping her to look after them. The last set of targets for Jenny looked to improve her memory and concentration, and her social skills, and to help her complete some life story work. The work involved in transferring these targets to the classroom setting was supported by each class team having fortnightly con-sultation with the therapeutic adviser, which provided an opportunity to discuss individual children or the class in general.

Having got to know the content of the curriculum, and having worked with it with the children for a few years, we felt it was important to begin to adapt it to make it more accessible and relevant to the particular groups of children we were working with, to increase the progress pupils were making. Whilst continuing to ensure all subjects were taught in all classes to provide a broad and balanced curriculum, it had become clear that some aspects of the National Curriculum were so far away from our children's own experiences that it made it very hard for them to learn and retain this learning. We had also learnt that by presenting aspects of the curriculum in a way that addressed a child's current emotional or social needs it was likely to make the learning much more meaningful and thus accessible to the child. So, for example, in our reception classes scientific teaching of changing properties, and map work and food production from the geography curriculum were taught via a topic about food. A topic on fairy tales included learning the seven times table using Snow White and the Seven Dwarfs, teaching counting in threes using the Three Little Pigs, and learning about fractions using ginger bread men. For some of the older children elements of the literacy strategy were taught in a project on managing our angry feelings, and another around boosting our self-esteem, and the history curriculum was brought to life in the class room by a visit from Bob the Builder, who had discovered some ancient artefacts whilst putting in some drains!

Alongside planning learning objectives that were more likely to accu-rately meet individual's needs, we looked to train and empower our learning support assistants, so they were able confidently to lead learning activities for small groups of children. This would mean that teachers would be able to dif-ferentiate the planning of children's learning further, again to the benefit of individual children.

The role of keyworkers in the school had always been highly significant to the progress of the children, as Cole, Vissor and Upton identified in effective residential schools for children with emotional and behavioural difficulties generally:

> Most important was the fact that RSW (residential social workers) appeared as dedicated people willing to make personal sacrifices on children's behalves. They were able, and willing, to form relationships and pay close attention to children's needs and were skilled in using the life-space to support a child's social, emotional and sometimes educational development. (Cole *et al.* p.163)

It seemed essential to find a way of including children keyworkers more clearly in their academic work, so we introduced termly teacher/keyworker meetings, where the child, teacher and keyworker would look together at the work the child had been doing in class. This was intended to ensure that the keyworker had a good knowledge of the child's abilities, particularly in literacy and numeracy, and to allow the child to receive praise from the teacher and keyworker. Later we introduced Basic Skills Plans for children who were not making sufficient progress, where class teams, keyworkers and parents/carers were all given suggested activities to help the child progress.

Reintegration work

Preparing to leave the school was something that seemed to preoccupy many children for months prior to the actual event. At Salzberger-Wittenberg explained:

> For any separation evokes earlier situations of being left by mother or father, and thus the fear of being once again exposed to feeling helpless, in a state of chaos and panic. By the nature of his role and/or personality the teacher may therefore be experienced as the person who holds the different parts of the mentality of each individual within the group as well as holding together in his mind the different aspects of the members who comprise the group. Without his containing presence, the group fears that it will fall apart, be lost, lose the link between its component parts and in addition lose the memory of the past good experiences. (Salzberger-Wittenberg 1999, p.141)

Children would often seem to regress during their last few months at the school. Behaviours that the child had not exhibited for some time might re-emerge, often becoming as problematic as when they first arrived at the school. This often would become a time of great stress, both for the children and staff working with them. Whilst trying to empathise with the child's situation, staff also tried to maintain appropriate expectations of the older children. However, children often seemed overwhelmed with anxiety and unable to maintain their higher levels of functioning and communication for periods during this time.

To help prepare the children for this big transition we set up links with a local mainstream school, a variety of clubs and societies, and some work experience placements. Children in our top class received a letter from a pen friend at the local school. After some exchanges of letters, the children were taken by their class team to visit their pen friends, who met them at the school door, and showed them around their school. The following week our children began to visit the school for half a day per week, sitting next to their pen friends. The staff from our school would be around to support them if they needed it, or help out in other ways. Sometimes this could be observing children from the mainstream school who were exhibiting emotional and behaviour difficulties, in order to assist their staff. After a few weeks the pen friends came to visit our school, where our children showed them around. We also arranged sporting fixtures and musical exchanges between the two schools.

Once a new school had been identified for a child from the Mulberry Bush School to move on to, we encouraged a similar type of transitional process to be put in place. Our teacher would visit and we would invite the teacher or learning support assistant from the next school to visit us. Information about the child's abilities, and the most effective ways to teach and manage them would be passed on, including the individual target-setting work we had in place for them. A series of visits would then be arranged for the child, which may well have been planned with additional weekends at home, to help prepare the child for moving back or spending more time at home.

Assessing progress

Throughout a child's time at the school the teachers would use the systems that we had developed for assessing and recording pupils' progress, which would inform the planning for the next step. Curriculum attainments would be assessed at the end of every term, and transferred into the child's individual record book. Individual education plan targets would be assessed termly, with the child's whole school targets assessed twice a year. We measured children's classroom on-task levels on a half-daily basis, and the number and severity of incidents of violence on a weekly basis. The information about the incidence of violence was analysed on a weekly basis by a group of senior managers from all areas of the school, where decisions would be taken about appropriate action. Data from all these records would be transferred to whole school tracking sheets, which enabled us to have a regular overview of progress of all the children, to be aware of the effectiveness of the provision.

Conclusion

Children placed in therapeutic schools and communities will always place huge demands on the people responsible for their education. However well organised and equipped the learning environment of schools and communities become, they will continue to require staff to cope with very high levels of challenging and disturbing behaviours, well in excess of what most people will experience in their lives. What has not changed for teachers teaching severely emotionally disturbed children during the last 20 years is the need to understand and manage their own feelings, evoked by working with people who find the challenge of learning new things very anxiety-provoking and threatening, and who communicate these feelings through powerful projections and antisocial behaviours.

The provision of good quality educational opportunity, which places realistic yet stretching expectations upon children and leads towards meeting their academic potential, is an important aspect of the task of therapeutic schools and communities. Educational success raises self-esteem and self-confidence, and helps individuals reframe how they see themselves and their place in the world. It is a positive pulling force that can be tremendously valuable in a young person's journey to a better future. Improving the quality of teaching and learning of therapeutic schools and communities should be a high priority within overall institutional development work. To aid a young person's transition from these specialised treatment settings back into the mainstream world of schools, colleges and work, it is advisable to base the structure of the education provision on the same systems used in mainstream education. These systems and structures can then be adapted to become more meaningful and accessible to individual pupils, where a therapeutic understanding of the underlying difficulties the young person is experiencing, and effective ways of working with these difficulties, can be integrated into the learning programme.

Therapeutic schools and communities provide the best hope for some of the very troubled and troublesome young people in our society. It is essential that all young people placed in these important national resources benefit from the positive aspects of the educational reforms that have been taking place throughout the United Kingdom over the last few years.

CHAPTER 12

Keeping Families in Mind

Jane Pooley

Introduction

'Oops, they fell to earth!' This chapter focuses on the inherent dilemmas of re-membering that children placed in alternative care settings actually have parents who hold a place in their minds, whether or not they can be active and present in their lives. We will explore some ways of working with the parents and families and with other significant people, often foster or grandparents.

Staff in residential settings work with some of the most damaged and vul-nerable children and young people in our society. In the wish to be helpful, it is easy to forget that the children have come from previous care experiences with their parents and often with experiences of foster and adoptive carers too. They will also return to their parents or alternative carers when they leave the therapeutic community and sometimes at holidays and weekends. It is vital to a productive outcome that working partnerships and relationships are forged with the families of origin, foster and adoptive carers. Making these connections helps us to understand the significance and influence of early re-lationships on the current behaviour and needs of the children. At a more general level family work contributes to planning viable and sustainable futures for all the children in residential settings.

Therapeutic residential settings are focused on creating a safe and nurturing environment in which the child can slowly begin to feel tolerated and cared for, and to learn anew how to respond to adults who set appropriate and thoughtful boundaries. These children need to believe that their thoughts and feelings are valued and of interest to those around them (Winnicott 1964). It is not surprising therefore that therapeutic settings have not histori-cally been good at remembering that the child will, whether we wish it or not, place a great importance upon his or her family of origin. When I refer to children I am talking about young people aged 5–20 years. Even though younger children and adolescents have different needs their families in their minds are intact. We find that whilst the adolescents who come to specialist settings may chronologically be a certain age they are often in need of staff to work with them and understand them at a much earlier developmental age. Most of these young people will never have experienced early attachment relationships of a quality upon which they could build their lives, so the therapeutic community gives them a chance to rework these experiences.

Messages from research and social policy

In Britain government departments have taken seriously the need to support the fabric of family life in our society. In the late 1990s there was a much welcomed surge of energy generated from central government to address the needs of children, young people and their families and to find ways of delivering appropriate services in order to support family life in its many configurations.

Many research reports have indicated that the needs of children are best met when they are cared for in a family environment that can give them a safe base for secure attachment relationships (Ainsworth and Salter 1978; Fonagy, Steele and Steele 1996; Main 2000).

David Utting's report highlights research evidence indicating the 'desirability, where possible, of maintaining parental contacts and continuing to work with families' of children placed in care. It states that: 'Clean breaks may work for adults, but they are not the answer for children.' (Utting 1995).

Working with children, young people and their families in therapeutic residential settings

The children

So, what about the children and young people who are unable to manage life in a family, the children who come to specialist residential care and schools? Children and young people referred to a residential setting (school, home or psychiatric unit), invariably present with multiple difficulties. They are likely to have experienced numerous disruptions and losses and to have had involvement with multiple agencies and professionals, e.g. foster carers, hospitals, social workers, community child psychiatric services, education and other residential units (Bowlby 1988).

The staff

Staff on the other hand are frequently confronted with a complex dilemma. This includes the need to hold both the hope of being able to help the young people and their families or carers solve the sometimes unbearably painful difficulties that have brought them into the service, whilst at the same time holding the often unacknowledged and unconscious wish for the therapeutic community unit to fail in bringing about change. Staff often wish to give up, stop trying to bring about change and new understanding in the child's network. The amount of energy and enthusiasm needed to find even the smallest solution or next step forward with the child takes over their focus and a wish to shield the child from further pain and disruption takes over. Unconscious processes are at play in the carer/child relationship that militate against knowing and thinking too much about the world that is external to the current environment. This dynamic is entirely understandable and yet needs to be worked with and understood in the team.

The parents and carers

Parents have often experienced their own difficulties, unresolved losses, trauma and disruption. These issues can surface in relation to their child needing a therapeutic community. A dreadful sense of loss, not being good enough or feeling to blame is very often carried by the parents and carers into their relationship with the therapeutic community. The hope is however that if parents and carers can be engaged in the work and focused on supporting change for the child, then issues that they have carried between themselves, often for many years, can be worked through at the same time (Bowlby 1969; 1973; 1980).

Understanding and healing hurts from previous generations and times can very often enhance the potential for the present relationships (Byng-Hall 1995). Thus, through engaging with each other's needs more fully, changes in relationships can occur that may allow living together, or at least being together in some way, in the future.

The task of the therapeutic unit

Those who work in the residential sector know that most of the children in their care have for one reason or another not been able to live successfully in a family environment. The children and young people have usually experienced multiple placement and family breakdowns. It is not uncommon for a 10-year-old child to have been through many family environments before he he or she arrives in a therapeutic community. The experience of repeated moves, often because the place of care has not been able to tolerate or understand the child's behaviour, exacerbates the child's sense of distrust of adults and heightens the fears and anxiety that precipitate the unmanageable behaviour. Therapeutic residential settings focus on creating a safe and caring environment in which the children begin to feel held, tolerated and cared for. When this happens they can begin to learn, often for the first time, that they need adults to set caring and thoughtful boundaries for them and that their thoughts and feelings are valid and of interest to those around them. It is not surprising, therefore, that staff with this focus have not historically been good at remembering that the child comes from another family and may well return to it, or to an alternative family, after treatment. It is a difficult task to require care staff to hold the child's network in mind when they necessarily have to be preoccupied with creating an environment, and relationships, that address the child's distress in such a way that it can eventually be thought about and reparation and healing can begin. Creating an environment in which the young person receives the message, 'we can bear you and we are committed to being alongside you in despair, struggles and joys', is after all central to the task.

Long histories of previous professional involvement with the young person and the family and carers may generate feelings of apathy, powerlessness, anger, mistrust, suspicion, disappointment, defiance, hopelessness and disillusionment – a stance that is commonly verbalised in 'what can you do?' or 'there is nothing that can be done'. At the same time, for some families and young people, the possibility of having an intense assessment, treatment or diagnosis can be experienced as a relief too. Some parents and professionals place a great trust in the therapeutic community, communicating a powerful feeling of hope that this may offer a solution to their troubles.

So what should be done with these dilemmas? How can work go on that attends to and develops these interfaces without blame and competition but with a genuine regard for all players? Having described and explored some of the dilemmas associated with the family/care network joining, and being joined, into the therapeutic community process, let us move on to discuss relevant theory and its clinical application in this area of work. We will do this through the use of four case studies from different contexts and involving children of different ages. These studies also raise another important question, namely, who should do the work? If it is the keyworkers, what are the inherent dilemmas for them?

Family work with a young child who returned to the family after placement in a residential school setting

Daniel's difficult behavior in his junior school was a cause for concern from the age of five. His behaviour was said to be inappropriate and disruptive in class and often violent in the playground. Shortly before Daniel started school his family experienced great emotional trauma when his uncle was convicted and imprisoned for sexually abusing Daniel's younger sister, Patricia. The family received counselling.

By the time Daniel was eight his behaviour had further deteriorated: he was underachieving, he required constant attention, did not respond to praise or instructions, was rude and defiant to staff and used abusive language. He also wet and soiled himself frequently. He was admitted to a residential school when he was nine.

The work with Daniel in his own right involved being part of the day-to-day integrated living and learning experience in the therapeutic and education milieu where he was encouraged and helped to look at his chaotic and aggressive behaviour, to make links with his feelings and to find different ways of expressing them. Later, when it was felt he could benefit from it, weekly play therapy was offered. Alongside this the family team worker began to connect with the family. Initially she found them still traumatised by the sexual abuse, and further traumatised by the previous counselling that perhaps had been carried out too early. However, over the two and a half years of Daniel's placement, the worker visited approximately every six weeks with telephone contact in between visits and the family slowly started to talk about the trauma and how it had affected each family member. Daniel had witnessed the abuse and was able to share with his mother his feelings of responsibility, and his fear that he, the only boy in the family, would be like his uncle. (Chapters 4 and 5 have addressed the questions about how Daniel will have been helped to think about his experience of being placed away from home and taught to understand how his troubled thoughts and feelings were being expressed through his behaviour.)

Daniel left the residential setting to attend a mainstream school and to live at home with his mother and sister. The family worker continued to support them, though family sessions were not as often as when Daniel was resident. The issues they worked on in the first year after he left were the inevitable shift in family members' roles brought about by Daniel's return there full-time. His mother had anxieties that Daniel's still fragile sense of appropriate behaviour would let him down at his new school, and she had feelings about having to 'fight' to get him the extra support he needed.

The family sessions continued to be experienced as supportive by the family. In school Daniel did very well academically, and his behaviour was within tolerable limits. Some 20 months after leaving the residential community Daniel was still doing well at school, and family members were living more harmoniously than they had done for many years.

The family worker in this case offered the family a chance to learn over a period of time to trust professionals. Using his supportive presence they were able to start talking to and hearing each other, instead of retreating into a 'safe' silence. Without this space, Daniel may never have been able to share his feelings of guilt and his fear of becoming an abuser, thus continuing to shoulder this burden on his own. Enabling the family to let go of some of their secrets is likely to have reduced the tension in the family and in this way made Daniel's return home full-time less likely to break down. A note of caution about facilitating the telling of secrets – there are times when the risks of telling can have the potential to be more damaging than not telling (although this was clearly not so with Daniel and his family). It is often helpful for this discussion to be part of the work with the family.

Family therapy with a 13-year-old girl in a psychiatric unit undertaken by a trained family therapist

A 13-year-old girl, Gemma, was taken into care after she had alleged sexual abuse by her father. Two younger siblings were also removed from the family and placed with foster carers. As a result several professionals became involved with Gemma and her family and began to adopt positions in relation to whether they believed Gemma or her father. Thus the professional network began to parallel the polarised positions of truth and lies held by the family members themselves. This situation remained stuck for two years with very little contact between Gemma and her parents.

Gemma was referred to a residential psychiatric unit where she elaborated on her accounts of her abuse, and fluctuated between wanting to see her parents on one hand and wanting nothing to do with them on the other. Her changing positions gave rise to much debate and difference within the clinical meetings. Family therapy appointments were planned and the workers were surprised to note that until then there had been no meetings with the parents to hear their views.

The first session was with the parents only. It became very confrontational and polarised with parents saying they felt marginalised, blamed and ostracised and that there had been very little consultation with them about Gemma's welfare. The therapist worked with their feelings of powerlessness and of not being believed. This acknowledgement allowed members to feel less under attack and to take more risks in their discussions, avoiding the need to hold an intractable position, a tactic most of us use when we feel cornered. The therapist was then able to acknowledge the differing views of people and how these had solidified into a debate about truth and lies. The parents could then be helped to use family therapy space not as a way of arriving at a decision as to who was telling the truth and who was lying, but to understand what had happened to them as a family as a result of the abuse, including the impact on their feelings and future relationships. Gradually Gemma was also able to join these discussions and remain involved in the family meetings and dialogues about relationships.

This example illustrates a concept in systemic thinking described by Gregory Bateson as the difference that makes a difference either in a relationship or the meaning that is ascribed to it (Bateson 1972). The differences were provided by the worker adopting a stance of interest and curiosity where blame and judgement were suspended and where family members could both comment on and hear others' comments about relationships in the family. In this way new information was able to emerge that made it possible to understand and try out 'old' relationships in new and different ways. Previous work had become stuck because the parents and professionals had been locked in dialogue that was about truth and lies. In this sort of conversation there is no possibility of change or more open discussion as all participants become further and further polarised in an attempt to 'prove' their point. Steering conversations away from the theme of 'truth versus lies' which had paralysed the family so far, to one about family relationships, allowed the parents, Gemma and professionals to have a common focus and diminished the other polarised positions, which they had previously all adopted. Bringing the parents into the frame allowed all the family members to begin to negotiate new ways of relating. (See Chapter 6 for more on systemic approaches to family therapy.)

Work with the adoptive family of a boy (12 years) placed in therapeutic community residential home

Thomas had been in intensive care as a premature baby. After much deliberation he was returned to his mother. Within weeks he was again in intensive care, near to the point of death, following extreme neglect by the mother, who had been deserted by the father. He was taken into foster care and a care order was granted. An adoptive placement was made with Rose and Richard when Thomas was three and a half years of age.

Richard was pleasant, jovial, practical and hard-working but emotionally rather distant. He found it difficult to allow himself or others to know how he felt. Rose was warm, sentimental and caring; at times she became over-whelmed and anxious.

Thomas was referred to a therapeutic community at the age of eleven. His behaviour had become more disruptive and aggressive, both at home and in school, and he was at risk of becoming drawn into the company of groups of young local delinquents. In the family home he was prone, when Richard was absent, to sudden violent outbursts of increasingly dangerous intensity, largely directed at Rose.

The adoptive parents were very positive toward the idea of placement in the therapeutic community and engaged eagerly with staff right from the beginning. After an apprehensive start, Thomas also engaged well with the team although it took some while for him to reveal the patterns of behaviour seen prior to admission.

The head of social work, who managed the referral, transferred the work to the treatment team once Thomas was admitted. The head of social work remained available to advise staff and to talk with Thomas's parents on occasions when communication became difficult between them. Thomas was often furious and upset when he was aware of his parents talking and thinking together with staff. This anger was seen as indicating how anxious Thomas was that adults would not be able to work things out together, which made it even more important to persist so that Thomas could experience adults as finding ways through situations without resorting to violence, walking out or other feared traumas.

The young woman who became his key worker quickly began to experi-ence, through the very powerful projections and transference from Thomas, just what his adoptive mother had been experiencing with him at home. Equally, it gradually became possible to understand the extreme quality of his anger and aggression in terms of the lack of attachment to his birth mother, her deliberate neglect and her final rejection of him because she saw him as re-sponsible for her partner's abandonment of her.

Rose had been so affected by this transference from Thomas that she began to feel that she was going mad herself, to the point where she had had to seek psychiatric help. The focus of support to the parents – but mainly to Rose, as Richard tried hard to remain on the periphery – was in the following areas:

- providing regular verbal updates of Thomas' progress to help with their guilt at 'sending him away'

- providing containment for Rose's overwhelming feelings of anxiety about her sense of failure as a mother and her fears for the future

- avoiding being drawn into a collusive relationship with the parents against the local authority social worker, who was in danger of being excluded from the process

- helping Rose and Richard adopt a more empathic and less punitive approach to Thomas, alongside helping Thomas to understand that he needed to regain their trust if being at home was to become a more positive experience for him

and later in the placement:

- helping Rose to deal with the huge emotional threat posed by Thomas wanting to respond to the wish of his older birth siblings to resume contact with him now that they were no longer in care.

There was powerful resistance to this latter issue from Rose even though it had been agreed during the original adoption proceedings. Helping both sides see and understand the other's point of view was a complex and delicate piece of work.

Most of this work had to be undertaken by Ruth, the key worker in the residential unit, because it was with her that the relationship existed. It was often conducted over the telephone because of the distance of the community from the family home. These calls usually took place late in the evening after Ruth had finished her residential shift and during a period when she was now experiencing from Thomas the full blast of hatred, anger and attack (frequently physical) which had previously been directed at Rose. It was not therefore surprising that Ruth was beginning to doubt her own sanity and needed the utmost understanding and support from her team, alongside skilled and insightful supervision from her manager.

Towards the end of his residential placement, Thomas had achieved much growth in his personality and in his capacity for self-reflection. Had the work not included the wider network of the family, progress would have been much more limited and would not have been sufficient to preserve this young person's place in his adoptive family.

This case demonstrates the scope for working with the families of children in residential treatment settings. However, had the community in question had the structure and resources to enable the social worker who managed the original referral, or a designated family worker, to undertake much of the direct work with Rose and Richard, the key worker would have been freed from an almost impossible task in terms of the stress and anxiety she had to carry. She would also have been freed from an equally difficult position of dual loyalty in relation to Thomas on the one hand and his parents on the other. Whilst it is possible for primary and keyworkers to work with families it is more efficacious to split the roles whilst maintaining good communication between workers. We must not forget the tremendous scope for engaging with families and supporting them at less obviously 'family work' times such as handovers at weekends and holidays, visits and telephone calls.

Family work with a 16-year-old girl in a psychiatric unit (undertaken by a trained family therapist)

Mandy, a 16-year-old girl referred to an adolescent inpatient psychiatric unit, had an extensive history of self-harm, and a diagnosis of 'Reactive Attachment Disorder'. She had lived her early childhood with her alcoholic mother, until receiving inpatient treatment for an eating disorder at age 13 (during which time she made an allegation that she had been sexually abused as a much younger child by her stepfather). Following this she had spent two years in foster care before moving to her paternal grandparents, from where she was admitted to the psychiatric unit.

Family work is a part of the contract of admission for many adolescent units. Initially the work with Mandy was carried out in two parts, first with Mandy, her father, his partner and paternal grandparents, and second with Mandy and her mother. The initial focus of the work was to enable Mandy to form sustainable relationships with her family which would be supportive for her after her discharge. It soon became clear that the timing of this future-orientated work was not appropriate; there was too much in Mandy's mind that was unresolved from the past. Her understanding of what occurred in the therapy room was embedded in experiences of abuse and so the conversations that were being attempted were ones in which she did not feel that she was being taken seriously (Jones 1993).

In response to this feedback the focus of the work changed to meetings between Mandy and her mother, and Mandy and her father. This took place in order to provide the opportunity for Mandy to address her experiences of the past with both her parents separately. Mandy struggled and finally succeeded in expressing her hurt and anger at not feeling protected, or even parented, by her parents as a child. Both parents attended regular meetings and in this way began to open up new possibilities for relationship with their daughter. In a 'debriefing' session with Mandy, after the work with her parents had finished, she said that, for the first time, she felt that she had been believed and thus able to see that her psychiatric difficulties were no longer the result of her being 'bad', but that they stemmed from the relationships with her family, for which her parents, as adults, had to take some responsibility.

The family worker was convinced that Mandy's sense of being believed at a profound level did not merely refer to what passed between her and the worker on that occasion, but to the total therapeutic experience. Through doing family work, Mandy was able to rewrite her understanding of her family's past. This original family script had been co-created throughout Mandy's childhood in the joint action of the everyday relations between her and her parents. It was only by re-entering those relationships at a different time and in a different context that her taken-for-granted beliefs about herself could be reviewed and revised so that she could move forward towards a more productive and satisfying life (Byng-Hall 1995).

Who should do this work?

There is no easy answer to this question. It is helpful to have staff dedicated to the task of working with families and networks as it frees up the keywork relationship to focus on understanding the child and working with his or her projections. Asking a keyworker also to work directly with the family dynamics can be overwhelming, as the work with Thomas illustrates. Issues of split loyalty and blame are hard to escape. However, the keyworker holds important information that is going to be helpful to the family work, such as his or her experience of what it is like caring for the child on a day-to-day basis and passing on ideas and models of working with the child. Systems need to be set up so that these experiences are understood by the family worker and can be woven into the work.

If family work is undertaken by staff external to the unit there is a very real danger of splitting, experiences not being connected up and mirroring of old patterns being played out in the family. It is a vital part of the healing for the child to experience adults working together and forming thinking alliances where difficult issues such as ambivalence, blame, hurt and so on can be talked about safely and connected with narratives about past histories and possible futures. Dedicated family staff need to ensure that they develop effective feedback to the unit and keyworker as well as ensuring that good communication channels are in place, particularly around the sharing of day-to-day issues. There is no easy way of doing this; those involved need to search for meaningful and workable solutions.

There are many opportunities for keyworkers to influence and link with the family – handovers at weekends and holidays, visits, telephone discussions. These moments have important potential for getting alongside the family and finding ways of supporting each other in the task of caring for the child. Keyworkers can embrace them as opportunities to model ways of thinking and caring (see Chapter 7 for more ideas on the 'opportunity led' approach to incorporating potential learning from everyday incidents and interactions into the therapeutic task). They will also need to be mindful of the, often unconscious, wish to be better than the parents or to blame the parents. These feelings are inevitable given the close working relationship that residential staff have with the children. A good supervisory process (see Chapter 14) and good links with the family workers ensure that these issues can be thought about but not played out.

Some final thoughts

No one would dispute that in an ideal world children should live, grow and mature to adulthood in a family environment. It is right that the Children Act 1989 encourages us to work in 'partnership' and maintain contact with 'birth families' wherever possible. However, we need to be careful that, when this has not been possible for multiple and complex reasons, the children who drop out of this ideal do not become refugees in our society, being moved aimlessly around, compounding their sense of isolation and worthlessness. For members of staff caring for these children who have been neglected and abused in their families, it is hard to think about, let alone work with, the family and care network in the child's home community. The natural desire is to want to protect the child from any further hurt and disappointment, and even to blame previous carers. It is hard to consider the possibility of the children returning to their home environments and what this means in terms of working towards the best possible transition.

Systemic, psychodynamic and attachment theories and practice offer frameworks for working with these challenges. It is helpful in this work to understand family patterns, relationships, beliefs, values, interactions and the context in which these are embedded. It is also important to consider how people construct ideas about themselves over time in order to make sense of life's events and experiences. Systems thinking also helps to look at the interfaces between the young person, the family and the social system of which they are a part, including extended family, peers, other agencies that may have been involved, and the unit itself. Psychodynamic theory enables us to use the thoughts and experiences that are evoked in the work to understand more fully the feelings and dynamics of individuals and their important relationships. It also helps us to sit with and digest sometimes very painful and evocative relationship dynamics. Attachment theory wonderfully bridges the two and reminds us of the vital importance to psychological well-being of having significant figures that are available to listen, respond and place thoughtful limits without judgement and blame.

Family work in residential units presents an opportunity for the young person, family and professionals involved to explore past, present and future issues in a different and perhaps more meaningful and connected way than previously possible whilst the placement institution and its staff hold and offer a reliable source of consistent, bounded and thoughtful experience of attachment, reparative care and graded learning opportunities.

We ignore at our peril, and the peril of children we hope to care for, the families who are alive in the children's and young people's minds, even if not present in their day-to-day lives in the residential setting. Working with families supports the prospects of a more satisfactory future for these children and young people, one in which they can in turn be good-enough parents to their own children.

With thanks to all the Charterhouse family work group who contributed to this chapter: especially to Lindsey Stephenson, Shila Khan, Chris Knight and Andrew Elliott for their case study material and to Jocelyn Avigad for her thoughts and feedback.

Part III

Management and Development

Introduction

It was proposed in a classic paper describing the work of one therapeutic community for young people that 'you can have management without therapy but you can't have therapy without management' (Butlin 1973). This axiom remains profoundly true, and indeed it could be argued that the best therapeutic community practice embodies a creative collaboration between the therapeutic impulse and the organising principle and that, in the treatment of these most chaotic and anxious young people, neither element will get very far without the other. In terms of mainstream residential practice these views find support in the results both of research findings (e.g. Sinclair and Gibbs 2000) and of inspection reports. One overview of a national inspection reported that:

> the effectiveness of staff in those homes where *good practice* was observed was based on:
>
> - clear leadership,
>
> - organised and consistent ways of working, *and*:
>
> - clarity of purpose.
>
> (Social Services Inspectorate 1993: 31)

There could be no clearer indication of the importance of good management in the residential care and treatment of children, although sadly both research and inspection frequently identifies serious deficits in the quality of residential practice and in the leadership and overall management of that practice.

It may be hoped that in matters of management, just as in the detail of everyday practice (as evidenced in Part 2), therapeutic communities may be able to offer a lead or inspiration to those engaged in mainstream residential practice – or at least that they may be able to suggest some of the appropriate thinking and structures which can contribute to the best management of practice. This is the focus of Part 3. We begin with the very personal account by Richard Rollinson of his experience as Director of the Mulberry Bush School. This account focuses first on the early days of his ten years as leader of that community, then takes us through to the issues facing him as he came to the end of that period. Peter Wilson describes the functions of supervision and consultancy and shows how, when taken together, these two mechanisms for staff support and development play an essential role in ensuring the quality and appropriateness of the therapeutic support offered to young people. Another truism in this work is that 'you can't provide good support for young people unless you have access to good support for yourself', and Peter shows how this works out in practice, again drawing on some of the unconscious elements in consultation. Peter's focus is primarily on individual consultancy and supervision, although there is also a strong case to be made for consultancy to whole staff teams, since it will be clear from elsewhere in the book that therapeutic community practice is strongly systemic in involving the whole team working together with the whole group of young people.

Andrew Collie focuses on the overlap between staff development and training for individual staff members and developmental issues for the whole team in his chapter on staff development and training, and he shows how opportunities for learning and growth may arise for staff in the course of everyday life, just as they do for young people.

We mentioned research findings earlier, showing how they indicate the need for effective management, and we have included in this section a chapter on the current state of research in this field. John Wright and Phil Richardson give an authoritative account of recent developments, indicating both the necessity but also the complexity of the task of researching the effectiveness of residential treatment of young people.

Shortage of space has meant that we feel we have not been able to do full justice in this section to the themes of management and leadership, and we would like to return to these topics in a future collection. There is also more that could be said on other aspects of research, and especially on the value in this field of the more qualitative approaches which seek to explore and explain the processes of treatment rather than attempting to prove connections between particular methods and their possible outcomes – again, this will have to wait for another time!

CHAPTER 13

Leadership in a Therapeutic Environment: 'What a Long, Strange Trip it is'

Richard Rollinson

Introduction

Frankly, in my view the last thing the world needs is another paper on leadership that is full of complicated and largely abstract ideas about theories, styles, strategies and skills. Of course such contributions are not unimportant or entirely without value. However, there are so many of these texts already available that their volume alone can come close to overwhelming us. At the same time the question 'what does it take to lead a therapeutic community?' is an important, indeed central, matter for us to address thoughtfully and rigorously. Only by doing so will we have any chance of developing and maintaining an environment that offers to very troubled children at least some hope for healthy recovery, change and growth. Therefore, this question is the focus of this chapter.

It may be of interest to know that in Latin 'focus' means fireplace, or more specifically 'domestic hearth'. Hence it was not entirely accidental, for example, that shortly after his election in 1932 Franklin Roosevelt gave a series of 'fireside chats' to a nation hugely anxious about its survival while in the grip of what was for many a remorseless depression. Whatever he said each week in his talk, the underlying message was always the same, 'Things may be terrible in families, towns, cities and the countryside across our nation, but at its hearth (and its heart!) things are calm, thoughtful and strong. So we will endure and recover to better times'. So too today a leader of a therapeutic community must attend to 'the hearth and the heart' in ways that preserve and develop further the good and goodness within the community itself and within its members, staff and residents alike.

Therefore, I offer a very personal account of and reflections on some of my own experiences while the Director of the Mulberry Bush, a residential therapeutic school in Oxfordshire for children aged 5–12, suffering from severe early emotional disturbance and deprivation. Inevitably it is impossible to cover all the important themes in one chapter, but I do believe that the ones I shall touch upon have a general application across a range of therapeutic environments and will resonate for many involved or interested in leadership in such settings. I believe from my own experiences and from the influence of others (e.g. Greenhalgh 1994; Obholzer 1994; Ward and McMahon 1998) that there are numerous vital aspects to this task of leadership. However, its unifying 'focus' in therapeutic communities is upon identifying ways of creating and maintaining a strong containing environment that holds/endures and that will help people develop relationships and ways of living that will facilitate emotional growth and learning. That is the primary task of the leader in support of the primary task of the entire community.

To begin with...

I propose to start with *endings*, that is my ending as Director, or even more precisely my telling the children in January 2001 that I would be leaving in the summer. I choose this route because in our field we know that good endings are the basis of good beginnings and good *carrying-ons*. We also recognise that it is at such times of major transition that what has been achieved or put in place strongly will often be most apparent or revealed.

In September 2000, the beginning of my tenth year as Director, I had decided that for a variety of reasons, personal and organisational, it would be best for me to move on. It was time to take up a new challenge elsewhere and to open the way for a new Director to take forward with renewed energy the next phase of the Bush's continuing development. The matter had been turning over in my mind for some weeks before I came to the decision, but once having made the decision I felt thereafter that it was the right one for everyone. The Chairman of Trustees, the Conducting Management Group (CMG), which included most senior staff, and then our consultant were the first I informed. With the latter we agreed a time in November to inform the staff, fixing it on a Friday of the children's weekend home so they had some space to absorb my message and its impact. Finally we decided that I would tell the children in late January by which time they would be settled back in from the Christmas holidays. It was also long enough before the February mid–term break so that they did not have to carry the impact of the message out with them before it could be worked on within the school.

Of the entire process, the prospect of telling the children was the hardest part for me to contemplate without feeling awful and anxious. As Director I had met each child first as part of their assessment process even before they visited the school, and I was there to receive them into the Bush and pass them on to the grown-ups who would be looking after them. Hence, while rarely involved in their day-to-day direct care and education thenceforth, I was still a significant figure for them and saw them for some time most days. I was anxious for different reasons (for them and for me) about declaring openly to them in a 'Gathering' (as we called our whole group forum) that I had decided to leave. Once done, deep down I could neither pretend any longer that it wasn't really so nor retract. For the first time I would have to acknowledge fully the final reality – I was leaving of my own volition.

As the day grew closer I became increasingly preoccupied with these worries, particularly about somehow saying the wrong thing or not being clear enough in what I was saying. I took this to our weekly CMG session with our consultant. He suggested that I might find it helpful first to write out what it was that I was so worried about saying or saying badly, and that this might help me to be clearer about what I needed to say in the context of our task, and to be heard as I wanted to be. I found this to be a very liberating and calming exercise. There on the paper were all my anxieties, diversions and false reassurances to them and to myself that my going did not really matter and would make no important difference. There too were my fears that I would be hurting them irreparably if I did not stay on now.

I was then able to write what I needed to say, keeping it to four basic points: everybody who comes to the Mulberry Bush eventually leaves, children and grown-ups; most often people leave because it is the right time, the work which a child or adult needed to do here had been done, at least well enough, even if there was more to be done somewhere else afterwards; I've been Director for ten years now and I've been helping people make lots of changes; and, now it was my time to plan my leaving and I have decided that I will leave in the summertime.

On the day of the Gathering I still felt nervous but was able both to convene the meeting and inform the children without seizing up. With all the grown-ups as usual in, amongst and alongside them, the children themselves paid full attention as I spoke, hearing me out soundlessly. When I finished, there was the almost classic pause of a few seconds, and although it seemed much longer to me I felt no overpowering tug to leap in and reassure. I was looking at them all carefully. Some looked startled, some blankly impassive, while others had snuggled up close or closer to a grown-up. Then Charleen called out, 'So who will be looking after us then?' All eyes were on me, and I replied, 'Well, I will be going, but I'm not taking all the other grown-ups with me. They will still be doing the real looking after you like they do already. The Managers (Trustees) whom you've met before have already been thinking about how to find someone who will become the next Director. As soon as we know anything we'll tell you so you know too.'

Jay then called out, 'I think John (Deputy Director and Head of Residential Therapy) should be the new Director. He's the one who really looks after us already because Richard goes out to meetings a lot.' Again all eyes on me, but before I could respond Asher said, 'Well, I think it should be Andy (Headteacher) because he already talks to us all together like this'. Eyes back to me and I replied, 'I can understand exactly why you children would think of John and Andy and perhaps other grown-ups whom you already know and trust becoming the new Director. I'm sure that the Managers know how important it is to you that whoever they choose to replace me will be a person whom all the children and grown-ups will be able to trust, whether you know the person already or will have to get to know him or her.'

The children began chattering amongst themselves so I called them back to attention and asked if there were any other questions for now. Lewis asked, 'Who do you think should take your place, Richard?' I replied to the fixed eyes of all (grown-ups included) that not only did I not have a person in mind, but it was also very important that I not suggest someone or even be part of choosing my replacement. My contribution had been deciding to leave and then helping the Managers to plan the way in which they would find a new Director. That didn't still the interest and several more children called out, 'Really, Richard, who do you think?' I said, 'Well, one person has come into my mind and he's right here in this room.' 'Who, who?' 'Dallas [one of the older children]; he's always telling me how to do my job or that I haven't done it properly!' Dallas, sitting right up front near me and as usual pretending that he was only half listening, immediately looked at me and said, 'What's the pay?' I said, '£5 pocket money per week and meals.' 'Right, I'll do it.'

There was some laughter and then Charleen stood up and said, 'Richard, if you're going, I think Rowan should have your baseball bat and hat because he really likes baseball, doesn't he?' George then called out, 'Well, I like baseball too. Can I have that poster in your office?' Other hands were now being raised to make bids for things of mine. I said, 'Look, I know that I've told you big news today, but remember I'm not disappearing immediately. I'm going in the summer. That's several months away so we have time to make plans. Whether that includes children having some things of mine remains to be seen, but we'll certainly have enough time to say proper goodbyes.'

Soon we had been together for over half an hour, with a collective 'focus' upon a matter hugely significant for all, and there hadn't been the slightest distraction, let alone disruption. Please remember the profile of this population: 34 children, aged 6–12, at the Bush for between four months and nearly four years. Prior to arriving most had been excluded entirely from school, many from several and the large majority were uncontainable in a family. Such were their levels of confusion and disruption. Those few who had remained in school or at home had only managed it due to the extraordinary effort of a teacher or headteacher and the devotion of a carer. Now here they were, attending to, thinking about and discussing a major transition, a leaving, an ending – an occasion which in their not too distant pasts had been synonymous with catastrophe, breakdown and disarray. They sat, their eyes on me – these very young and troubled children in amongst, leaning against, holding the hands of grown-ups, who while they themselves were still working on the reality of my moving on, were nevertheless at this time entirely available to the children around them. And out of that scene or experience came important questions, put in such a way that they highlight fundamental issues that apply to our primary task regardless of whether a leader is announcing his or her departure. 'Who will look after us?' not 'Who will be the next Director?' or 'Where are you going?' Because of the containment provided by thoughtful planning and by caring adults physically and emotionally alongside the children the fundamental question could be asked directly. It did not need to be 'acted out'. Then some thoughts about possible resolutions could be entertained (or played with) instead of there being a desperate drive to impose an absolute certainty.

Surely these questions and thoughts reveal something very important – namely, the features of a leader that are key in the eyes/minds/hearts of the children themselves, and I am sure that these are high on the grown-ups' list of priorities too. So, 'from the mouths of babes', a leader looks after them/everyone (us) and he or she talks (and listens) to and with them. In both activities a leader treats each of them as a human being capable of hearing important things, of feeling strong feelings and of talking and thinking about such things. This occurs in the presence of others, children and adults, living and learning together not just *in* a group but even more *as* a group. Moreover, a leader has to be able to cope with uncertainty so that the children can too and he or she has to be clear about the limits of what even a leader can do. Finally, for now, a leader knows and ensures in the work of emotional healing that time, thought and planning must be at the heart and hearth of our activity.

With these in place transitions and change can be managed, whether they be arrivals and departures or ones that occur naturally through day-to-day living.

Where otherwise anxiety and uncertainty become acted out in, for example, violence, our experience tells us that continual, daily hard work in the areas of care, communication and containment (undertaken by grown-ups with passion and compassion for these children) ensures that violence and disruption will become unnecessary. This is because there is no breakdown of communication, as the founder of the Mulberry Bush, Dockar-Drysdale (1990), always insisted. However, if the hard work that will realise and retain this state is to be available reliably then there must be a leader who will do his or her own hard work in service to these goals and this state. I think that the event I have described illustrates that this hard work was being carried out to a positive effect in the Bush in 2001, but now I want to scroll back – to the time of my arrival as Director in August 1991.

Beginnings

I had worked previously at the Mulberry Bush, first as a care worker (1974–81) and then as an Assistant Principal (1983–86). When in 1991 the managers were unsuccessful in securing a successor to the outgoing Principal, they asked if I would consider applying for the post. The combination of my great love and respect for the Bush, and my ego being polished by the invitation, prompted me to put my name forward. This was a crucial period in the history of the Bush. The outgoing Principal had advised the managers two years previously that without major root and branch transformation it was unlikely that the school would be able to continue. This was due to internal and external changes that had already occurred and the prospect of further imminent developments in policies and procedures in child care, child protection and education. In response managers and staff had adopted a vision for the school that involved just such a fundamental transformation. The community based on the large group would change to a therapeutic school living in small groups, with a more clearly differentiated education area and experience and a specific area of activity focused on work with families. The new post of Director was established in order to lead the task of turning this vision into a physical, organisational and cultural reality.

Flushed with enthusiasm for the place and the task (and with just the slightest fantasy of arriving as the 'great leader on a white charger'), I began my tenure by meeting with the staff for two days before the children returned from their summer break. What I found was a staff team that was in disarray and near to despair. They had not only lost a head but also, it seemed, heart and hope. With my arrival they had to face a huge agenda for change and, perhaps not surprisingly, quite a few were ambivalent about setting off on this challenging journey. Nevertheless, the reality now was that many of the ways of living and working with the children that had emotionally contained their disturbance over so many years were no longer doing so. Indeed they were sometimes amplifying that disturbance now, forcing the grown-ups to make ever more Herculean efforts to hold everything together. One of the major consequences of this predicament was that staff seemed immersed in simply surviving, finding it impossible to make space to think, not only about a way forward but even about what it was they needed to be doing in the present. The combination of their losses and the prospect of the enormous changes ahead had traumatised many of them in important areas of their functioning.

In particular, the senior staff immediately beneath the Principal felt that for a number of years the model of a community held from its centre by one person had bestowed upon them many responsibilities, but little to no (perceived) authority or power to act effectively. Whether they actually did or didn't have such authority was another matter by this time. There was a wide-spread feeling from staff that they didn't know why they were there, or what it was they were supposed to be doing with the children (who, remember, were returning in two days!): 'Would it have been better had the managers closed the place?' This sense of hopelessness and of feeling overwhelmed of course had an immense impact on me, and one feeling was that, for that very moment at least, I wanted to retaliate in kind. I also knew that it had been a gruelling few years of uncertainty for everyone and whatever the levels of confusion, distress and impotence that currently gripped them, there remained a long history and enduring core of commitment and creativity. I also realised just enough that my own feelings were about myself and my not having calculated at all realistically in advance the powerful impact on me of taking up a position of leadership in a community, and particularly a community in transition, and that with so much going on there would be wave after wave of strong feelings breaking over my head. Yet somehow until then I hadn't let myself anticipate either the enormity of the responsibility I had assumed, or the deep levels at which it would affect me. Instead I had believed naively that since I understood, I would somehow be spared having actually to experience the intense reality itself. Now I was learning fast and also questioning even faster my own ability to be a leader in a therapeutic environment.

In the midst of this, one member of staff finally broke free of the collective depression and said tentatively: 'I'm certainly very afraid of all these changes we're facing, but I'm even more afraid that we might stay the same.' That one timely statement tipped the balance and kept me thinking not just then but for many days ahead. It also led me to suggest to everyone that we allow ourselves to go back and 'start at the very beginning'. Who are these children that we are trying to help? What has happened to them? What has been the powerful impact on them of these experiences? How do they express this impact even to this day? Then what do we try to do with and for them once they come into our care? Finally, to what end or outcome, for what purpose do we undertake this extraordinary effort? In short, what is our primary task? Out of this came what remains in largest part to this very day the 'Statement of Primary Task' of the Mulberry Bush. It remained of course a struggle, but there was the beginning of a process of re-energising taking place, of looking at how to change and adapt, while preserving the things that help children learn, change and grow, and of realising the vision that would meet the changed circumstances and new challenges in our work.

Quite regularly in the following months, as key issues were discussed sometimes late into the night, our heads would feel as if they were spinning and while resistances didn't cease entirely thereafter, there was a sense that a Rubicon had been crossed by all of us. I felt that I had resisted the temptation or invitation to despair and belief that things could only ever be the way they had been. In addition the staff – so many of whom did excellent work, cared deeply about the children and had already been working to introduce changes before my arrival – henceforth seemed to accept that the only way was forward, but together we could make it. Moreover, I am not suggesting for one moment that I was able entirely of my own accord always to maintain a thinking perspective in these difficult circumstances, and my feelings and frustrations must have shown. Without the active encouragement of the trustees, the foresight and insights of our therapeutic consultant and the understanding support of several key staff over this time, I most certainly would have lost myself entirely in the fury, fears and fantasies that periodically coursed through our team and our meetings.

Gradually too, the staff regained their capacity to think in support of each other. For example, when we were thinking about how we could adapt the old school building, a classic late 1960s style – open plan and acres of glass, another staff member said, 'This whole building is totally useless. It needs pulling down and bulldozing over. Then we can start all over.' This time I didn't have to respond myself. A colleague reminded him that for children over many years this building had been a very special place. It had worked for them and others right up to recent years. It could still be adapted as part of the changes; we don't have to pretend that nothing of value ever happened there.

For quite some time still all the grown-ups could feel very persecuted and nearly overwhelmed by trying to work in between two systems, old and new.

The children too felt and expressed this tension, most powerfully through disruptive and destructive behaviours. At one point, after a few days of relentless violence and distress from them, the grown-ups met together with the Deputy, while a colleague and I showed a video to the children, having told them the reasons why the grown-ups were all together. After little debate the staff decided unanimously that devolving into small groups could not and need not wait for new houses to be built. Without much difficulty they then divided the current large group into three groups, largely according to degrees of integration and unintegration. (Two years later a fourth group was established.) Staff members were then attached to groups with a senior member being designated team leader. These decisions were then presented to the children, with those few who were not with their special grown-up being reassured that this important relationship would continue to be supported by specific adaptations already familiar to them.

So many other changes, both large and small but each important in its own right, occurred before, during and after that move into small groups. However, that was a vital cornerstone of the new structures that had needed so desperately to be introduced in order to develop the integrated programme of care and education. Up until then our adult actions and responses to situations were often based on contingency – treating as important whatever it was that happened next. Now there was recognition that structure in our work was crucial. Moreover, people realised that they didn't have to blame others or themselves for the difficulties with which they had been struggling. The school had needed to introduce new structures in order to grow and change with the times. Once in place, even in rudimentary form, they could commence again using their skills in identifying and meeting the emotional needs of the children.

As our consultant observed, initially the school had seemed much like a roll-on-roll-off ferry (RO-RO): very vulnerable to being destabilised and sunk by relatively small amounts of water (anxiety) pouring into it because there were no internal walls (structures) once the outer hull (boundary) was breached. This was much like the ill-fated *Herald of Free Enterprise*, which sank just off the Belgian coast in 1987. Now the school as ship was sailing much more reliably even in sometimes rather tempest-tossed conditions. Other internal boundaries and spaces followed – small group meetings, team and senior management meetings, daily morning meetings, school/living group meetings, etc. Thinking at all levels became more reliably present, ensuring that the developing structures matched the task. Progressively I myself was 'allowed' first and then encouraged to move back and forth across the school boundary, as I, the Director, saw fit. I was no longer regularly being pulled in to decide day-to-day issues or adjudicate over disagreements. These responsibilities were being held and exercised more and more at the right levels and in the appropriate spaces. Even better, in time people began to remind me, kindly but firmly, of my own position when I sometimes drifted into too great an internal involvement or when I suddenly parachuted into a situation that did not require my direct management.

Themes and issues that emerge

Many important issues and interesting thoughts on the subject of leadership emerge from the preceding personal narrative. Nevertheless, it seems clear to me that 'containment' – as we understand the concept from a psychodynamic perspective – represents an overarching theme. Anxiety is often writ large in organisations, especially those within the helping professions and even more especially within therapeutic communities where, as an integral part of treatment, feelings have permission to exist and be expressed. Uncontained, anxiety can do much to undermine, divert and sometimes pervert the primary task. At the Mulberry Bush it was a regular presence throughout my time as leader. It was never a case of ridding ourselves of it as a phenomenon, however much we may have wished this could be so at times. Instead it was a daily task to try to recognise anxiety wherever it was gaining a foothold and once recognised it could be thought about – particularly with regard to its source – and then worked on until ultimately contained. In this way anxiety becomes material for our work rather than something persecutory to be repelled or a distraction to be ignored, in effect denied.

Therefore a leader must try to ensure that anxiety management is happening regularly and reliably at all levels of the organisation or community. However, as senior staff in the Bush had pointed out to me, to take on responsibility effectively requires authority and power. As Obholzer observes: 'Responsibility without adequate authority and power often leads to work related stress and burnout' (Obholzer 1994: p.43) – both organisationally and personally, I would want to add. Nor can one simply have one or the other: to be assigned authority without power is to be continually subject to demoralised impotence, while to exercise power without authority too often gives rein to omnipotence. In the former predicament the leader or leadership can begin to believe that the lack of hope that is being felt so intensely is actually the institution itself losing its heart: 'We've tried that. We've done that. Nothing works any more. This place has lost its heart.' In the latter the leader can come to believe that the community and he or she are one and the same. The largely unspoken refrain, 'What's good or bad for me is good or bad for the community', becomes the dominant stance for tyrannical decisions and arbitrary actions.

As is so often the case, leaders should be seeking a healthy balance. It is Obholzer's judicious mix of authority and power that will take the work forward even in difficult times. This is why 'good enough authority' requires the regulating attention of a leader, monitoring and maintaining the mixture at or close to such a balance. Of course, in human affairs there is never complete equilibrium or perfect harmony. Nevertheless, if this process of regulation is operating reliably under a leader's direction, then these inevitable tensions between the two can be much more creative than disabling. This key regulating activity, which in my view lies at the heart of a leader's responsibilities, can usefully be characterised as 'holding in mind and holding the line'. While in the context of our work the analogy is not exact, it is true to observe that a leader must maintain (and be helped to do so) a maternal-like reverie that will afford a live feel both for the various parts of the community and for the whole. Like that reverie, it is not a position or state that one can take on or put aside too casually, always confident that if set down it will be easy to pick up again. In the absence of the leader and of any well-established structure for maintaining a focused oversight, residents (and sometimes staff too) can shift very quickly from feeling held in mind to feeling or fearing dropped out of mind. They then begin to produce behaviours to get, if not back *in* the mind of the leader then at least *on* that mind. Putting the dynamic into words it reads something like:

> If I can't be held healthily in mind and feel safely contained, then I'll have to settle for being on someone's mind. Even if I can achieve this best by becoming a continual problem, nuisance or risk, that's better than feeling dropped out of mind because for me/us that feels exactly like being out of my/our own mind. I want good attachment, but I'll take attention for being bad when the only other option is feeling 'mad'.

The need of children and grown-ups alike to be held in mind and the actual task of holding confer a deep responsibility on a leader. Some months after becoming Director, I was leaving my office (which was alongside the living areas), heading home in the late autumn dark. As I walked down the drive I suddenly stopped and looked back, overtaken at that moment by an extremely powerful sensation that I was 'leaving the baby'. Then immediately the words 'this baby must be saved' sprang into my mind – words spoken some weeks before by a young mum at a family centre where I was offering consultation and who had been struggling for some time to accept that while she loved her infant dearly she could not reliably offer him loving care. On that day she had agreed that her child be placed with foster carers, bravely summing up the painful reality with those words that had just returned to me as I looked back at the school. It was an important experience and sentiment highlighting the truly deep nature of our world of work. The task then was, and remains, to ensure that this genuine sentiment about the children and the work did not drift into a false sentimentality.

This is where and why the need to 'hold the line' comes to the fore in leadership. Too sensitive a belief that these children have suffered too much already can produce a sentimental environment in which firm limits and boundaries (that also serve to define healthy spaces) are too little in evidence. Unconsciously, they are seen as the cruel repetition in the present of earlier harsh and punitive treatment, whereas, along with positive encouragement and sympathetic reminding, leadership must also incorporate firm challenging or 'stern love' as it was called by Fred Lennhoff (1960), one of the pioneers of work with maladjusted children. Sensitivity, sensibility and firmness in leadership – again in the right mix – support much-needed structure. Recognising this reality during his time at the Cotswold Community, John Whitwell says that 'in some respects the therapy (for the children) is the order of the community' (Whitwell 2001). The ego functioning and task-directed behaviours of the grown-ups underpin and express this order and support the vitally important activity of forming lasting and meaningful relationships. With such order and structure (and relationships) there can develop in the children a healthy sense of being and belonging. Without it they remain emotionally rootless or disconnected, 'in' but not truly 'of' the community.

Having been established, this order is not simply self-sustaining either. It requires constant management at all levels, up to and including the leader, where managing oneself (and one's feelings) can sometimes be the toughest challenge of all, especially as you need to be and feel on top of everything since you hold ultimate responsibility. It is easy to break the very boundaries you otherwise expect all others to honour always, as I now illustrate.

In an effort further to reduce contingency as the primary determinant of how we organised ourselves at the Mulberry Bush, the CMG, then newly formed, affirmed that we would no longer allow our weekly session with our consultant to be interrupted for any reason. In the first several weeks this 'no disruption' rule had been fully respected by staff. Then the big test came, not from without the meeting but from within, from me! Just as we convened we were told that a child had struck and injured a member of staff. An ambulance had been summoned, as the worker may have been seriously concussed or worse. The (very able) team leader of the group was attending to the situation.

After some discussion we agreed to proceed with our meeting. From the start my mind was 'outside' and I struggled unsuccessfully to attend to the work of the meeting. Then I noticed the ambulance arrive. After a few more agitated minutes I interrupted the meeting and said that I was too preoccupied with what might be going on outside. I felt that as Director I should be overseeing the situation directly.

Following a brief silence, one member reminded me that the matter was in capable hands. There really was nothing I could do there that was not being done already. My presence out there would only interrupt from within our meeting what we had worked so hard to establish in relation to impingement from without. I declared that I was still of a mind on this occasion to make an exception. This prompted our consultant to suggest that we use this occasion as a test – of our trust, discipline and principles. We could remain together and see what happened. Very reluctantly I agreed, and while the pull to be out there felt a strong physical tug at times, with the support of my colleagues we made it. Well, I made it (just) and immediately afterwards I discovered that, as I had been reassured, the situation had been well managed. Child and children were contained in a group meeting, the adult was attended to, no serious injury was found and our meeting had continued. On this occasion the right space and level had dealt with what not long before would have been a drama that 'successfully' pulled everyone under its all-enveloping grip – to the detriment of therapeutic task and order.

This was an event long remembered by us all and especially me. It gave a vivid lesson in how challenging it often is and even how physical it can feel to really do the work of creating and sustaining appropriate structures and a culture in the community in which the tasks of holding together living, feeling and thinking can proceed without diversion. Openness and enquiry are readily presented as key expressions of a true community; yet they are rarely found being practised except where the hard work behind the phrase 'holding in mind and holding the line' is happening.

Hardest of all in this respect is when things are not known and, as above, outcomes are uncertain. The relief, whether in an individual, a group or the entire community, is very apparent, palpable even, when something important becomes known or understood. Often less apparent is the destabilising impact which not knowing can have on communities. This can be the source of enormous anxiety that floods into every area of our daily activities. People can feel as if in an intolerable limbo, described by Winnicott as 'the unthinkable anxiety of annihilation' (1965, p.47). In these circumstances we risk dealing with uncertainties and not knowing by becoming absolutely certain. In effect we deny our ignorance and can kill off the complexity that we need to be working with, by insisting that things really are simple. Unfortunately, treating the complex as simple in order to deal with anxiety invariably yields a simplistic, and wrong, certainty or response.

Unlike the infant about whom Winnicott was writing – developmentally unable as yet to think – we have the capacity to do just that. So long as we continue to think, even about these 'unthinkable' anxiety-inducing things, we will be more able to contain the potentially damaging risks of not knowing as well as the need to pretend we know when we don't.

Mrs Dockar-Drysdale gave a talk to the Managers and Friends of the Mulberry Bush in 1971, shortly after the move from the original farmhouse to a new building on the same site. Needless to say everyone was very pleased, and perhaps she sensed an elevated level of confidence that with a newly con-structed environment we had found the solution that would make the work much easier. She spoke to them about the dangers of becoming complacent or certain. She declared that the work must always proceed in a way that can tolerate doubt or not knowing. Only in this way we can hope to ensure that we are carrying on thinking. It is in absolutist or crisis cultures that there is no doubt; there is only absolute certainty. A culture with structures, boundaries and spaces will support thought. Thought will contain uncertainty and, thus, thoughtful responses can be made to the children, not only when adults are supporting healthy functioning but even when they are managing break-down. The emotional 'mess' can be tolerated, and dealing with it can remain at the core of our work. It need not be driven out. Of course the sufferings of uncertainty are real, but nothing like the eventual suffering born of absolute certainty.

Most often in our communities this desire for certainty will be expressed through a demand for clear answers to what appear at least to be straightfor-ward and important questions. Sometimes the effort of trying to produce ab-solutely clear answers comes close to becoming a near mythic venture like the search for the philosopher's stone. In the first Harry Potter book, Hermione discovers that the stone will transform any metal into pure gold and the person possesing it will live forever (Rowling 1997, p.161). She accurately presents the popular understanding of the philosopher's stone. However, in alchemy long ago the search was for something rather different. For the true alchemic masters the search for the 'lapis exilis' was in fact their efforts to discover the value that lay deep in what was despised and rejected. It was a quest to uncover value, not to find unimaginable wealth, eternal life or absolute answers. In important respects that is the true nature of our work today with our troubled residents. Our focus should be less upon getting answers for someone and more about identifying (and helping the person to identify) the value that lies deep within each child, a child who almost always feels entirely worthless and unwantable on joining us. And in a community based on learning from experience and enquiry, perhaps our modern quest should be continually to raise and refine the questions that will assist our enquiring into the true value of each person. Answers, when they do appear, can come along in their own good time and way. Our work needn't stand or fall only on finding them.

So containment, holding in mind and holding the line represent a complex and sometimes surprising set of responsibilities for a leader. With the right support from within our communities, on the boundary (especially in the shape of consultation) and from the outside, we will more likely be able to provide 'good enough leadership'. Then we may also be able to hold the hope: for children who for now can only see their presents and futures as a continual repetition of their catastrophic pasts; for staff who must face ferocious emotional and sometimes physical onslaughts in a very hostile social climate, and for society which, when not sentimentalising them, still too often regards troubled children merely as trouble, to be dealt with as mad, bad or out on the streets. If we have hope we can resist falling completely prey to cynicism or despair. Moreover, this hope which is grounded in our belief of the potential for even the most damaged children to grow towards health is probably our greatest gift. Bolstered, therefore, with a robust hope we can carry on, however long and strange the trip has been, is and will be. It is marked by times of happiness and sadness, with difficult decisions to make and therefore necessarily lonely at times, with some regrets, but always interesting and definitely of great value.

CHAPTER 14

Consultation and Supervision

Peter Wilson

Consultation and supervision are crucial activities in the process and development of any organisation, not least in therapeutic communities. Both are fundamentally concerned with enhancing and widening the competency of staff in the interests of meeting the aims and objectives of the organisation. In therapeutic communities, the overriding purpose is to provide a safe, containing environment in which young people can learn, through relationships, the nature of their disturbance and the prospect of improvement in their lives. Both activities have a responsibility to develop a state of effectiveness of staff in their work with young people and with each other – sufficient to enable them to learn on the job, to encourage their capacity to draw on their training and to build on their personal experience. Equally, consultation and supervision may each be delivered at both an individual and team/group or even organisational level, according to needs and focus. Indeed part of the strategy for staff support and development in any therapeutic community will include planning for an appropriate mix of these different levels and types of intervention.

Despite much that is similar, each activity has its own distinctive place in an organisation, and it is important for all concerned – employers, senior and junior staff and young people – to understand the difference in role and function. In many respects, supervision is more straightforward. It exists within the mainstream of the organisation; it is an integral part of the effective management of the organisation. All organisations need a clear structure, a comprehensible framework in which staff know more or less where they stand and what they are required to do. This is particularly important for the optimum running of therapeutic communities working with young people. Above all, supervision safeguards this structure, taking care that staff are doing and are helped to be doing what they are supposed to be doing. This involves monitoring their performance, reviewing their job descriptions, assessing their training and resource needs and appraising, in general, their work position in the organisation. It has to take into account too the requirements on the organisation from external agencies in relation to legislation, (e.g. the Children Act, the Health and Safety Act) inspections (e.g. OFSTED) and working procedures of referring agencies (e.g. Social Services, care management).

Supervision thus plays a central role in any organisation. The supervisor is in many respects the linchpin, connecting the broad objectives and strategies of the organisation with the actual practice that is carried out day by day. He or she sits clearly within a hierarchical line management structure, accountable to those more senior and responsible for the work of those more junior. He or she has the authority to tell the supervisee what to do, both in terms of management and practice/therapeutic work, and it is incumbent on the supervisee to follow the advice or instructions given. It may well be argued that, in ideal circumstances where such supervisory resources exist within a well-delineated and well-funded organisation, there is, in fact, no need for any further organisational provision; sufficient support, encouragement and understanding can be provided well enough within the established functioning of the organisation. Theoretically, this may be possible; in reality, however, it is rarely the case. All organisations, by virtue of the uncertainty inherent in their growth and development, have a way of becoming unstuck, however well run, in different ways at different times at different levels of their operation. Communication between various parts of the organisation may not work or policy and strategy objectives may become confused or contradictory. Staff may become discontent, ill or absent from work; and in therapeutic communities young people may suddenly manifest their anxiety through increasingly disturbing behaviour – more runaways, more self-harming, more sexual acting-out and violence. Whatever the signs, there arises a sense of things coming adrift, without any clear, obvious understanding within the organisation of why or how to find a way through. It is at this point of acknowledgement of inevitable limitation that consultation makes its entry.

The essential virtue of consultation is that it exists 'outside', or rather, 'on the edge' of an organisation. As Silveira puts it, the consultant in a residential institution is 'the nonresident crossing the boundary every time he visits, looking in and looking out' (Silveira 1991). The strength of his or her contribution resides in being slightly at odds with the organisation; a part of and yet apart from the living goings-on of the organisation. This is the very element that the organisation needs because of temporary or prolonged moments of blindness that occur, inherent in its involvement with its own working. The directors, trustees and management may lose sight of their mission or strategy and staff may become over-embroiled in their practice. The consultant offers, from a special place of difference, something relatively uncompromised or cloyed by institutional pressures – a bird's eye view, without, as it were, having too much institutional wool being pulled over it.

Consultation of course comes in many forms and there is great difficulty in defining exactly what it consists of or should consist of in different settings (Dare 1982). For many, the term 'consultant' takes on a rather weighty, even pompous tone – management and organisation consultants, consultant psychiatrists, surgeons and so forth. All conjure up notions of heightened esteem, superior knowledge and mysterious power and a promise of bringing about rapid change and remedy. These, of course, may as much reside in the eye of the beholder as in the claim of the provider. But nevertheless, too often, a fantasy prevails, fostered on all sides that something near magical might happen – a fantasy that does not serve well the ordinary purpose and necessity of consultation in any organisation.

According to Skeat's etymological dictionary of the English language, the root of the word, 'consult' is probably allied to Latin 'sedere', to sit. 'Con' has an interesting ambiguity – being an adverb meaning 'against' as well as a prefix indicating 'with'. At a most fundamental level, then, consultation is about someone, 'the consultant' sitting with and against another person (consultee); or conversely, someone seeking someone else to be by their side, but contrary. This understanding of the term can of course be applied to many forms of creative human interaction, but in essence, it particularly captures the specific nature of consultation – that it is a supportive, yet challenging process; affirming, validating, drawing on strengths, yet critical, questioning, alert to resistances and weaknesses. In many of these respects, consultation is akin to supervision. The major and crucial difference, however, revolves around the question of professional responsibility. Unlike the supervisor, the consultant does not have managerial or clinical therapeutic responsibility for the work of the consultee. This remains firmly with the consultee, who is ultimately answerable to his or her supervisor. The consultee is free to accept or reject the thoughts or ideas of the consultant. Unlike the supervision relationship, the arrangement between consultant and consultee should be voluntary, and the spirit of engagement collaborative – both parties being involved on a more equal footing with the each other in a process of learning. This basic principle is well enshrined in an important definition of consultation provided by Caplan:

> A process of interaction between two professionals – the consultant who is a specialist and the consultee who invokes the consultant's help with a

current work problem, with which he or she is having difficulty and which is within the consultant's area of expertise. The work problem involves the management or treatment of one or more clients or patients. The consultant takes no direct responsibility for the implementation of the remedial action for the client. (Caplan 1970)

With this understanding of the process of consultation, there is the possibility of both the consultant and consultee being to some extent liberated in effect from the demands or constraints of the supervisory management process – freed to work with each other on a problem beyond the reach of formal institutional processes. At the same time, of course, neither can lose sight of their accountability to the organisation for which and in which they work.

Not all forms of consultation hold so clearly to the aspiration of impartiality that is implicit in this definition. In the medical tradition, for example, a consultant basically makes a diagnosis on the basis of direct observation or report of consultee and gives clear recommendations and practical advice on the treatment of the patient. Where this occurs, as it invariably does within the same profession, consultation draws close to the process of supervision. Similarly, many behavioural approaches to consultation (Bergan and Kratochwill 1990; Erchul and Martens 1997) involve a significant amount of direct instruction (for example, in classroom management), teaching problem-solving techniques and mobilising of additional resources for the consultee. These may be well suited to the aims and objectives of particular organisations, but the consultative stance is decidedly active, bearing heavily on the autonomy of the consultee, not dissimilar in fact from supervision or a form of in-service training.

In those organisations that work more broadly within a psychodynamic framework, as in the majority of therapeutic communities with young people, the style of consultation that is generally adopted is more consistent with the principle suggested by Caplan (1964, 1970). The purpose of such consultation in such therapeutic communities is to enable the residential staff to think about their experience and observation in their work with children and young people and with each other (Wilson 1999). It is to foster an understanding of children's and young people's lives and the ways in which they express themselves in their behaviour, attitude and relationships. Most importantly, it is to provide an opportunity for residential staff to reflect on the emotional demands of the children and young people upon themselves as well as the pressures of the organisation. The focus of this work is always on the difficulties and personal anxieties that arise or might occur in the course of everyday work, such as to interfere with the primary task of helping the children and young people. Caplan conceptualised these anxieties in terms of 'theme inter-ferences', certain patterns of personal preoccupation within staff that distort the 'professional objectivity' that is required of them to work effectively. Much depends on the consultant's capacity to provide a setting in which the consultees feel safe enough to explore and to understand the nature of their feelings and reactions to children and young people with whom they are working.

Consultation and supervision therefore sit alongside each other in thera-peutic communities as indispensable forms of support and provision for resi-dential staff. Both contribute to the structuring and containment of staff – the one more managerial, directive; the other, more consultative, reflective. Both offer ideas and thoughts to help clarify problems and ways of dealing with them – the supervisor, from the basis of his or her own knowledge of the or-ganisation and professional skills; the consultant, by virtue of his or her spe-cialist experience in the field and external view point. It is important that the consultant and supervisor are seen as complementary – in recognition that the supervisory process may not be able to encompass the full range of feelings permitted in consultation; and that consultation should never be used as a re-placement for the organisational and practice responsibilities of supervision. The consultant augments the supervisory experience. He or she is more able to be open to and to bear the anguish and uncertainty that residential staff often feel and to help them sort out the words and thoughts to free them to make sense of their experiences and develop more appropriate ways of coping. In large measure, the consultant enables the consultee to discover what in a sense the consultee may already know or has known; to mobilise, with greater clarity, the consultee's own resources and capacity to think creatively about his or her problem; and to formulate relevant questions and ideas that need to be clarified in the organisation as a whole and through supervision. In line with my opening remarks, it should also be borne in mind in the following discussion that when I refer to the 'consultee' I may be referring to either an individual member of staff, or a team or sub-group of staff, or even to the whole staff team including the director, since consultancy may operate at each of these levels.

Within a therapeutic community, it is the day-to-day living interaction between residential staff, children and young people that constitutes the core of therapeutic work (Polksy 1962). It is in the interplay of relationships and in the midst of the everyday life of the communities – the waking, dressing, feeding, cleaning, studying, working, resting, sleeping – that numerous moments of experiences and thought occur that over time accumulate into a potentially profound therapeutic experience (Rose 1990). Both residential staff and young people encounter feelings and responses that are often intense and bewildering because of this element of sheer immediacy and proximity. The level of individual and group emotional disturbance amongst children and young people in most therapeutic communities is generally high. Young people invariably bring with them the residues of their past painful experiences and tend to relive these experiences in different ways in the community. The therapeutic community becomes, in effect, an arena of transference re-enactment – of both transference and countertransference. 'The essence of residential treatment is that each child projects its inner world against the macrocosm of the residence' (Ekstein and Wallerstein 1959).

Residential staff are all too readily perceived by young people at various times, as a result, as depriving, abusive, neglectful or seductive. Staff inevitably respond in ways that reflect these perceptions as well as their own sensibilities in relation to intimacy and authority. They face a stiff task, all too often exposed to their own personal vulnerabilities as well as to experiences which may or may not have resonance in their lives. A young person may react at times to a residential worker with such defiance and hatred that the residential worker's own memories of comparable feelings within him or herself, both to and from his parents, may be reawakened; or it may be that such hostility is of such quality and intensity as to lie beyond the emotional comprehension of the residential worker (so adding to his or her sense of confusion and feeling out of depth). Whatever the circumstances, the residential worker finds him or herself often unaccountably and unpredictably in various kinds of involvements in which he or she may feel humiliated, beguiled, attacked, disarmed, seduced, excited, disgusted.

Bruno Bettelheim, one the most influential pioneers in the field of therapeutic work with children and young people, made it very clear that, 'to become a childcare worker means first and foremost to become oneself because only then can one become a self to others' (Bettelheim 1966). This in many respects is a tall order. Some staff are more threatened than others by the direct expression of emotion and find ways of insulating themselves, avoiding possible loss of control in conflictual and intense situations. Others have a greater need to be loved and suffer the consequences of setting firm and unpopular boundaries. Others particularly resent authority and may too easily find themselves identifying or colluding with the delinquent tendencies within the community. There are those too who are more threatened by intimidation or attack and respond prematurely in a punitive and judgemental way. Always, there is the danger of staff becoming immobilised by their anxieties or acting them out in an unthinking and random way, through inappropriate and destructive activity.

The style and approach of the consultant varies considerably according to his or her experience and personality and the general values and objectives of the organisation. A great deal depends on the manner in which the consultation is introduced and how the consultant is used. In some organisations, consultation is an accepted and respected activity, well sanctioned by those responsible for running the organisation and by senior management. There is a reasonably clear understanding of the consultant's role as well as his or her relationship to senior management and supervisors. Other organisations may be less well informed and invite consultants in with greater uncertainty and ambivalence. Both at an organisational level and amongst staff many fears may be aroused by the prospect of the arrival of a consultant – fears of scrutiny, of being misunderstood, of criticism, of loss of credibility or reputation or of exposure to the discomfort of issues that may have been personally and institutionally kept well under wraps. Alternatively, and in large part in defence against these kinds of anxieties, there may be an idealisation of the coming of the consultant as a potential saviour, a solver of all the organisation's problems, at both an individual and organisational level.

Different organisations find their own ways of inviting consultants in. Many initially may invite external help at a practical, clinical, client-centred level – seeking advice on how to understand and deal with particular children. The consultant may well be expected to see children directly for assessment as well as meeting relevant staff. In many instances, if the consultant earns sufficient credibility and trust on this basis, he or she may be asked to help further with staff relationships, enabling staff to understand the impact of the children's and young people's disturbance on them and to work better on the tensions and blockages that exist between them. This may be done at a group or individual level or both. It is not uncommon too for consultants then to be further invited to address broader management issues of the organisation.

Consultation can then occur at three main levels – client-centred, staff-centred and organisational. In some organisations, the same consultant may well be asked to involve himself at all three levels. This may occur over time – as Silveira puts it, the consultant is 'graduated' by the organisation. It is the organisation that 'dictates the pace' (Silveira 1991). He describes a gradual process of the consultant becoming accepted and emphasises the importance of the consultant being prepared initially simply to 'be there' and 'be available' – being reliable, consistent, punctual and ready to tune in to the 'need for an ear'. Some organisations may be more clear in the differentiation of consultant practice and invite a consultant with specialist organisational and group work skills specifically to provide organisational consultation. Others may not be ready at all and resist any offering of consultation at an organisational

level. Obholzer, in discussing institutional defences, describes his own introduction as consultant to a residential school; he gives an account of one
memorable occasion when he was told by the head teacher, 'please don't come
today – we are having a problem' (Obholzer 1994)!

Case illustration: Consultation with an individual staff member in a therapeutic community

The context for the following illustration was a therapeutic community (for
very disturbed adolescents) whose attitude to consultation was positive and
long established. The consultant had been in place for several years, working
primarily with staff, with little formal direct contact with the adolescents
themselves. All the staff met with the consultant weekly on an individual basis
and in staff meetings in which the consultant sat as observer or facilitator. The
consultant met with the senior managers and supervisors on a regular basis to
discuss general issues relating to the progress of the community.

Major issues that arose in the therapeutic community revolved around
central conflicts concerning care and control. The community by and large
did well to contain the tension of these conflicts and hold the line between
being over-punitive and over-tolerant. Inevitably, as in similar organisations, it
was not always able to hold the balance as steadily as it would like, buffeted as
it was by the continual emotional pressures and behavioural attacks of the adolescents. Inevitably, too, it had to deal with sudden and unplanned events. At
this particular time, two important changes had occurred in the community
that had an unsettling effect. Several key senior staff had recently left; at the
same time, an unusually large number of new adolescents had been admitted
to the community. The community was thus in a state of significant emotional
loss and yet faced with a barrage of new demand from a group of highly
anxious and as yet unassimilated delinquent adolescents.

All of the staff were on edge, some feeling the departure of their colleagues more deeply than others, but most angry with the senior management
for allowing in so many new residents at the same time. One staff member in
particular was very angry, complaining especially about his feeling at the butt
end of what he regarded as bad decisions on the part of management – leaving
him in effect having to deal single-handedly, as he saw it, with the worst
excesses of some of the adolescents' behaviour. He was responsible as
keyworker to one of the senior boys, who was behaving in a particularly challenging and violent way. In the midst of so much change, it was clear that the
boy was reacting strongly to feeling abandoned by certain significant staff
members. Rather than help the community hold the boundaries, he allied

himself with the hostilities of the new boys and targeted his anger and frustration onto his keyworker. He was, for several weeks, unremittingly nasty, swearing, spitting, ignoring the keyworker's remonstrations, walking off, ridiculing and mocking amongst his friends. Many in the community thought he should be expelled, but the management had held back from making any hurried decision.

The staff member felt furious – furious that he was in receipt of so much anger, furious with the organisation for not doing something about the situation and furious at his colleagues for standing by and not helping. He wanted the adolescent to be punished and thrown out – 'leave him to his own madness'. He was at times beside himself with anger, finding it difficult to restrain himself from shouting at and berating the boy, at times almost coming to blows. He was frightened by how strongly he felt and knew that he was close to doing something unacceptable – and that the intensity of how he felt was interfering with his other duties. His supervisor gave due warning that this behaviour was becoming unprofessional and encouraged him to discuss the matter further in consultation. This, he did, but not without some impatience and readiness to extend his fight. In one consultation session, for example, he was particularly agitated and appealed to the consultant 'what do I do – don't just sit there, tell me what to do'. When the consultant refrained from giving direct advice, the staff member got up to leave – contemptuous of the consultant's lack of competence; 'see what you feel like at the end of this' (his anger and walking out). Eventually, he calmed down, although it took some time for him to reflect on how much of his own experience, especially in the past, was being caught up in the pressures of the present.

The consultation sessions provided a necessary space for the staff member to take stock of himself, to understand the nature of his feelings and to find other ways of approaching and working with the boy. A wide range of issues was covered, including the nature of the boy's own emotional predicament and behaviour, the particular meaning of all of this for the staff member himself and the prevailing dynamic that existed within the staff group and the organisation as a whole. The staff member could readily understand, once in a position to consider it, the anguish and the vulnerability that lay behind the boy's behaviour in the light of his childhood exacerbated by his sense of loss of key staff and perception of the anxieties of the new residents. He could also come closer, though with greater difficulty, to facing the acute sense of humiliation and impotence he felt in relation to the boy's attacks on him and in particular the boy's apparent indifference and ridicule. This touched on the staff member's memories of his own relationship with his father, which in many respects had not been so dissimilar from the boy's. His disappointment and dissatisfaction with his own father who had been at times very close and yet at other times belittling and ultimately rejecting was a part of his life that had caused him great distress and he could see how much he shared in this respect emotionally with the boy. He, too, had felt let down and betrayed by his staff colleagues who had left, one of whom he had worked particularly closely with in setting and maintaining limits within the community.

The effect of this kind of work in consultation was positive over time – the staff member feeling less alone and frightened of how he felt (less abandoned to his own 'madness') and with better understanding of the behaviour of both himself and the boy. This process of understanding was in no way easy or comfortable and clearly there were many moments when the staff member transferred onto the consultant a great deal of feeling that belonged to the organisation and his past and current experience. The consultant's understanding of the transference was crucial to the survival of the consultation process, and to the continuation of the staff's learning and working in the community.

The problem, however, did not lie only within the staff member concerned. It was clear that the boy's abusive behaviour and the staff member's desperation reflected anxieties that preoccupied the whole community at that time. The staff member resented being put into the position of the 'hard man', 'the heavy', the one that that would take on more than others the aggressive behaviour in the community and take the knocks as well. He recognised his own sense of excitement in being so engaged and prided himself on his ability to appear strong – and yet he understood his resentment in feeling pushed into a position of being the very kind of punitive father in the community that in his own experience he had not been able to bear and did not wish to re-experience.

In consultation, the staff member was enabled to take a firmer grasp of these issues and better mobilised to bring his concerns more clearly to the whole staff. In addition, the consultant himself, with the full knowledge and permission of the staff member, raised the matter generally of the staff group's responsibility in one of his regular meetings with the supervisor. In subsequent staff meetings and through staff supervisions, a comprehensive discussion took place about the disruptive behaviour of a number of the boys in the community and of the need for all staff to share equitably the burden of the challenging behaviour. The staff meetings were chaired by the supervisor and the consultant served as facilitator. This required the consultant to hold clear boundaries within himself as to what he could permissibly share in the group of what he knew of the problem and what he held confidentially in relation to the staff member's personal life. A decision in the end was taken not to exclude the boy from the community and, although clearly difficulties continued, the staff member himself felt better able to work with the boy and the staff more committed to work co-operatively.

Discussion

In this illustration, the focus of the consultation was on the interplay between the life of the organisation, the young people, the staff and the individual staff member himself. The consultant was well established, positioned at some distance from the everyday life of the community, yet sanctioned by the director and trustees and in an openly acknowledged association with the supervisor. The consultation consisted of meeting with the staff member and staff group on an ongoing, regular basis. In many respects, this was a satisfactory arrangement, allowing time for the consultant to gain credibility and for staff to build up trust.

The issue of trust is critical. The consultee looks to the consultant for good judgement, sufficient maturity and strength to contain anxiety and enough independence to keep 'clean' enough to hold confidences. Much depends on the personality, knowledge and integrity of the consultant and trust is not something easily or quickly earned. In all organisations, there is always the danger of the consultant becoming drawn into the internal preoccupations and allegiances of the organisation and losing the essential element of objectivity that defines the core of consultation. The consultant may well forget his proper sense of place and inappropriately usurp the role of supervisor or manager. It is not surprising that Caplan (1970) and others warn against consultations of long duration in any given community that might encourage dependency; to safeguard against this more short-term interventions with a defined emphasis on problem solving are recommended. Much can be said for the proposition that a 'successful consultation is a no more than a means of enabling a consultee to define the problem that led the consultee to seek consultation in the first place. Once the problem is defined the consultation is complete' (Wilson 1991). There is no doubt that this idea comes close to capturing the essence of consultation and may well serve as the basis of a legitimate rationale for short-term consultation. Equally, however, it can be said that in therapeutic communities with disturbed adolescents, consultee staff present a series of problems in response to an array of challenges and surprises within a constantly changing therapeutic environment that renders the consultation process, in effect, continuous and never complete.

The nature of the consultant's impartiality, so central to the concept of consultation, does nevertheless raise a number of interesting issues about the extent of his or her influence. Consultants are invoked for various reasons, largely determined by the needs and understanding of the organisations themselves. Some organisations may clearly be looking for a child mental health specialist, with sound knowledge of child and adolescent development and disturbance. Others may be looking for consultants with training and expertise in group and organisational dynamics. Whatever the requirements, there is an expectation that consultants will make a difference either to the quality of understanding or the functioning of the staff and organisation. However much it may be a principle of consultation primarily to facilitate and enable rather than to direct or 'impose' views, few consultants practise with such pristine neutrality – responding as they do to the appeals of the organisation and carrying with them, by virtue of their expertise, their ability and wish to bring about change.

In the case illustration, the consultant was in fact particularly influential, not least because of his relationship to the personal life of the staff member. The process of consultation in this instance ranked close to that of psychotherapy, engaged as it was with the impact of the problems of the community and of the boy on the staff member's own emotional sensibilities. Some consultants argue against treading over the fine line from consultation and into psychotherapy – particularly in the sense of uncovering private, personal problems and interpreting connections between a consultee's private and professional life. Clearly there are dangers in consultation becoming absorbed within itself, insulated from the rest of the community and entering into areas of the internal life of staff members that are not within the province of the organisation. Equally, however, in therapeutic communities, staff are often overwhelmed by the emotional impact of community life on their very sense of being and seek to understand better their difficulties in working with the aggressive and sexual nature of their adolescents and in dealing with issues of rivalry, competitiveness and authority in their working relationship with staff. For a consultant not to have the capacity and interest to address these essential personal issues in the context of therapeutic community is tantamount to failure in his or her fundamental task to enable consultees to carry out their work effectively.

Conclusion

Consultation and supervision play complementary but separate roles in any organisation; in therapeutic communities, they are vital in working together to constitute a working base for the ongoing management and containment of the anxieties of those, both staff and young people, who are residents. Much of the caring and healing in a therapeutic community exists within the living experience of everyday group life and in the interactions of staff and residents. Staff are inevitably exposed to a variety of powerful experiences, some of which they may be able to understand and cope with but many of which they cannot make sense of at all without help. It is the function of both consultant and supervisor to 'help the helper to help'. The value of the supervisor resides in his or her greater knowledge and experience of the community and of general practice and authority within it; that of the consultant is his or her particular specialism and external perspective. The consultant has an unique relationship to the organisation, being invoked from outside, rather than employed from within. The life of the consultant can be, in fact, a lonely one, positioned always on the boundary, usually not up to date with the fast-moving currents of community life, and often weighed down with the volume of community anxiety that is deposited in the consultation. It is not uncommon for consultants to feel uncertain of their usefulness, just as staff do. Consultants frequently carry the very same feelings that staff experience in relation to young people in the community. In order to sustain objectivity and some degree of sanity, it is important that the consultant have access to support for him or herself or preferably work with another colleague as co-consultants in the same community.

The style and approach of consultants may be very different; so too, the work of therapeutic communities. There is no question that the art of the consultation takes many forms, as idiosyncratic as the consultant and consultee who take part in it and as varied as the cultures of the therapeutic communities in which it takes place. Silveira suggests that the determinant of good outcome depends on 'the gestalt of the person (the consultant), the approach (the style) and the institution (the consultees), coming together in some kind of chemistry' (Silveira 1991). Consultation should be an integral part of any healthy organisation – the acknowledgement of the need for it and indeed the call for it, being a sign of robustness within an organisation, a capacity and willingness to take opportunities for new learning and creative work. As Furnivall (1991) puts it, 'consultation is not in fact about rescue but about the empowerment of staff'.

CHAPTER 15

Staff Development
and Training

Andrew Collie

Effective, relevant, staff development and training programmes[1] can make a vital contribution to therapeutic organisations for children and young people. They play an essential role in helping staff, individually and collectively, to gain an understanding of the complex conscious and unconscious processes inherent in therapeutic work. I will argue that external training provided by institutes of further or higher education must be geared directly to the residential therapeutic task. Training programmes will only be effective if they contain three elements: theory and research directly linked to practice; practice evaluation and assessment in which the student demonstrates the use of training in the development of professional or therapeutic skills and understanding; reflective space in which students are helped to make the necessary links between what they learn, what the learning means to them and how they make use of the learning in practice.

I will also argue that training gives therapeutic staff the opportunity to experience a process similar to the therapeutic process they are attempting to provide for the children or young people, namely, to gain a degree of ego mastery over potentially overwhelming experiences. Appropriate training will provide staff with an experience of identification with mentors (tutors, senior colleagues, line managers or clinical supervisors) which will replicate the therapeutic experience of the children they are working with. Training in this context must include psychodynamic, systemic, social learning and other concepts which help to build a vocabulary of unconscious emotional life. If it meets these criteria, the model of training I am proposing will enable staff to articulate and symbolise experiences which may otherwise be nameless, terrifying and overwhelming.

Finally, training programmes benefit workers most (and contribute to ego mastery) when they are accredited, either professionally or academically. Existing professional training in social work rarely meets all of the criteria suggested here as being appropriate to the therapeutic task. We will look critically at this aspect of training later, but first we will look at training in relation to new and inexperienced workers, who have specific training needs arising from their position of relative unfamiliarity with the therapeutic task.

Training for staff new to psychotherapeutic work

The transmission of organisational culture

It is a common experience for new staff working in therapeutic communities and therapeutic children's homes to feel lost, deskilled, overwhelmed and helpless. They may feel envious of more experienced colleagues who appear able to cope with almost any situation, and be vilified by the children for their incompetence. Training, clinical supervision and the sympathy of friends and family seem to have only a limited ameliorating influence on these painful experiences. Some people leave therapeutic work forever in their first year. Part of the reason for the disturbing nature of this early experience is that the new staff member finds that his or her ego is not fully up to the task of surviving, digesting, and transforming the primitive, hostile and chaotic projections which come with the professional territory. They are faced with experiences which they may not have had to contend with since their own early childhood or infancy, and which seem alien and terrifying. Gradually, through a process of ego development and a developing capacity to process experience (Bion 1991), the staff member begins to gain a degree of mastery over unconscious processes, becoming increasingly able to perform the role of 'transformational object' (Bollas 1990) that the professional role requires. Appropriate induction training and staff support takes this process into account, with more experienced workers taking a central role in lending ego support to their inexperienced colleagues.

The first stage in this phase of professional development has been described as 'unconscious incompetence' (Shohet and Hawkins 2000). Experienced workers from other fields (including other therapeutic work) may have functioned well in these settings, and attribute their initial bewilderment to organisational inadequacies, the ingratitude of the children or a host of other external factors. People with less experience are more likely to blame themselves and their own inadequacies. In fact, this early stage can be understood as the worker's ego ideal (Chasseguet-Schmirgel 1984) or idealised self-image, coming into conflict with the reality of their ego limitations, which challenges and threatens the ideal. Ego defences are mobilised, often from a superego position, and the worker typically develops relationships with the children or young people that are characterised either by retaliation or emotional withdrawal. Both stances are counter-therapeutic, as they are obstacles to the development of the worker's potential transformational capacity.

How the organisation (or external training programme) responds to such defensive behaviour is critical. The new worker needs help to make sense of what is happening. Help takes either the form of support for an essentially defensive position, or of opportunities to explore the nature of the defences, and the reasons for them. The latter requires a willingness and ability by the organisation (or external trainers) to engage with the worker in a process of reflective thought about how he or she occupies the professional role. Trainers are similarly engaged in a reflective process about their own professional role. The worker needs help to move out of a defensive position and into a position where he or she can acknowledge the limits of competence, and tolerate a position of partial incompetence. 'Conscious incompetence' is the next phase of professional development, and is usually achieved with the help of senior colleagues within the organisation. The next section looks at some examples of this process in action in an organisation which understands the process.

Internal Staff Development

The primary purpose of internal staff development programmes for residential and therapeutic community staff is to transmit the culture, values and working practices of the organisation. At its best, this is a complex process of internalisation, in which a new generation of staff, through a process of critical evaluation, take into their internal world the living culture of the organisation, and help to develop the culture in line with changing organisational and external circumstances. For example, in the therapeutic community setting, new staff might be assisted through clinical supervision or guidance from senior or more experienced colleagues to make sense of unconscious processes that can be bewildering and disabling when they are first experienced. Tom Main (1990) describes the process of culture transmission and warns of the dangers of taking this process for granted. If the organisation does not pay careful attention to the way in which it transmits the understanding and knowledge underpinning working practices, new staff may work in a ritualised way, with practice being stripped of some of its original meaning. New staff may develop an unconscious resistance and hostility towards accepted practice when its underlying meaning has not been communicated in a form which can be internalised.

> It was the practice in the adolescent therapeutic community to make a clear distinction between coffee mugs for daily use, and coffee cups used for more formal occasions such as meals or 'high teas'. This distinction was re-inforced by an insistence that mugs should only be used in the buttery area of the dining room, and cups should only be used in their own designated area. The young people enforced this rule themselves. One evening, after the young people's bedtime, two new members of staff were observed drinking coffee from mugs in the 'wrong' area and laughing about the ab-surdity of the rule they were breaking.

> A senior member of staff intervened and told them to take their drinks over to the appropriate area. She then sat with them and explained that the practice was an important part of the design of the therapeutic environ-ment. It provided an experience of boundary and standards for a group of young people who had little previous experience of either. The fact that the young people themselves enforced the rule showed that they attached considerable importance to it. She said that some young people would be very distressed if they thought that staff were ignoring this practice, as they relied on adults to help them develop their own fragile internal boundaries.

The new staff members were manifesting a number of defensive manoeuvres. They were adopting a hostile attitude to a working practice they did not un-derstand, and which threatened their ego ideal. They colluded in denigrating the practice, and supporting each other's defensive position. At a deeper level, they were operating from what Klein (1946) describes as the para-noid-schizoid position, a primitive defensive state originating in early infancy. The primary characteristic of this state is splitting of experience into its good and bad aspects (good resided in the collusive relationship, bad feelings were projected into the 'absurd' ritual). Their actions indicated further examples of primitive defensive functioning: hostile attacking of the therapeutic process, and a collusive denial of potentially damaging behaviour. Their attitudes and actions, if left unchallenged, threatened to be counter-therapeutic because they would have (consciously or unconsciously) communicated their attack on a therapeutic strategy to the young people.

The senior staff member, who understood the potential danger in their behaviour, gave them the opportunity to think about the underlying psychosocial significance of an apparently absurd ritual, and to understand an aspect of the therapeutic environment. More than this though, they were experiencing an aspect of the therapeutic process for themselves. By having their behaviour challenged, and then being invited to think about the significance of their actions, they were given the opportunity to internalise new professional boundaries of their own, and to reflect on why they had not been able to understand this without external help.

Another important aspect of the learning process experienced by the two new staff members was that they identified themselves with the senior staff member, whom they both respected, having worked a number of evening and weekend shifts with her, and whom they knew to be reliable, skilled and devoted to the well-being of the young people in her care. She gave them the opportunity and the support to move to a more mature and reflective emotional state, described by Klein as the 'depressive position'. In so doing she acted as a transformational object. Again, we see a parallel with the therapeutic process of young people in therapeutic environments. Developmentally, children up to the period of early adolescence identify with the values, capacities and interests of their parents and other significant adults, in order to develop the attributes of a successful member of their social group. They can do this most successfully if they are helped therapeutically to move to the depressive position, tolerate the sadness and pain that this implies, and establish a more mature reflective capacity. Professional development follows the same pattern, with senior colleagues being role models for newer members of staff, who can internalise, both consciously and unconsciously, the professional and personal aspects of the person they admire or respect.

The effectiveness of the identification process depends on the capacity of the staff group to tolerate and survive paranoid-schizoid processes which are both internal to each individual (we all contain primitive internal objects), and also projected powerfully into staff by children or young people in residential environments. This in turn depends on the organisation's ability to offer suitable senior role models to a staff team that is likely to be mixed in gender, age, culture, sexual orientation and personality structure. Gender identification is one example. If a senior staff team is composed mainly of one sex, it will potentially be more difficult for staff of the other sex to form identification relationships with senior colleagues. Managers need to be aware of the significance of the balance of their middle management team, and senior staff members may need help in developing their capacity to be effective role models.

Transmission of culture to more experienced workers

Possibly the most significant area of organisational life in terms of transmission of culture is the way in which authority is held by one generation of staff members and managers, and is passed on to the next generation. Menzies-Lyth (1988) argues that senior staff need to be able to judge the maximum amount of responsibility they can delegate downwards to less senior staff, in order to help the next generation to internalise their own sense of authority. She describes this process, following Klein, as 'introjective identification'. The children in turn will be able to introject their own sense of personal authority if they see adults operating autonomously. An early stage of the identification process can take the form of junior staff idealising senior colleagues, and projecting their own authority *into* the senior colleague, at the same time denying their own capacity to hold authority. The junior staff member will only be able to reclaim his or her projected authority by having it returned by senior colleagues.

> John had worked at the therapeutic community for three years, and was for the first time leading a group of five adolescent boys on a caving expedition in Yorkshire. Gordon was a senior member of staff who was in the process of leaving after six years, and was on his last expedition. He had been a significant figure for John, and had been a role model and mentor.
>
> One of the boys, Craig, was very attached to Gordon and was finding his impending loss almost unbearable. He repeatedly challenged John's authority, insisting that Gordon should be leading the group. One evening, Craig produced a knife, defying John's instructions to hand it in. The situation was tense, and John looked to Gordon for guidance. Gordon remained silent, and John realised that it was up to him to deal with the situation. He called a group meeting (in a tent) to deal with the situation. He insisted that nothing else could happen until Craig handed in the knife. Craig became increasingly threatening, but John held his ground. After a tense stand-off, Craig handed over the knife, and rushed out of the meeting in a distressed state. John followed him and they talked thoughtfully for an hour about how upset Craig was at Gordon's departure. Later, John and Gordon discussed the episode, and Gordon congratulated John for the way he exercised his authority. John told Gordon that he had hoped he would take charge, but that it had been essential that he had not. He felt that he had moved into a 'senior staff' position.

John, as a relatively experienced worker, had reached a position of 'unconscious competence' at the start of the camping trip, particularly in relation to his ability to hold appropriate authority. Some of his potential as a leader was still being projected into Gordon, who was attempting to give up authority as part of his leaving process. John knew what needed to be done about a boy with a knife, but attempted to hand authority back to Gordon, who resisted the offer. After successfully managing the situation himself, John moved to a position of 'conscious competence', only possible once he had actually managed, been seen to manage, and felt himself to have managed a difficult and anxiety-laden episode. In so doing he was able to identify more fully with his own capacity to hold appropriate authority.

I hope these examples make clear that informal transmission of organisational culture and values lies at the heart of staff development right through a worker's involvement with the organisation from induction through to occupation of senior roles, and that the process is not simply an intellectual one. The worker has to be given the opportunity to internalise the living culture of the therapeutic process into his or her own internal world of object relations through a process of introjective identification with more experienced colleagues. However, there are limits to the capacity of organisations to meet all the training needs of their workers. In the next section we will look at the particular contribution external training programmes can make to the professional development of therapeutic workers, and to therapeutic organisations.

External training

The role of external training is, I believe, to transmit meaning through a process of linkage between theory and practice. The linking process is an inner world process and is the responsibility of the student within a facilitating learning environment. The significant difference from internal training, which can also provide a facilitating learning environment, lies in the connecting process between the student, the employing organisation and the wider community of thoughts and ideas which good external training can provide. It is only through external input that organisations and individual workers can fully appreciate that the unconscious processes that engage them within the organisational frame are knowable, and known about, outside the organisational frame. Students often express amazement when they realise that their experiences have been shared by others, thought about, given meaning, and been articulated in a theoretical context. One student, after a day discussing the concept of projective identification (Ogden 1982) said, 'This makes sense of the last fifteen years of my life'. Another, after being introduced to the concept of the 'frozen child' (Dockar-Drysdale 1990) was in tears, having been the keyworker of such a child, who had exhausted all his and the organisation's emotional resources over an 18-month period, and where no help to understand this child had been available.

Those who design and deliver courses for workers in therapeutic settings have roles and responsibilities similar to those of the small group leader or senior member of staff. That role is, to resist the students' wish to be protected from the reality that the work is complex, difficult and demanding, whilst holding the possibility that reality can be understood and survived. The example of Gordon and John, above, illustrates how two workers managed a highly stressful event without compromising their different responsibilities, and without denying the distress behind the knife boy's aggressive hostility. They jointly modelled ego mastery over the boy's chaos and anxiety, and enabled him to move temporarily beyond his aggressive/defensive posture. It was only some years later that John systematically studied psychodynamic theory, and was able to understand and articulate the incident fully, and to feel confident that he could share its meaning with other professionals from outside his organisation.

External training can provide a stimulus to new thinking within organisations by offering reflective thinking space independent of thinking focused on day-to-day crises or medium-term strategic organisational requirements. It is a truism that the more anxious one is, the less one is able to think reflectively. Organisations which do not make good use of external thinking often find themselves caught in anxiety-driven unconscious assumptions, where old solutions based on ritualised thinking are applied to new problems. Training, like organisational consultancy, can act as a shock or a catalyst to introduce new ways of thinking, and contribute to an organisation's capacity to adapt and develop to meet changing circumstances. To follow Tom Main's (1990) argument, meaning can be restored to ritualised practice, and so restore creativity and flexibility of thought and action.

Academic and professional qualifications

There are other dimensions to external training programmes which distinguish them from internal staff development programmes. All residential child care provision is now governed by national occupational standards, and professional training must meet academic and professional criteria which do not have the transmission of culture as a primary goal. Rather, the validity of professional training is now defined in terms of its conformity to competency outcomes linked to occupational standards.

Mainstream social work training at qualifying and, to a lesser extent, post-qualifying level, provides training in professional values, competence, skills and knowledge that arise from occupational standards relevant to field social work. Only at post-qualifying level is there a focus on child care social work, and only to a limited extent is this aimed at the specific training needs of residential child care practice. Any relevance to therapeutic residential care or treatment is coincidental, and Diploma in Social Work courses as currently designed may actually damage the competence of therapeutic child care workers by giving them a false sense of competence. In post-qualifying courses in therapeutic child care it is not unusual to see good professionally qualified students struggling to unlearn some of the values and practices which inhibit therapeutic work. One sees this most clearly in heads of homes who have attempted to implement policies based (for example) on empowerment, confidentiality or children's rights, which have fed into the children's omnipotent fantasies and achieved the opposite results to those intended. Skills in therapeutic management and communication, organisational dynamics and strategic thinking and planning were not taught, leaving students with clear goals and values but no help in implementing them effectively in this setting.

The national picture is even further from the approach suggested here at basic grade level. The new training requirement (under the National Minimum Care Standards introduced in 2002) is for National Vocational Qualification (NVQ) level 3. This is a competence-assessed qualification with no specified training input requirements. If candidates (they are not thought of as students) can complete a portfolio that demonstrates a range of relevant competences, validated by internal and external assessors, they will be deemed to be trained to minimum standards. There are some knowledge requirements, but candidates are not required to demonstrate that they *understand* anything. The lack of quality assurance standards for the training input into NVQ3 means that large numbers of staff can be trained relatively cheaply, without employers being required to demonstrate a commitment to good quality training (still possible within an NVQ framework). One can criticise the NVQ structure for allowing employers to deny the complexity of the task, and thereby preserve the status quo of residential work being the poor relation of social work, and one can criticise it for being a one-size-fits-all solution to the complex training needs of the whole residential child care/therapeutic community/secure estate/special school workforce.

NVQ represents an advance on the previous situation, where no minimum training was specified in this field. It does provide employers with the opportunity to train workers if they choose NVQ programmes which attempt to meet real training needs, and which begin a process of helping workers to think about the work in a reflective way. It is possible to do this, but is not a requirement. In a limited way, the NVQ structure can introduce elements of relevant training and learning experiences that do justice to the professional task.

The training college where I work was asked by a local authority to provide an NVQ programme for its residential child care workers. The brief was to provide 12 taught days introducing the workers to therapeutic methods and understanding, in keeping with the philosophy of the Social Services Department. The course designers were faced with a difficult task, as the NVQ knowledge elements did not fit comfortably into appropriate theoretical frameworks. In addition, these elements seemed exactly that – elements – fragmented bits of knowledge, or value statements or examples of good practice. There were between 22 and 54 of these elements in each one-day unit.

We decided that we would try to identify key therapeutic themes which we thought had a bearing on each of the units, and modify the syllabus accordingly. In addition, we wrote assignments for each unit which drew together as many of the elements as possible into coherent questions linking theory and practice. The students then had the task of working through the assignments with their practice assessor, who helped them to link the written work with what they actually did at work. At the time of writing the course is still in progress, but initial feedback seems to suggest that the course is both stimulating for the students, and is helping them demonstrate the practice skills required of the NVQ programme.

Conclusion – an ideal training programme?

Appropriate training must preserve the positive elements of mainstream training – professional and academic accreditation, having one's practice scrutinised closely, the development of a professional identity – whilst recognising that effective therapeutic work relies crucially on the worker's ability to experience, tolerate, understand and make sense of complex unconscious processes at both individual and group levels. If workers and their employing organisations are to be helped by external training programmes, there is a number of interrelated elements which need to be in place, related to each other through appropriate teaching and learning methods and structures. These elements are:

- theory and research which help workers to make sense of their own and the young people's experiences, especially theories from child and adolescent development; psychodynamic theories of individual and group behaviour; theories of organisation, especially systemic theory and therapeutic community methods.

- therapeutic goals and values, and how these might be reconciled with social work values

- forums (such as case study sessions and young child observation) which provide opportunities to link theory, use of self in role and practice skills

- a 'reflective space' in which students can experience and learn about themselves as group members and develop their capacity to make sense of their experience

- an assessment method which measures understanding and knowledge, and the influence these have on professional practice, as well as the more normative assessment criteria based on assessment of competence.

The single most important factor once a course has been designed is the quality, skill and personality of the trainers, and their inevitable limitations. How a course is implemented, taught and psychologically managed by the trainers, and how the students relate to the trainers, will determine how the knowledge is both transmitted and received. Tom Main deserves the final words on this approach to training:

> Identification being a wide-ranging matter, trainees learn not merely from what their trainers teach or preach, but from what they practise, and not only from what they do, but what they imply; from what they love and what they hate; and what they do not do; and what they take for granted. (Main 1990, p.67)

Endnote

1   For the purposes of this chapter, I am taking 'staff development' to mean those aspects of the professional learning process that take place primarily within the organisation (such as induction training), and 'training' to mean those aspects which take place externally to the organisation in the form of training programmes provided by external bodies (such as professional training at a university or other institute of higher education). The distinction is somewhat artificial, as the two clearly overlap. For example, induction training programmes are almost always provided internally, and reflective space similar to internal case supervision sessions is provided by good training courses. Nevertheless, the distinction is important, because organisations can only take the training and development of their staff so far, and training programmes can never provide all the learning opportunities that staff will have access to.

CHAPTER 16

The Challenge of Research

John C. Wright and Phil Richardson

Introduction

Perhaps for many readers of this chapter a first question may be 'So what actually is research?' Research is 'any honest attempt to study a problem systematically or to add to our knowledge of a problem' (Reber and Reber 2001). However, while clear, this does not go far enough to address the concerns and questions facing researchers and those informed by research in the field of residential therapeutic work with children and young people. The more psychosocial therapies are established as bona fide within mainstream social and healthcare services, the greater the demand for evidence-based practice in these fields. In this context research is more broadly defined as an approach which uses the scientific method of observation, data collection and interpretation, and specifically focuses upon issues such as treatment safety and effectiveness, whether those offered help may deteriorate as a result, what the minimum standards of good practice are and the most cost-effective way of delivering the service. These concerns are equally relevant for service provision for young people whether it be in health, education or social contexts. In this chapter we intend to review the demand for an evidence base from the perspective of policymakers and funders, then look at the kinds of evidence currently available and what it tells us about good practice, and finally identify some future challenges for research development in this field.

Why the current demand for an evidence base: Policy makers and funders

Evidence-based practice currently occupies a central role in public policymaking. In the UK attempts to modernise government (HMSO 1999a,

1999b, 2000) emphasise the importance of using evidence of the effectiveness of interventions as part of a drive towards higher quality policymaking.

Take for example the recent message from government for the redevelopment and improvement of NHS services. While funding has been acknowledged as a significant factor, other key areas of concern have also been identified. These have been summed up as follows:

> The NHS is a 1940s system operating in a 21st century world. It has: a lack of national standards, old-fashioned demarcations between staff and barriers between services, a lack of clear incentives and levers to improve performance, and over-centralisation and disempowered patients. (Secretary of State for Health 2000)

While addressed at a national level, these concerns are of equal relevance to and require examination at the local level.

The message is clear that the context in which therapeutic work takes place is not a dyadic one, between care staff and managers or care staff and clients. It is a three-way transaction, involving management, clinical staff and service users. This structure, the key driving force for evidence, aims to increase accountability for providing an effective service to those in need, while keeping costs to a minimum. The two major influences are clinical governance and cost effectiveness. Clinical governance – the mechanism for the local delivery of high quality clinical services by systematically focusing on the activities involved in delivering high quality care to patients is seen as the linchpin for ensuring improvements occur and are maintained. The five essential building blocks of clinical governance are clinical audit, risk management, quality assurance, clinical effectiveness, and staff and organisational development. Clearly research has a potential role to play in each of these activities. Cost effectiveness, in addition, aims to discover best treatment options through adding costs into the equation. Here we would emphasise that identification of the cost of a service not only involves the money spent on it but also what is lost by not implementing the most effective alternative. For example, a provider may decide that costs can be reduced by centralising adolescent services from three district-based units to a single regional one. However, there are inevitably hidden costs to this move which need to be calculated for a true comparison to be made, such as the added travelling times for family and the possible impact on treatment engagement and alliance. In conclusion, clinical governance is what we need to focus on to improve services and evidence-based practice is one of the methods we use for evaluating such improvements. As residential treatments are potentially powerful interventions with high costs they are often the focus of such enquiries.

However, despite the developments in evidence-based practice and clinical governance, many practitioners remain sceptical, if not cynical. It may be a long time before we can expect to see any investment in meaningful research which looks at the therapeutic value of a young person having a caring adult available at 3 a.m. to discuss his or her terrifying nightmare and worries about the family, let alone the potential experiential learning fostered through socially structured meal times. Consequently, there are anxieties about over-simplistic models of therapy being clumsily applied to complex human relationships which might even go as far as producing detrimental effects. An anxiety is that ultimately this approach leads to nowhere but management by targets born of a culture of chasing quick fixes and easy solutions, e.g. waiting list initiatives. An organisation such as a therapeutic community is a complex, dynamic and evolving system. Setting goals in the above sense might only lead to managing what is measured and ignoring what isn't – a downward quality spiral.

So, are we faced with a brave new evidence-based world that we should embrace or one from which we should run? The demand for more, and better, evidence on which to develop public policy requires providers of services to reflect upon existing and new sources of valid, reliable and relevant evidence. This will be the focus of the next section.

The state of contemporary research evidence

One important source of evidence for informing practice, commissioning and policymaking is the use of systematic collations and appraisals of findings. Traditional narrative reviews offer a personal interpretation of the expert's overview of the most salient aspects of relevant literature. This means that, to the extent that experts differ in their personal views, their interpretation of the literature may also differ. In a systematic review every step of the review process is defined with sufficient transparency and specificity to ensure that a second reviewer approaching the task in the same way will arrive at the same conclusions. Thus systematic reviews specify their search terms for identifying relevant literature, their inclusion and exclusion criteria for the studies they consider, and the precise basis on which they draw conclusions from the data reported in the included studies.

However, evaluating the quality or reliability of research data is not an easy task and poor quality reviews can be grossly misleading. One needs to hold in mind the dictum 'garbage in, garbage out' – i.e. a high quality review cannot improve the quality of the poor research which went into it. Important developments in the thinking about this area includes the work by Oxman and Guyatt (1988) who produced guidelines for reading literature reviews. They point out that, just as flawed methods in a study of therapy can invalidate the results, so too an unsystematic literature review can come to incorrect conclusions based on subjective biases. The danger is that, in attempting to make informed decisions in an expanding body of literature, we rely on reviews to guide us – without considering their quality.

A case example: in 1990 a special review article was published by Pfeiffer and Strzelecki on outcome studies of residential treatment of children and adolescents. The publication was in a highly eminent journal with a rigorous peer-reviewed publication policy. The review claims to consider all outcome studies of residential treatment reported in the literature from 1975 to 1990. The conclusions and recommendations from the review focus upon ten variables predicting good or poor outcome including higher IQ, healthier family functioning, and good quality aftercare being positively related to outcome, and 'organicity', 'bizarre, antisocial and primitive symptoms' predicting poorer outcomes. It is an influential paper which is often quoted by care staff, researchers and those who commission services. However, when this publication is examined in detail it can be seen to have some serious flaws. First, the methodology of the review itself is insufficiently reported so there is no easy way to replicate the findings. Second, when nonetheless a best guess is made to do just that, one of the present authors found four publications not mentioned in the review and yet could discern no obvious reason for their exclusion. Third, when the original studies included in the review were traced, something which happens less and less, with increasing reliance being placed on the ready-made overview, some of what qualified for inclusion in this important review was of an alarmingly poor quality. For example, a five-year follow-up study of a residential school for behaviourally and emotionally disturbed boys included vague and subjective outcome variables (one 'poor' outcome was defined partly on the basis of the fact that the patient 'married a woman twice his age' and a second included 'suspected homosexual').

Finally, the reviewers employed a mathematical formula for combining studies to produce an overall 'effect size' for different treatment variables, such as treatment age and outcome (to indicate to what extent these factors were generally predictive of good or poor clinical outcomes). While on the face of it this seems rigorous, the reality is that much of the original data was collected without using reliable or valid measures; the follow-up time frames varied from two months to eleven years; and sources of outcome varied from IQ tests to case note reviews. In this respect we would concur with the views expressed by Blotcky and Dimperio (1991) that while this type of review provides a useful job in describing up-to-date follow-up studies of residential treatments, any conclusions which can be drawn are probably more interesting than meaningful and carry the potential for misleading us into a false sense of confidence about the findings.

By and large similar criticisms to those described above continue to be consistently echoed throughout the published and unpublished literature (e.g. Burns 1996; Cornsweet 1990; Curry 1991; Imrie and Green 1998; Jensen, Hoagwood and Petti 1996).

Although studies of residential treatments are not of sufficient quality to address the issue of effectiveness further, we might look towards broader relevant research for evidence. In the field of child psychotherapy there have been four broad-based meta-analyses (i.e. attempts to combine the findings of several studies) to date which, in total, encompass more than 300 separate treatment outcome studies. These were recently reviewed by Weisz (1998) who found that the mean treatment effect sizes (i.e. the estimate of the overall average effect of the treatments in improving scores on the relevant outcome measures on a scale from 0 to 1) across the four studies ranged from 0.71 to 0.88, which points to a consistent beneficial treatment effect. This finding is also roughly within the same range as found in adult psychotherapy meta-analyses.

However, most child psychotherapy research is not very representative of clinical practice cases or conditions. Given the current emphasis on moving towards empirically supported treatments we need to ask what relevance research-based studies have in the real world. Weisz *et al.* (1995) went some way towards addressing this in a study which specifically compared clinic-based treatment outcomes. They found that in these cases the overall estimate of the treatments' effectiveness (effect size (ES) was 0.01) fell well below that of the research-based therapy studies described above (ES = 0.77). This suggests that the results of clinical practice may be less positive than those obtained in research settings (for many reasons). Similar failures to replicate the outcomes of research have also emerged from studies of improvements in the integrity of systems of care (Bickman, Noser and Summerfelt 1999). To summarise, the evidence for the efficacy of research-based child psychotherapy has not been matched in the outcomes of clinic-based treatments. These conclusions clearly point towards the increased need for practice-based evidence as much as for evidence-based practice, that is, better research designed towards helping us clearly identify and establish what treatment approaches produce sound outcomes with the specific client groups worked with in a day-to-day practice.

One recent study which has gone some way towards addressing such criticisms is Chamberlain and Reid's (1998) randomised controlled trial comparing multidimensional treatment foster care (MTFC) with group treatment residential care (GC). The participants were adolescent boys detained under the juvenile justice system, many with a history of multiple previous out-of-home placements. All had concordant high risk factors including history of sexual abuse, drug abuse and fire setting. The study indicated that MTFC produced more favourable outcomes than GC and emphasised the therapeutic value of placing such troubled children in long-term stable specialist foster homes. However, the true effect of this comparison (i.e. of the supposed active ingredients) is difficult to discern because of a number of confounding variables. For example, the two treatment groups received different amounts of professional help with regard to both family therapy (85% vs 50%) and individual therapy (100% vs 67%) – both in favour of MTFC, which could account for the difference found, rather than the group treatment versus foster care comparison per se. This example serves to demonstrate that while the researchers took care in the design of their study, research in this field faces many challenges, often compounded by the multi-dimensional and overlapping nature of the comparative treatment programmes. Clearly further research is needed to identify the individual components which contribute to the outcomes.

A related question concerns what the preferred outcomes are among stakeholder groups for child mental health services. Burns (1996, citing Rugs and Kutash 1994) was only able to identify one published paper in this area but its identified outcome priority is informative – the safety of the child (from others, from self, and of others from the child). Burns also emphasised the need for greater stakeholder consultation in service delivery and priority setting with the aim of greater concordance between the different priorities of different groups (e.g. purchasers, care staff, users and carers).

In conclusion, despite some broadly encouraging findings concerning their value, to date there has not been a prospective randomised well-controlled trial of residential treatments compared with best possible community alternatives. More optimistically, the methodology and synthesis of literature reviews for psychological treatments has been improving in recent years as evidenced by the growth in high-quality reviews of psychological treatments on the Cochrane database (www.cochrane.org). This has included several reviews relevant to residential treatments (e.g. Lees, Manning and Rawlings' (1999) review of therapeutic communities for people with personality disorders; Woolfenden, Williams and Peat's (2001) review of family and parenting interventions). More recent, and inspired by Cochrane, is the Campbell Collaboration (www.campbellcollaboration.org). This latter group disseminates systematic reviews of the effectiveness of social and behavioural interventions in education, crime and justice, and social welfare.

What can we conclude from the evidence regarding good practice?

So, what can recent research tell us about the efficacy and effectiveness of residential treatments for children and young people? The most consistently reliable message from the available research reports is that when rigorous quality controls are introduced in reviewing findings, there are as yet too few studies to draw any aggregated conclusions. Perhaps the clearest qualified statement would be that there is low-level evidence that some residential therapeutic placements produce changes in the mental and social functioning of some young people who have been unable to cope with family life. Little, who derives his views from a more qualitative approach, similarly comments:

> The answer is likely to be complicated. It is likely to be the case that therapeutic communities can hold some children but not others; at certain moments in time but not others; in some areas of the child's life but not in others. But such a complicated answer would advance our understanding of children in need beyond all recognition. (Little 2000, p.106)

Challenging questions for future research

In this section we try to identify important areas for future consideration by care staff and researchers alike and, where possible, offer suggestions for clinical units who wish to embrace the evidence-based practice agenda whilst suffering from the commonplace resource limitations.

1.   One challenge which follows from the above points concerns the vital need to develop better practice-based research. This can be achieved through activities such as the development of 'lowest common denominator' measurements for routine clinical evaluations. An example of just such an initiative is the CORE-OM – an outcome measure developed by Barkham, Evans and colleagues (Barkham *et al.* in press; Evans *et al.* 2000). This approach has the added advantage of facilitating the systematic collection of significant data on clients through treatment, which in itself often serves a helpful reflective and discursive function for a group of professionals organised around a single client.

2. A second promising development and one which follows from the first is the formation of practice research networks, where members agree to gather and pool data relating to clinical outcomes, using the same measures, in order to enable analysis of national and regional datasets. Such networks can help practitioners to take a research-based approach to exploring outcomes in their own services, sharing the findings, which can be compared with results obtained in more controlled experimental conditions. Thus, individual residential therapeutic settings for young people could contribute an important source of evidence on the effectiveness of services as delivered.

3. The incorporation of a user and carer perspective on outcomes is also a key challenge in our attempts to broaden and deepen our understanding of treatment effectiveness. For example, a recent study of how users of mental health services conceptualise outcomes found that considerations of the entire course and experience of 'becoming ill' and 'being well', as well as encounters with services and treatments, all contributed to perceptions of outcomes (Godfrey 1996). This shift in the outcome research agenda towards embracing users as 'experts' in their own difficulties has also been applied in a study of young people at a therapeutic community (Little 1995).

4. A further important challenge concerns the identification of optimal treatment interventions – by addressing such questions as whether some young people may need a period in a residential group setting prior to a successful foster placement or, alternatively, need periods of both in order to sustain an ongoing placement. For example, a young person who has a history of sexual abuse may be both thriving and sufficiently contained within a foster placement during latency but develop significantly more difficult-to-manage behaviours (e.g. promiscuity, eating disorders) during early adolescence with the onset of puberty (and all that this implies for issues around attachment when sexuality is more overtly added to the equation). Similar trends have also been noted through studies of boys with a history of significant physical abuse and later levels of delinquency (see, for example, Fanshel, Finch and Grundy 1990).

5. Research could also usefully move away from the direct head-to-head approach of outcome research on 'brand name therapies' and move more towards the study of basic psychological processes common to all approaches. Global concepts such as treatment engagement, the therapeutic alliance (between care staff and service user), and 'phases of change' (an approach which attempts to identify a universal series of stages in the change process when someone benefits from therapy) could usefully be investigated. One example of such an approach is the assimilation model (Stiles *et al.* 1991) which uses a qualitative approach to 'dissecting' outcome into changes in specific ideas, attitudes, or themes across treatment. See also Kroll and Green (1997) for an interesting account of the development of a therapeutic alliance measure in a residential setting. Another idea would be to investigate 'therapeutic moments' or, in the educational setting, 'teachable moments': points at which young people are more available to the influence of new or alternative ideas and ways of experiencing and relating to their world. Here we would be interested in what fosters, inhibits or blocks such moments and how best to exploit such moments when they do occur. For those who are unable to carry out such research on groups of clients the single case methodology approach can offer ways to investigate these processes systematically in individual cases. An important general point here is that psychotherapy research should include process and outcome together in order for us to get closer to understanding what is effective and why.

6. Finally, when considering the most cost-effective treatment options for emotionally and behaviourally disturbed young people, a blanket statement such as 'day treatment programmes cost less than hospitalisation' (Seyegh and Grizenko 1991) is only likely to be sustained if the costs are limited to the specific setting (Beecham 1998). One should, in fact, also include costs to criminal justice, health and education, social services, etc., all of which may be utilised with varying levels of intensity for this client group. In this case it is not difficult to envisage that an intensive day treatment programme, plus foster care, plus attending special educational provision may quickly begin to exceed the costs of a residential placement. The issue here is that unless a comprehensive approach to costing is taken, any claims to

difference may be due to unmeasured shifts in the burden of costs rather than a true reduction. Cost shifting issues can occur contemporaneously, during an individual's life course ('sleeper effects') or across family members or generations ('spill-over effects'). A summation will produce a 'cost-per-client-per-day', although this level of detail may need separating out for individuals, in order to pick up on important variations in the costs of care within a single institution or community. For example, an adolescent presenting with extremely high risk of self-harm in the context of brittle diabetes and a very unstable family background will inevitably have much higher costs for a unit than a more typically depressed young person. Costings also need to be sensitive to specific indicators of higher costs; for example being located in London (or other proportionally expensive location), managing high levels of self-harm, and requiring specific drug and alcohol services have specific increased costing implications (Beecham, Knapp and Asbury 1996). Again, the point is to ensure we are comparing like with like across services. In summary, while there is still much work to be done in the provision of reliable and valid cost information there have been some useful developments in these methodologies and techniques in recent years (Beecham 1998; Stiffman *et al.* 2000).

Summary

The drive towards increasing quality in public sector health, education and social services combined with the ongoing demands of managing limited resources have jointly contributed to a shift in emphasis towards research addressing efficacy, clinical effectiveness and cost effectiveness of interventions. For evidence-based practice to be a basis for the day-to-day provision of care it is axiomatic that high-quality research findings be available. Where therapeutic communities for young people are concerned the evidence base is scant. The real challenge for researchers in this field is to provide the basic building blocks of such an evidence base and the present chapter has addressed some key areas in which the challenges of this research agenda may be taken up by residential units working alone or in partnership.

Part IV

Applications
and the Future

Introduction

Our aim in assembling this book has been not only to explore and explain current practice in therapeutic communities for young people, but also to show how these ideas about practice may be applicable in other settings. In the past the therapeutic communities may sometimes have been viewed with some suspicion as 'rare and rarefied' or even as 'precious' (in all its various meanings), although the reality historically has also been that some of the most influential writing on residential practice (by authors such as Dockar-Drysdale, Balbernie and Winnicott) derived directly from their experience in therapeutic community settings. We are committed to promoting this exchange and development of ideas, and we have therefore included a number of chapters which discuss various ways in which therapeutic community ideas may connect with other arenas for child care practice.

In Chapter 17, Linnet McMahon makes the important point that, for ideas to be transplanted from one setting to another, there needs to be some context – usually in the form of staff training or development programmes – through which this process can be actively promoted and the necessary learning achieved. She then offers a number of examples of ways in which experienced practitioners on one training programme have been able to use ideas and principles from the therapeutic community approach to inform and develop their practice in other settings, including residential work with autistic children, and fieldwork with children in foster care. In Chapter 18 Michael Maher discusses the creative tensions which may arise from trying to establish more explicitly therapeutically oriented practice within a local authority context. Very few local authorities in the UK have successfully managed to achieve this therapeutic orientation, and Michael Maher is clear and forthright in his analysis of the reasons why this may be, whilst also offering some indications of the benefits to young people when such changes can be achieved.

Chapter 19 is a case study of another – perhaps surprising – setting in which one aspect of therapeutic community practice has been applied. David Hartman shows how the idea of the daily community meeting has been used in the setting of a secure unit for young people who have committed serious offences. Since the therapeutic community approach is about promoting change and learning in those youngsters who have experienced great trauma and distress in their lives, the 'secure estate' seems an especially suitable arena within which this approach might be expanded.

All of these chapters acknowledge that it may not be straightforward at all to translate ideas from one specialised field to other settings (whether within other specialisms or in more mainstream provision), and all of the authors offer their reflections on the learning which they have derived in attempting these connections. We would like to see more work in this field, and especially to promote a greater two-way exchange, since no part of the field can claim to have 'solved' all the problems.

CHAPTER 17

Applying the Therapeutic Community Model in Other Settings

Linnet McMahon

Introduction

It is probably axiomatic these days that work with an emotionally disturbed child can be most effective when it is located within an understanding of the child's experiences of attachment and identity, of separation and loss, and of the way these affect the child's inner world and its externalisation in behaviour. There will be attention to the family system and often work with the child's family, also taking account of social influences – ethnic and racial issues, poverty, and so on.

What is often less well understood is the capacity of the most emotionally damaged children for attacking the very help they are offered, because they find hope of change at first unthinkable and later unbearable. Hence the exclusions from school, the foster placement breakdowns and the moves from one residential placement to another, leaving a wake of confusion, anger, conflict, division and despair which threatens to engulf those who try to help. The disturbing feelings raised by working with these children need to be both understood and managed for the therapeutic task to be achieved. It is here that ideas based in the therapeutic community approach can be helpful to workers in other settings.

The therapeutic community approach and the 'holding environment' in child care

Perhaps one of the key distinguishing features of the therapeutic community approach is the emphasis on the daily living experience. While a specific therapy session may be part of the provision for a child, what happens in the 'other 23 hours' (Trieschmann, Whittaker and Bendtro 1969) is viewed as equally important. Further, the events of the day take place within a group of people living and working together. How people relate to one another and deal with difficulties and conflicts which inevitably arise is key. Much work is 'opportunity led', a thoughtful responding to events as they arise, and seizing an opportunity for helpful intervention. There is commitment to a 'culture of enquiry', an expectation of openness of communication, and a recognition that feelings are better expressed rather than repressed. Here one of the major misunderstandings of the 'permissiveness' of therapeutic communities arises – the belief that therapeutic communities encourage an unbridled acting out. On the contrary, 'reality confrontation' with discussion of the consequences of behaviour and of feelings openly within a group, with encouragement to work at and work out difficulties, to understand feelings rather than merely act on them, is extremely demanding. The aim of work with the child is, in Melvyn Rose's (1990) words, to turn 'thoughtless acts into actless thoughts'. The emotional containment and the 'holding environment' (Winnicott 1965) provided by the staff as a whole is crucial to this process.

It is difficult work, requiring attention to managing emotional boundaries which are likely to be under constant attack. The work makes extraordinary demands on the self of the worker, requiring a personal engagement with the feelings arising, feelings which need to be thought about rather than defended against through avoidance, projection and splitting. It requires a willingness to start from a stance of not knowing and not understanding but using the capacity to think and to integrate thinking and feeling – another aspect of the 'culture of enquiry'. It is a democratic stance in which only a limited amount of authority derives from position and the greater amount from how a worker is in informal relationships within the group.

It is not only the children who need a holding environment. So too do their workers and carers, since effective work requires the provision of a mental space in which it is possible to think about the meaning of a child's behaviour and to respond accordingly, and in a co-ordinated way with other people in the child's life. The therapeutic community culture of openness, participation and communication both within a staff team and more generally within the community as a whole, through clear leadership, the use of meetings, a trust in working together in facing and sticking with a problem, offers a helpful model for such work.

Effective work depends on a worker and a staff team having a way of making sense together of what takes place – that is, they need a theory base for the work. The therapeutic community approach draws on a psychodynamic and psychoanalytic understanding of relationships, whether between individuals and family members, groups, or organisations, but perhaps with a special emphasis on group process. Used in conjunction with systems thinking, the emphasis on understanding unconscious processes can help the reflective staff team find a way of making sense of and managing otherwise apparently inexplicable events.

Applying the therapeutic community model in work with children and young people

An overview

Child care that takes place within a setting which works at providing the 'holding environment' of the therapeutic community model, whether explicitly or implicitly, has a better chance of being achieved and sustained.

The recognition of the importance of early preventive intervention in families has led to a flurry of developments in providing both education and support for parents and children. Family centres and similar early years services which can draw on therapeutic community thinking and provide an integrated and coherent service, in which the whole is greater than the sum of its parts, have the possibility of working in a way which can lead to real change in some of the most troubled families. The difficulties are great since there is often a tension between meeting the needs of the parent and the immediate needs of the child. Such splits can be acted out unconsciously by a staff team. The need for leadership which works with the whole team to explore such a reflection process (Mattinson 1975) is crucial. Some of this work is discussed in McMahon and Ward (2001).

A number of other education and care settings have the potential to act according to therapeutic community principles or to graft them onto existing practice. These include work with emotionally disturbed (EBD) children or with physically and learning disabled children and young people in group care settings such as schools, including special schools and pupil referral units, or in different kinds of day care, respite and residential child care. In schools there is a long history of using whole school assemblies or meetings and a more recent interest in nurture groups (Boxall 2002) and classroom 'circle times' (Mosley 1996/2000) (where children work at communicating feelings rather than acting them out) where a community meeting model could be useful. Much work is opportunity led, a response to events as they arise during the day, where understanding of unconscious processes can inform the task, even when the task is not specifically therapeutic.

Aspects of the therapeutic community approach can be relevant to work with troubled young people in adolescent mental health units, secure units and young offender institutions. For example, restorative justice involves the young offender, and his parents, meeting the victim of the offence, being confronted with the consequences of his actions and helped to think about the victim's feelings, and to make some kind of reparation. The community meetings of some therapeutic communities can offer a helpful model for working with the difficult feelings and conflicts engendered. Within a framework of what has been called 'tough love', in which all seek to understand behaviour rather than attribute blame, there is nevertheless no avoiding the reality of what has happened and the need for some kind of atonement. Family Group Conferences are similarly set up to bring together members of a family network to work at finding a solution to a problem. Here too the skills involved in leading a productive therapeutic community meeting are relevant.

In some of these settings, for example education or youth justice, the primary task of the unit may apparently be at odds with the therapeutic community approach, yet the successful attainment of the task may in fact depend on some ability to make sense of a child's behaviour and work with this in a productive way. This includes the attention to understanding unconscious processes within a meeting or an interaction but also within the staff team. In group care settings the work is carried out by whole staff teams, often under excellent and dedicated leadership, where commitment to open communication and good teamwork can go a long way towards providing a holding environment. However, there are probably few such teams or leaders with experience of understanding and attending to unconscious communication, containing anxiety and managing processes such as projective splits: thus there is an urgent need for staff training (see below). Reflective staff teams have the potential to work in a deeper way.

It is perhaps less obvious that some who work in relative isolation – for example in field social work, adoption and foster caring, and child and adolescent mental health nursing – may yet draw on therapeutic community ideas. Yet the notion of the holding environment and related concepts such as the 'transitional family' offer helpful insights which can provide some real stability and support to those most troubled children who would otherwise ricochet through numerous placements only to end up in penal or mental health institutions as they reach adulthood.

It is not possible to do justice here to the application of the therapeutic community approach in all these settings. However, I hope to pick out some broad themes from some specific examples, drawing on the work of a number of experienced child care workers and managers, all of whom have completed a two-year training course in therapeutic child care, which itself draws on the therapeutic community model.

Using a therapeutic community model in training and higher education

The range of professional backgrounds of students on the MA in Therapeutic Child Care at the University of Reading includes social work, teaching and nursing. Multi-professional working and learning brings its own tensions as different working cultures meet and potentially collide. However, there are also rich benefits from a diverse group of people sharing experience and working together towards a common goal of helping emotionally troubled children and young people. Moreover, there seems to be a positive value to learning which takes place away from the workplace and its hierarchies and relationships, and which offers the possibilities of learning from and about other settings. The task of the course is to find a way of working together which maximises the possibilities for learning, including those arising out of the recognition of and respect for difference. As well as differences in professional and agency background, differences of race, gender, class and so on also need to be worked with. These reflect the social and cultural context of the work and provide many opportunities for understanding the operation of power and prejudice, for valuing diversity, and for recognising and striving against oppression.

If a 'holding environment' supports the worker in practice it is arguable that the worker in training needs similar emotional holding. Bringing together theory and practice, connecting thinking and feeling, and reflecting from a position of 'not knowing' requires an immense personal engagement and a willingness to explore how our own earlier experiences feed into our response. In 1990 a working group led by Adrian Ward drew up a model for training in therapeutic child care to match the model for practice. This became the MA in Therapeutic Child Care course which he led for ten years at the University of Reading, work described in Ward and McMahon (1998). The 'matching principle' means that the working methods of the group of students and staff reflect some of the working methods in the therapeutic community. Thus there is an emphasis on working together as a whole group, sharing experiences and learning from one another, in all aspects of the course including course management and decision-making. The day's work is designed with this principle in mind. It starts with an opening meeting of staff and students, usually chaired by a student, for sharing important issues from each person's work and life in the previous week and discussing and deciding on any issues related to the work of the course. Similarly there is a closing meeting at the end of the day for attending to any 'unfinished business' and making the transition back into the outside world. 'Teaching' takes the form of discussion seminars, based on the reading of a paper the previous week, in which reflection on current practice situations and attention to process is key. The weekly experiential group helps peel back further layers of connection between personal history and professional practice. The staff meeting at the end of the day is a crucial time for piecing together and understanding the day's events.

In the accounts which follow, I draw on the work of a number of former course members as they examined and developed their practice, applying their learning to their own specific settings in therapeutic child care. Their broad themes include the provision of emotional holding and containment for children and for workers; the use of meetings, understanding unconscious communication between individuals and in groups, especially defences against anxiety; a particular emphasis on the reflective staff team and its management; and include above all the informed and thoughtful use of self in the work.

The first part explores the very difficult task of providing a holding environment in field social work settings, particularly for fostered and adoptive children and their carers. Later examples are drawn from group care and residential settings for children in public care and for children with severe learning disabilities.

Providing a holding environment in fostering and adoption

Many field social workers report that the organisations for which they work seem unable to offer much in the way of emotional holding for the work. Social service agencies are at the sharp end of society's projections – its discomfort with the existence of children and families in distress – where painful feelings are avoided in a culture of blame, so that social workers are 'damned if they do and damned if they don't'. Such a defensive culture may arise from an institutional defence against anxiety within the organisation, in which the need for the workers to be supported if they are to support others is lost sight of. It can help the individual social worker avoid a sense of failure and self-blame if she can understand the origin and operation of such unconscious processes, and so feel freed to seek supervision or consultancy, or use the team as a holding environment where the work and the feelings it arouses can be thought about (Obholzer and Roberts 1994). The worker who can then hold the child in mind over a long period, who can advocate for the child, and co-ordinate work with families, foster carers and schools so that together they provide a good enough 'holding environment' is the person whom the child will see as a 'helpful adult' (Farnfield and Kaszap 1998). What this entails is shown in the following examples.

Holding the child in mind

The social worker's task involves providing emotional holding as well as practical services to children and families. Where children are in transition between birth families and substitute care, or in foster and adoptive placements, a social worker who can hold the child in mind, and demonstrate this to the child, often over a long period of time and through a number of life changes, can help the child in turn to become a container, able to think about rather than simply react to events. This is shown in Simon Peacock's (1997) work with Bobbie.

> Bobbie and her sisters suffered severe neglect in infancy and by the age of 10 Bobbie had experienced more than 20 moves of home and changes of carer. Their lives were presented to me in a huge cardboard box, equivalent to one full filing cabinet drawer for each child. This Pandora's box created an unforgettable moment of emotional anxiety before I was able to get down to the task of piecing together Bobbie's life story. I decided to call a meeting of the numerous professionals involved, at which all expressed anxiety to 'do something now'. I felt , however, that in the first place the anxiety needed to be contained rather than immediately acted on. I would try to create some stability in Bobbie's life, which in turn could begin to enable her to construct some meaning to it. Meanwhile, realising I would need someone to provide some containment for me, I sought supervision from a colleague.

> Two years on I had achieved a more settled period for Bobbie in one placement and eventually, after another struggle with the organisation, obtained a place for her in a residential special school offering a good holding environment, that is, a culture which could tolerate her aggressive and disruptive

behaviour, providing containment not only through rules and boundaries but through a relationship for Bobbie with the teaching and care staff. However, her foster placement had to end and Bobbie's belongings ended up in boxes in my house…

After a few weeks an excellent new foster placement was found. Things were looking up, except that I was told that the schools transport would not pick Bobbie up from the new foster home because 'it was not in the contract'. The contract said to pick her up from Town A and take her to school but not from Town B where she was now, and which was a further 20 miles up the road. This meant I had to get up at 6 a.m. to pick her up at 7 a.m. every Monday morning to take her to Town A to meet her school taxi. I did the reverse journey on Friday evenings. Now I could quite easily have ordered a social services taxi to do the 20 miles from Town A to Town B and back – Parcel Force could probably do the job just as easily. What was important in this apparently minor piece of transport management was ' a response to the actor and not to the act' (David Howe's (1996) phrase). Bobbie needed a person who could carry her both literally and emotionally along the road from one part of her life to the next. I was making a tangible link for her and I was also making it with her.

The journey from school to foster placement mirrored the story of Bobbie's life. The anxiety about whether the two cars would meet up in the right place at the right time on each journey went a long way in demonstrating my reliability to Bobbie. It also demonstrated that the disparate parts of her life could be held together in me and by me. I believe it also demonstrated that I was holding *her* in mind and not just the task of getting her to school.

Once the task of holding things together for Bobbie was seen to be done reliably then she could begin an attempt at containing painful and anxious feelings for herself. One day she told me that her favourite song was 'All By Myself'. The realisation that the song had meaning for her was one of her first steps.

Holding the carers to hold the fostered child

While the social worker may directly provide holding and containment he or she is usually only one person among a constellation of other professionals concerned. Meetings for taking decisions and planning interventions are commonplace, but as the last example showed, such meetings are often overtaken by anxiety and the urge to rescue. More productive may be the idea of professionals meeting regularly as a 'transitional family' (Hey, Leheup and Almudevar 1995) simply to hold the child in mind and provide continuity between their past and future families. There is growing evidence that even some quite unintegrated children do well if they have a social worker, foster carer and teacher who are committed to them and thinking together about them (Farnfield and Kaszap 1998). This is close to the therapeutic community emphasis on a reflective staff team working to understand unconscious processes and providing a holding environment. Where the child is also present at a meeting there is an even closer parallel to the therapeutic community model of a community meeting whose task is to work at existing difficulties and conflicts. Social worker Debbie Mead describes how she provided a holding environment for Annie, a troubled and difficult adolescent returning from a residential placement, and for her rejecting birth mother, her foster carers and the school.

> A stressed (and departing) social worker gave me a scanty verbal handover in the car on the way to meet Annie. The case certainly did not feel 'held' on paper – there were great gaps in the files about Annie's relationships and residential experience but I gleaned what I could. I concluded that Annie needed a safe and stable environment where some order could be given to the chaos of her life. A weekend respite foster care placement proved successful and I worked hard to support its becoming permanent. My role was to coordinate resources and ensure regular communication between all concerned – home, school, foster carer and myself. We shared information and learned about how others experienced Annie, ensuring that the boundaries around her were consistent. Annie was an integral part of these meetings, able to express her views freely, and aware of expectations of her.
>
> My relationship with the foster carer proved to be the most important part of the success of the 'holding environment' for Annie. We were in touch almost daily. I helped her make use of her own emotional reactions to gain more insight into Annie's destructiveness and enable her to continue to provide a containing but not a withholding environment, giving Annie lots of good experiences to hold onto. The foster carer communicated well with school, and with Annie's mother. School provided a one-to-one support worker and Annie developed positive relationships with her teacher and other staff, and made carefully managed visits home. We all worked towards maximum clarity in communicating with each other, enabling all profes-

sionals to feel held – we all knew what we were doing and were all working together for the same end.

To hold this situation required tremendous energy on everyone's part. We aimed to respond immediately to any difficult situation, letting Annie know we were concerned and cared about her but also confronting her with the realities of the situation and what she could do to effect change. Over the next three years Annie's relationships gradually improved and she began to achieve academically. Although she would frequently regress to periods of more unacceptable behaviour, her resilience and self-worth grew.

Working with groups of foster carers

The model of the therapeutic community meeting has much to offer in working with groups of foster carers. Social worker Jenni McRae led a group foster carers who met to share difficulties and learn together about attachment, separation and loss, and the need for emotional holding.

Some felt guilty at past failures to understand a foster child and sometimes defensive and angry. I tried to stay with the task of understanding the unconscious processes involved in the group, paying attention to my own counter-transference feelings, to help group members think about painful feelings, often about their own childhood and parenting losses as well as about present difficulties, and which went to the heart of their motivation for fostering. Meeting together gave foster carers a cathartic sense of all being in the same boat and able to draw hope and inspiration from those who had experienced similar difficulties and feelings of failure when placements broke down. They could play with new ideas in the safety of the group, laugh at themselves and with each other, and test out new possibilities. (McRae 2000)

Holding an adopted child and the adoptive family

There will always be a need to provide emotional holding for the families and foster or adoptive carers, to enable them in turn to provide the same for the child, able to think about, make sense of and so manage difficult behaviour which might otherwise destroy a placement. The previous case studies concerned fostering. In a further example I return to the role of the social worker in the provision of a holding environment for a child in his adoptive family. This account is from social worker Sally Woods.

As a caseworker to a child placed with adoptive parents, apart from the statutory and administrative aspects of my role, I also had a role **'holding the child in mind'**. I had known Cameron over some years initially trying to rehabilitate him with his mother; then followed several foster placements before finding adoptive parents. This holding in mind is an emotionally involved process, not a detached or distant one, involving a lot of reflection, and exposed me to the child's painful emotions as I sought to understand his inner world and offer him continuity. Children in care for more than a short while often experience many changes of worker and also many placement moves, so that it is hard for them to be known and understood as individuals over time and their needs held in mind by any one constant person. My role was to transfer this 'holding in mind', and also to transfer my understanding of him, and knowledge of his life story, to his new parents who would keep this role. The foster carers were also involved in this transfer.

This leads to my second role, that of **supporting the placement**. I tried to offer a 'holding environment' for the adoptive parents while they sought to provide this for Cameron and his sister. Caring for emotionally damaged children who project their painful feelings onto those close to them is stressful. To be able to cope and continue responding helpfully the carers need a sense of being 'held' by the worker(s) as well as by their other support networks. I made myself available in a reliable and responsive way through visits and by telephone. I spent time thinking with the adoptive mother, and in between visits, about what was going on for Cameron, linking it back to my previous knowledge of him. I also used my knowledge of research and therapeutic processes, for example to explain what was going on when he regressed and to encourage them in the primary experience which the mother was intuitively offering. The school too may need to be reminded over time about Cameron's early deprivation so that they do not have unrealistic expectations if concentration and restlessness continue to be problems.

My third role was that of being a **bridge to Cameron's past**, based on my knowledge and understanding of his birth mother and his two older siblings. The siblings' relationships with him had, in my view, made a huge contribution to his ability to make a new attachment in adoption and to make good peer relationships. My insistence that the adoptive parents meet the siblings, which had been agreed pre-placement but delayed, put a strain on my relationship with the adoptive parents. However, the meeting went well, helping their better understanding of the birth family, and may enable face-to-face contact to continue sooner rather than later.

As the child's social worker there were times when I was more identified with the needs of the birth family, which led to tensions, but I had the advantage over a family placement social worker of detailed knowledge of the child's relationships and life story to assist the understanding of him in his new home. I view it as helpful to the child and adoptive parents to have access to two workers, so that different knowledge and perspectives can be offered and there can be an element of choice if there is a clash of personalities or views. At the same time the two workers need to be aware of the risk of splitting – and to manage this we conducted a number of joint visits and were both involved in the regular reviews.

My final role with Cameron, a child who has played a big part in my life, will be to 'let go'. This will need to include a positive ending of the relationship for Cameron, after the adoption order is made. This is a task still to complete. My visits have become less frequent and focused more on empowering the adoptive parents in their new role, and helping them through the uncertain time before the adoption hearing. I anticipate making myself available for discussion after my formal case holding role ends. (Woods 2000)

Working as a staff team at understanding unconscious communication

Workers in day care, schools and residential settings are usually part of a staff team. The way a team works and is managed varies greatly. Therapeutic community principles of working in a open and democratic way can go a long way to establishing good communication within a team. However, when conflicts arise they can be puzzling or their origins misunderstood unless there is attention to unconscious aspects of communication. Jeanette Langfeld here explains the need for a staff team as a whole to work at understanding the meaning of a child's behaviour in the local authority children's home of which she was then manager.

> In order to develop a meaningful treatment programme for a child it is necessary for all members of a staff team to contribute towards 'getting to know' a child and developing the insight to find meaning in their behaviour. What one person misses another will notice. What one person per-

ceives in one way will be viewed differently by another. Nevertheless it will also be through the preoccupation of the child's key worker that the significance of certain things can be understood. The maintenance of the team's capacity to understand behaviour as communication is ultimately a task for the home's manager, as this can be very difficult for staff to do when they are on the receiving end of the behaviour.

Understanding Kevin

Recently Kevin panicked when he was told that his key worker had some good news for him. He became quite distraught, saying that he guessed his worker was pregnant and would be leaving. He was reassured once he knew the news was instead about an exciting trip. Later this episode was discussed in terms of the importance of the key worker to the child. We then 'remembered' that Kevin's mother had died shortly after giving birth to his younger sister, when he was three years old. We were then able to think in more depth about Kevin's response and needs. (Langfeld 2000)

This helpful piece of reflection in the staff team was not the only way in which therapeutic community principles were grafted onto practice in this local authority residential children's home. The manager had long been using weekly meetings of children and staff, and helped both children and staff use them in a increasingly sophisticated and reflective way.

Managing Jo's bedtime: The provision of primary experience in a local authority children's home

The following account by Pete Grady, then a senior staff member in a local authority children's home, demonstrates how therapeutic care becomes possible when a staff team works together at understanding the meaning of a child's behaviour.

> The team were using staff meetings to try to understand the behaviour of a 13-year-old so that they had better options for managing him than either doing what they had always done or each working on gut feeling alone. Jo, a child who had experienced over 20 foster placements in the previous two years, was threatening and violent towards staff mixed with periods of wanting to please at any costs. These vacillations matched shift changes so that some teams were left feeling like 'bad objects' (Valentine 1994) while others revelled in the good behaviour that they experienced. Staff were split and some, unfamiliar with the concept of projective identification – of de-

fending against pain by subjecting someone else to it (Canham 1998), felt it was a personal attack.

From quite early on Jo's bedtime was a trigger for nightly disruption. He was unable to settle and made sure that others were not allowed to settle as well. Initial discussion in staff meetings focused upon Jo's aggressiveness and staff's feeling of being out of control; they saw his splitting between teams as manipulation. The team's major concern was how to put boundaries quickly into place so that he could settle down – a phrase that may be significant not only to bedtime. The need for boundaries may be seen as a physical expression of the staff's perception of a need to emotionally contain this unintegrated child who was explicit about wanting to destroy his placement. Jo's key workers were given the task of bringing to the next week's meeting a plan to deal with some of his behaviour. They came up with a 'novel' proposal which was to allow Jo time to settle based upon an agreed routine. He would have a bath or shower just before bedtime to help him calm down, then take a mug of hot chocolate to bed and drink this while reading a story, and he could have his door open slightly and a nightlight on, because he was afraid of the dark. The staff team readily agreed and within days Jo settled quickly and said he was having better nights' sleep than he ever remembered. Meanwhile Jo also became insistent that his towel remain on his radiator throughout the day and that he would wash it and return it himself. Once when the domestic staff forgot and washed his towel he insisted on washing it again before he used it. On returning to the unit he would always check that it was still there.

The team's provision of a bedtime routine normally appropriate to a much younger child was a therapeutic experience for Jo. However, it was not discussed by the team in terms of therapy or psychodynamics, although as team leader I was familiar with Winnicott's theory of the need for primary experiences for unintegrated children. The use of a transitional object was only apparent with hindsight; at the time no one could see why the towel was central to the process but there was a distinct feeling that it was. (Later it emerged that Jo's mother, who had been in care herself and not ready for a baby, had often left Jo crying because she could not bear to pick him up.) That is not to underestimate the way in which the team had thought about Jo and used their ability to work together both in meetings and in the public arena of daily living. A staff team without much by way of formal training in therapeutic care, but with the capacity to be reflective and use real involvement – the ability and willingness to put themselves in Jo's shoes – succeeded in providing good primary experience to help him towards integration. (Grady 2000)

Unconscious processes in staff teams working with children with learning disability and their families

It might be assumed that there is little in common between the experience of an emotionally damaged child and a child with learning disabilities. Certainly there is no reason to suppose that a learning disabled child is necessarily insecurely attached or emotionally unintegrated. However the effect on the child and their family of a severe learning disability – a 'primary handicap' – may involve what Sinason (1992) calls a 'secondary handicap', feelings of worthlessness, anger and despair, often all the stronger when difficulties in thinking and in verbal communication may be limited and prevent articulation of feelings. Then much communication is through behaviour, with its concomitant processes of projective identification and potential for splitting. The provision of a 'holding environment' benefits from attention to the unconscious processes involved in relationships within families, between staff and children, between staff and families, and within a staff team. The setting may variously be the child's family, a foster family, a playgroup or play scheme, the school, or a short or longer-term residential setting.

My own experience of leading a therapeutic play group for developmentally delayed very young children and their families, within a child development centre, together with my experience of being a parent of a learning disabled child, taught me the need to understand that a parent's anger with me or with other aspects of the service they received, while sometimes entirely justifiable anger, was also a projection of unbearable distress at having a disabled child. What helped a parent was their distress being understood, rather than colluded with – with all its risks of projective splits between different hospital staff teams, splits which were real enough in any case. Even more helpful was the mutual understanding and support that parents gave to one another in the course of the daily activities of the group, together with the respect for parents' views accorded by the staff team. This fits well with the current emphasis on a family's strengths and the empowerment model for work with such families, which is itself a good match with a therapeutic community model. The parent who feels accepted and understood within the holding environment of the playgroup is more able to manage his or her child's difficult and distressed behaviour.

The power of the therapeutic community approach lies in its ability to combine a positive and respectful appreciation of individual children or parents and their potential to help one another within a group, together with an ability to engage with difficult feelings and behaviour, seeking to understand their meaning, rather than gloss over them or react in an unthinking way. It also provides models for leadership which can help a staff team manage and learn from conflict, as the next examples, the first from Paula Stacey and the second from Denise Jolly, show.

A staff team working with the difficult behaviour of a learning disabled child in a local authority community home

Carl could not use speech but communicated through body language and gesture. He responded differently to staff members, for example, playful with one and serious with another. He had spells eating cigarette ends, often going into the street to search for them, and at the same time becoming distant and detached. Staff feared for his safety and they were split as to who would and would not take him out for his regular routine of activities, giving rise to heated arguments between 'good staff' who were willing to try anything and 'bad staff' who were perceived as punitive and intolerant.

The manager was able to see all sides, openly acknowledging the difficulties and remaining clear that they had to find ways of managing Carl's behaviour. The staff team began to realise that Carl's obsession with cigarette ends coincided with his keyworker's annual leave. The keyworker used to provide Carl with a simple and clear routine, explaining to him every step of the plans for the evening, what activities would be undertaken with whom. He acknowledged that his absence affected Carl, which helped the staff team recognise the importance of this relationship. Not only were the staff eventually able to manage Carl's behaviour and their own anxiety but also to build in more sensitivity to the potential impact of regular staff absences on other young people. The staff team were engaged in this process over many months, discussing and influencing each other and creating a living and learning experience in their work.

Understanding unconscious processes in a staff team in a residential school for children with autism

Whatever the underlying causes of autism, the autistic child's inability to communicate feelings in words means that a more primal communication takes place. The worker feels the child's anxiety through projective identification, mixed up with her own anxiety if the behaviour is aggressive. Unless the child's anxiety as well as the worker's is understood the child may then be isolated or separated, escalating the child's anxiety and strengthening the autistic shell of internal comfort routines.

One of the residential teams at the school was upset and openly divided in team meetings about their difficulties in working with a particular autistic child. Only the nominated individual worker and the team leader felt safe enough to spend time alone with him. The individual worker felt that she could not ask for a break from the intensity of her relationship with the child without placing undue stress on the rest of the team. The other teams began to regard this team as dysfunctional. Mature professional concern was abandoned as the teams seemed unable to focus on the reality of the child who at times presented as deliberately provocative (he would greet people by raising his hand and 'threatening' to slap), sexually aggressive (he had pushed female staff over and groped breasts and groin), and aware of his actions (he would verbally describe his assault as it was carried out). It became a matter of 'good' or 'bad' handling of the child ('he's OK when he's with me') or whether the organisation was strong enough to maintain his placement ('but where else would cope with him?'). There seemed no place for 'the hatred children can arouse, which must be coped with by everyone who looks after them. It allowed for no confrontation with the child's or their own hatred, an important maturational experience for both' (Menzies-Lyth 1989, p.225).

The beginnings of a resolution occurred in meetings called by myself as unit leader, when staff aired their perceptions of this child in a structured brainstorm. Both positive and negative comments appeared – the first honest appraisal of a staff team's relationship with this child. As the words came the boy's power seemed to diminish. When asked to think about what the boy might be feeling, in direct parallel to their feelings, the answer came through loud and clear. He was asking for safety, to be contained, to improve his poor image of himself. These conclusions were not delivered to the staff team – they discovered for themselves that what they had been demanding from each other the boy had been demanding of them. The projection was beginning to be understood. From this point the team could move forward to accept the reality of the work involved. It was still going to be demanding and often daunting work. However, staff felt enabled to discuss the process of the work more effectively, their role became clearer and they could begin to strengthen themselves against the child's defences of autism, and his particular way of expressing his own anxiety and poor self-esteem. By examination of some of the unconscious processes, often clouded by practical as-

sociation and submerged in habitual working method, it has been possible
to create a greater understanding and a more holistic approach to the task
of care.

Conclusion

Workers in a range of agencies and professions, both in group care and in
more individually based work, can draw on an understanding of unconscious
processes operating not only between individuals but also within groups and
organisations. By working at understanding the meanings underlying
behaviour they are able to provide a version of a holding environment for the
children for whom they are responsible. At times this may be very close to the
therapeutic community model, with everyone staying with the problem and
working at it together in the course of daily living. At other times the match is
less exact, as when a holding environment is provided by a reflective staff
team. In either case the quality of leadership is crucial – it must be both containing and enabling as well as discerning about the operation of the unconscious 'reflection process' (Mattinson 1975). Other versions of a holding environment may be compared to a set of Russian dolls, the individual worker
providing emotional holding for parents and carers, who in turn 'hold' the
child at its centre. This image raises the important question of how the organisation holds the worker.

One aspect remains crucial and that is training. The manager and worker
who is providing a holding environment needs to have experienced it herself.
This brings me back to the importance of the learning experience matching
the model for practice. Learning in a context which draws on the principles of
the therapeutic community means experiencing personally the interplay of
painful emotions arising from one's own and others' experience, working to
find meaning in it, and then exploring ways of responding helpfully, using the
self in the service of the child.

CHAPTER 18

Therapeutic Childcare and the Local Authority

Michael Maher

The 1990s and the beginning of the new century have seen great changes in how residential childcare and treatment is organised. Over this time a series of investigations and reports have resulted in an era of much greater scrutiny, in which it is more difficult for malignantly motivated people to organise an institution around the gratification of their perverse appetites, and the way that this has been approached has come from an emphasis on the individual child's needs, rather than the overall needs of the organisation, as this could be motivated by exactly these perverse or malign motives. The reports come from this perspective; the Children Act is written throughout with the individual child's needs given paramount status. The sector has moved from one of relatively loose regulation to one which is governed by highly developed and all-encompassing regulation, and is an area in which the functions of scrutiny, complaint, inspection and rights compete in an ever more crowded field. All the foregoing has been enacted in the name of care, and I believe that it has had the effect of making it much more difficult to run group living institutions in ways which are shoddy, neglectful or actively abusive. So far, two cheers for progress, then.

But there is always a price. As in child development, every advance is only attained at the cost of giving up a previous state of being. So, what has been gained and what has been lost? Another way of thinking about this is to ask a particular question, and it relates to the following. I wonder what my experience would have been if I had had to go into residential care when I was a child, and what it would be like now for my children if that fate befell them? I wonder what it would have been like if I had been deeply damaged and

277

disturbed by my experiences, what chances I would have had, and what chances I (or my children) would have now?

These are not easy questions to attempt to answer. To try, I look for research undertaken into trends in the field of residential care, and of course I quickly find that there is not much that helps. One book, which came out in 2000, provided some material on which to base some views. *Providing Residential Services for Children and Young People: A Multidisciplinary Perspective*, by Catherine Street, looks at the current state of business across children's homes, therapeutic communities and adolescent psychiatric units. It contained the following findings: 'A decline in belief. Ideals…have been replaced by pragmatism'; 'requests for emergency placements had increased by 30% compared to earlier years'. What lay behind the above trends? – interestingly, something about 'a shift in the emotional quality of professional relationships' – that agencies, and individuals in agencies could not afford to be as closely invested in the children for whom they bore responsibility, that practice had become more defensive, and that a 'climate of non-exoneration' existed, whereby residential staff never felt exonerated of allegations (which were increasingly commonplace), irrespective of the findings of investigations.

Residential units are soft targets, open to being maligned by any critic, and there is no shortage of hostile observers to exploit these opportunities. It seems then that in this climate both sides – the referrers and the providers – have taken a step back from some of their most difficult and needy children. What happens in the space so created? What does this gap mean to the children so retreated from? How are the residential resources changing to cope with this shift?

The Street book only provides an answer to the last of the above questions (the first two are even more important and I want to come back to them). Most of the organisations involved in the research expressed the intention to improve their screening of referrals – in the health units, this was expressed as screening out conduct disorders on the basis of poor residential treatment prognosis. Other resources expressed it as a wish to screen out referrals inappropriately displaced from other areas. The issue for me here is that everyone is trying to screen out the same referrals – the violent, conduct disordered, borderline, 'ungroupable', angry, chaotic child. If everywhere is trying to avoid these children, jockeying for position to deny responsibility for them ('intersectoral territorialism'), where do they end up? I will return to this later in the chapter.

So, let me provide an answer to the questions I started with. As I read it, for most children and young people in residential care, things have improved since a generation ago. For the most damaged and difficult, with the stepping back and the resultant psychic no-go areas, things may be worse. This, perhaps then, is the price. Clearer professional boundaries (good thing) have led to greater emotional distance (bad thing). More scrutiny and regulation (good thing) has led to more defensive practice (bad thing). A greater emphasis on care and safety and child protection (all good things) has led to a loss of commitment to treatment and an unwillingness to take necessary risks (bad things). The emphasis on the individual (good) has led to a loss of belief in the potential and importance of the use of the group (bad). These are some of the prices – there are others also, and they relate to the other questions raised and unanswered so far in the course of this chapter. I will turn to these next.

Local authority social services are driven by twin imperatives: the need to manage increasing levels of need and expectation within generally static or diminishing budgets and the need to avoid unacceptable levels of risk. Social policy shifts usually occur when research or fashion suggests improved outcomes whilst at the same time offering a cheaper way of going about business. Recent examples of this at work include the current emphasis on inclusion in education and the emphasis on family placements as the first and last word in placements for all children to be looked after by the state. It is often a process whereby a sound principle can get pushed too far for what become rather cynical reasons. What is remarkable in child care in the last decade has been the opposite trend in placement type for the very disturbed child. As often in such situations, we start with a dualistic tension – the need to make good value, cost-effective placements versus the need to keep the child safe. We might also add another tension – the need to treat versus the need to avoid risk.

Let me cite a brief example from a recent (composite) case. Laura is just 15; she is angry, confused and often violent. Recently her specialist foster carer placement broke down in an emergency when she set a fire in her bedroom. With some considerable difficulty she was found a bed (despite these being no legitimate space available) in one of the local authority's children's homes. The team responsible for out-of-county placements scoured the south of England for an emergency bed. It became clear that when possible placements in the private and voluntary sector – including therapeutic communities – were told about her behaviour nowhere was willing to take her. The one potential place could be in a couple of weeks. This response was from a provider that specialises in placements of young people on their own. They had a project that a young person was leaving and there would be a vacancy in that timescale. It would cost around £180,000 a year; she would leave the area (to go about 100 miles away) and lose her school place. The team continued to look, the unit continued to be overstretched and under pressure from this intractable problem. The manager offered to keep her over the weekend, rather than she and the staff continuing to live with the uncertainty. By this time her behaviour was deteriorating and secure accommodation was considered: there were no beds in the south of England. The following week an internal solution was engineered; a young man was moved to another unit to release a vacancy at the unit where Laura had been 'lodging'. This was by no means ideal, or even acceptable, but it was the least bad alternative.

The main issue that I want to raise from the foregoing is that of containment, both in the system and in the unit. There are no 'bad guys' in the story I have just told; the social services department did everything it could to provide for this girl, and was willing to fund an out-of-county place which was hugely expensive and which would provide a questionable service with no evidence to show positive outcomes. The private provider that places children on their own is offering a service that few others are prepared to, and for good reason: the stakes are too high; it's too risky. The level of risk is not intrinsic to the case; it has become so because we have made it so. Such expensive responses, which bleed social services departments dry and compromise their ability to intervene earlier and more positively, are the consequence of the paranoid atmosphere created by the uncovering of all the abuses of the past 20 years. It has passed into the culture of the young people – 'if you touch me I'll get you done'; staff feel understandably vulnerable and back off; the resultant gap feeds the loneliness and desperation and the narcissistic defence against these feelings.

What happens to these young people? Some of them still get referred to therapeutic communities. More of them, however, bypass this sector and are placed in ones or twos in houses over the south of England, maintained through having a staff team, often recruited through agencies, devoted entirely to keeping them 'safe', by virtue of keeping them apart from other young people. They have been deemed impossible to live in a group, and the result is that the powerful forces mobilised by group living and group educating are removed – envy, conflict, sexual attraction, adolescent destructive group processes. Their teeth are pulled. When this happens, the chances of moving them on to somewhere where treatment can happen become remote indeed. Treatment is risky, difficult and painful for everyone involved – and often too risky, difficult and painful to attempt.

Historically most of the children who came to therapeutic communities had been deemed unmanageable and ineducable in a group, so the task of the therapeutic community was constructed as teaching them how to live, and be educated, in groups. The way that this was taught was by throwing them into the group at the deep end (there is no shallow end) and then helping them swim, knowing that they would struggle for the first two or three years or so. The difference was that the therapeutic community tradition saw group processes as essential, as things that could be harnessed to make the experience a joint undertaking with the young people. Such an approach inevitably brings problems – in fact the problems are an inherent part of the approach.

Perhaps the thing that has changed most is the willingness to live with problems and see problems as potentially productive, that disturbed children and adolescents could help each other as much as they can damage each other. The climate tends now more to equating such issues with badness, and equating smoothness with goodness. Hence placing these young people on their own, and educating them on their own. Big is bad, because there are too many problems that ensue when too many of these personality types are placed together – and of course that is true; it's just how many, of what type, that I would debate. Therefore, small is good, and smaller is better and single is best. This satisfies our current societal and institutional needs to defend ourselves from risk. It is a kind of condom culture, whereby the difficult unruly child is sheathed and the world around is protected from catching anything terrible from them, like violence or madness. It is also a very angry, or perhaps a guilty response.

These children are living insults to the values we tell ourselves we live by and permit others to live by. They refuse to behave, conform, get better and stop impinging on others and us. We (by 'we' I refer to the dominant perception of the age, the way in which the majority of people within a culture make sense of their experience of living) hate them, deny the reality of hating and murderous feelings in ourselves and project them into those who attempt to work with them, and place them in highly expensive and uncertain places on their own. This has had a dual effect over time.

Children like Laura are placed on their own often because no group care living situation will accept them. We should not have to search our minds for long to wonder why this might be. Referring agencies have placed such children in therapeutic communities and other, often lower quality, group-based care and breathed a sigh of relief. Then, some way down the line, a child protection issue will crop up. I am not referring to paedophiles here, or systematic abuse. I mean the types of things that inevitably ensue when disturbed and aggressive children are placed together. A child hits another child, or is found in another child's bed, or an allegation is made. The ambivalence towards these victim/aggressor children then comes out in a critical attack on the residential establishment. The ground that all residential units – good and bad – stand on is eroded by such attacks, which have become commonplace. The necessary confidence, the ability to act with proper authority in the knowledge that actions taken in the best interest of the children will be seen as they are and not misconstrued has been increasingly lost from the residential sector. The attitude – fuelled by a multiplicity of well-known cases of appalling abuse – that residential homes are places you send children for them to be abused, is now embedded so firmly in the collective psyche that adventurous, flexible, impassioned, imaginative, creative work with these children – the work that most characterised the therapeutic community tradition – is harder to achieve than it used to be, and it was always difficult.

What happens to them now then? Many are 'kept safe' until they are 16 years old then cast forth into some cynical arrangement of 'semi-independence'; their care and education complete. They have learnt that they are untouchable, that they cannot live or be taught in groups, that they can break systems and people, that they are dangerous and to be feared. They do not belong anywhere. If one definition of culture is all the things you don't have to do, then this way of working with this kind of child is the antithesis of culture – child care through isolation. In this small and rare example, we have reached the apotheosis of individual materialism.

So, what is the way out of this trap? How can we avoid the pointless and despairing waste of potential that such a social trend represents? If only a few of these children get into therapeutic communities, is there anything that can be learned from that tradition that could be transferred to other settings that might survive the translocation? What essentially happens in successful therapeutic community work, and how is it so essentially different from the work that is possible when a child is placed alone?

The difference is, of course, the group. I have written elsewhere about what happens in group analysis, and how this treatment offers something different from individual therapy.

> The individual 'gives up' the sense of separateness, and there is a merging with the group. The neurotic patterns that individuate and isolate are challenged by the processes of communication; there is a process whereby patterns of relating and self-concepts (how one relates to one's own internal object relation constellations) are dissolved, then assimilated and finally metabolised. Merging is followed by redifferentiation in an altered state. Others' differing perceptions of the individual's self allow for the possibility of giving up attitudes which had become fixed. More things become possible through the group's belief that each member of the group has more options than he or she realises. 'On reflection, in both senses of the word, an individual member is helped to explore what he is not and,

therefore, among other things, what he is' (Pines 1981). There is a move from isolation to connectedness, to becoming a part of a greater whole. 'Getting lost in others is the way to becoming oneself' (Van der Kleij 1985). Maher (2000)

Of course the setting and process of group analysis is very different from that of a therapeutic community, but the two worlds have a common ancestry, and the above description holds equally for a successful treatment in a therapeutic community, where the container and the contained is the community itself. It is my contention that some of the above processes can be translocated to other settings and survive, in an altered form, within the statutory setting of a social services run service, and in my own work I have been identified with this endeavour.

Before I look at what aspects of this can be achieved, I want to revisit the old established tenets of what makes for therapeutic community practice. The most well known of all descriptions of what defines the 'therapeutic community proper' was attempted by Rapoport in 1960. He came up with the four main themes of therapeutic community life. They were:

- democratization

- permissiveness

- communalism

- reality confrontation.

By democratization he meant that each member of the community should share equally in the exercise of power and decision-making. By permissiveness he meant that the community should be able to tolerate the deviant or abnormal behaviour of its members without suppression – the understanding and the expression of reactions to it were the things that mattered most. By communalism he meant that all events in the community should be a shared experience with the maximum of interrelationship, participation and openness. Reality confrontation does not need a gloss from me.

This was based on adult communities and it was written more than 40 years ago, and it shows. I can imagine the reaction I would get if I were to propose a new residential treatment facility for adolescents based on these principles. Permissiveness and communalism are concepts that had their heyday in the 1960s, and are now viewed at best as quaint, at worst as dangerously sloppy and neglectful. They just do not fit in the highly regulated world of the twenty-first century. Even democratization seems debased as a concept. Yet I would argue that embedded in the tradition that these terms represent there is something of great value, and highly pertinent to the current situation. A translation is needed, a recasting of these ideals into language which fits the modern palate. A suggestion of what this might be like follows:

- *Power sharing* – feelings of power, effectiveness, expertise, insight and outsight as well as those of impotence, frustration, ineffectiveness and blindness should be shared across groups and roles, without denying issues of training, experience, skill and actual role and power differentials.

- *Tolerance* – the need to express and understand behaviour is balanced by a recognition of there being limits to permissiveness, and continued gross acting out may threaten the integrity of the group, even the institution, and actions have to be taken in order to underline boundaries and restore order, but this should be in the context of an underlying tolerant ethic where punitive responses are resisted whenever possible.

- *Interdependence* – the work of the community is about learning how to live in groups, and problems affecting the whole will be reflected by various disturbances in the parts, and problems arising in a part would affect the well-being of the whole.

- *Reality Confrontation* – the basic dynamic remains the same: an individual's behaviour would be constantly reflected back to him or her – 'when you do this, it makes me feel like this'.

So, how much of the above can translate to 'ordinary' children's homes? Can a local authority use these principles to provide therapeutic childcare direct? Do they want to?

To address the last question first: in my experience the staff in most local authority children's homes would like to consider the work they undertake as essentially therapeutic in its nature. However, these same staff are extremely wary of identifying their work in this way. How can we account for this paradox? The main causes that I can identify are ignorance about what makes for therapeutic childcare and anxiety about being attacked if they presume to make such a claim for their work. Yet what does it mean for a residential establishment if it does not make such a claim? Many establishments give the impression that they deliver care in a sort of neutral way, that they emphasise the importance of the values contained in anti-discriminatory and anti-oppressive practices, but beyond these constructs they do not adhere to any particular philosophy. They often style themselves as 'eclectic', in the vague belief that if you believe in enough things, you offend nobody. Actually, if you believe everything, you believe nothing. None of this bears much scrutiny. There can be no such thing as a neutral transaction in this field. Every home has an ethos, formed from the sum of the dynamics between the managers, the team and the children resident, and influenced by the prevailing social, legislative, professional, political and economic context. The question is rather, 'Can staff articulate a shared ethos, and what impact does being able to do that have on the atmosphere in the home?'

I want to come at this by way of some research that is not into residential care, but has important implications for all kinds of establishments. Most of the Newcastle 1000 Family Study, published as *Continuities of Deprivation* (Kolvin *et al.* 1990) concentrates on links between multiple deprivation and offending behaviour in young men. It also looks at the obverse side of this picture, and reaches some conclusions about protective factors that seem to be at play in avoiding this outcome for those who do not offend. One phrase leaps out of the research, and that is the part played by 'effective parenting', and how this is a very important factor in all of this. What does this mean? What is this Holy Grail of social work? In an interview in *The Guardian* Kolvin expanded on what his research team had isolated from this phrase 'effective parenting':

> Unsurprisingly the attitude of the mother was found to be overwhelmingly important. Non-offenders were more likely to come from homes where the mother, although in bad circumstances, felt able to cope. 'Where families did not understand their problems, or had a general sense of helplessness, bad behaviour rapidly developed in the children. The more the mother felt life was beyond her control, and the lower her self-esteem, the worse the behaviour of the children.' In homes where the parents worked together as a couple, where there was good communication, intimacy, affection and minimal quarrelling, children were also less likely to offend. (Kolvin, in *The Guardian*, date unknown)

Here we have two principles – straightforward, unsurprising. Parent or parents who feel they can cope; parents who can communicate openly, with respect and affection. This latter is particularly important when it relates to parents addressing differences between them with respect to how they bring up their children.

I want to make a leap from the above research and bring these principles to bear on residential care. Frankly, it's not much of a leap. If these principles stand as protective factors in families, which, complex as they are, are not as complex as group living and working situations, then they must be all the more important in all kinds of residential care. Ergo, staff need to feel that they can cope. And staff need to be able to communicate openly, at depth, address differences and as a group achieve a necessary level of intimacy. By this I mean deepening and widening communication, so that more things become openly talkable about, and fewer things need to be gossiped about. In order to communicate successfully, you have to be able to say what is on your mind and be able to listen to different points of view. If powerful and primitive emotional forces are at play, this is incredibly difficult. If it is between professionals, it is harder still. It is acceptable for a parent to feel distressed, envious, and hateful towards a residential social worker. It is hard to own up to the fact that residential social workers in a team may harbour similar feelings in relation to each other. It is remarkably hard as a worker even to admit to the fact that there are times when you might hate the children you are caring for and have murderous feelings towards them, as well as wanting the best for them and even loving them.

For the past four years I have worked closely with Surrey Social Services' own children's homes to encourage the expression of such emotions, in the belief that not only are they understandable, they are sane and necessary and need to be understood in context. Many of the children I am thinking about are intensely provocative and will push people to their very limits of restraint. When a worker needs to express frustration and anger, when he or she has been spat upon or been assaulted or insulted, they may need to say something like 'I could murder him'. This is part of a communication. The other part of the communication is the person who receives this. If it is another worker on shift, and the two are used to each other and close, and have been pushed to their limits before, they can with confidence understand exactly what is being said, and can act accordingly. If it is to a manager, who knows the worker well, who is close, who has been there before with this worker and this child, likewise.

If there are unaddressed problems in the relationships in the team, however, then things might go wrong. First, and most commonly, the worker does not express his or her frustration to anyone, because it is not safe to. In this case then the chances of acting out the frustration – maybe hitting the annoying child or saying something cruel – are increased. Second, the recipient of the communication may misinterpret the expression of feeling for a declaration of intent – a very common mistake – and could over-react. Finally, the recipient may not hear that this time the feeling of desperate frustration is different – 'unless I get help now I may do something desperate' – and may be blasé and not act when action is required.

These then are what I would argue are the foundations for any therapeutic child care service – one based on maximising the protective factors that can be mobilised and enhanced in this setting. For staff to feel they can cope they have to feel heard, feel they have some influence over critical decisions and feel that they will be supported and backed up when they are under fire from children, families, other professionals. This will also be enhanced by the pursuit of the other principle – of expanding the field of discourse between staff team members. If these foundations are established then other things can follow – the articulation and elaboration of an ethos and culture; a modelling of similar communicative principles with families and other professionals; the increased possibility of long-term personality change in resident young people.

In the effort of thinking together, and using their feelings in the service of understanding, and trying to think about the experience of the child in the middle of this experience, the network can come together enough to hold the child and provide a secure base. It will not happen on its own. It has to be encouraged and rewarded with respect. It has to cut both ways – those who question and challenge have to be prepared to be questioned and challenged, and be wrong, and admit to it. This has to be modelled throughout the organisation. Such attitudes, if cultivated over time, could lead to a belief that such exchanges are not about being bolshie, difficult residential social workers, but are the very heart of the work, and those that are not doing it are not doing an essential – perhaps the essential – part of the work. What this means in practice – between adults – can be summed up in a phrase: 'Take responsibility for what you don't say'. If you feel something, and say something about how you feel – particularly in the group setting – something can be done about it. If you say nothing, nothing can be done. In an atmosphere of trust and respect, if you say something out of line or rude, then you can be told, and you can think about it, maybe realise that you had made a mistake and apologise. (This applies particularly to those in positions of authority and power.) If you are not able to do this, then you need to think hard about whether this is because you are in a hostile environment where everything you say will be taken down and used in evidence against you, or whether such paranoia is a convenient excuse for not engaging in the difficult work of speaking directly to people rather than feeling aggrieved and gossiping about them.

I am describing the building of a culture of enquiry, where the question 'why' becomes as important as the question 'what'. In such a culture behaviour is seen as having meaning, and feelings are considered as indicative of evidence outside the 'owner' of the feelings – so if you are upset when in close contact with a child, it is not a sign of weakness or unprofessionalism, but telling us something about that child's own upset and the absolute necessity to be in contact with it. I am not making an unreasonable claim for

Surrey's Children's Services children's homes when I say that such a culture has grown, over time, to the point where we can honestly claim that therapeutic work takes place.

For this to have happened, the senior managers of the organisation had to believe in a structure that would allow it to develop in this way. They had to believe that 'work' with the staff groups would help them deliver better child care. But what type of work works? As far as my role of internal consultancy goes, it depends on my being involved, and being regular, reliable and accessible. I have to keep going back, keep listening, hearing, bearing the secondary distress borne by the carers for distressed children. I have to allow them to pass on projections that are placed into them by the children and help them think about their feelings. It is also important for me to be part of the distinguishing process between what is bearable and what is not.

If we are thinking about achieving an optimal level of anxiety for a group to manage, then external boundary issues are as important as internal dynamics. Traditionally one set of issues has been dealt with by line management and the other by consultation. My role crosses those boundaries and the resultant tension could either be productive or open the way for splitting. In some ways I represent the maternal function: containing, listening, attending to, worrying about, holding in mind. My colleague – the operational manager of the homes – represents the paternal function: keeping to task, reminding of limitations and boundaries, reminding of the outside world, being slightly less worried. The trick then lies not in neutrality but in how he and I negotiate the boundaries of what is real and what is fantasy, what can be borne and what cannot, and so on. They need the 'father' to hear and act on their behalf, to be close, available and responsive, to protect when necessary and to push a bit when the home threatens to withdraw, regress or sulk. They need the 'mother' to know how it makes them feel to be up against it with violent and abusive children, to intercede on their behalf, to keep in close touch with the elements necessary to be 'good enough'. They then need the mother to be paternal and the father to be maternal. They need the mother role and the father role to discuss the home and come together in a joint response and continue to be available, whether that response has been a cause for relief or for pain. They need to be helped to develop their ability to talk together about differences, to share their common experiences, to be honest about how these children make them feel, to stop pretending that they are untouched by the work.

This point brings me to my conclusion. An organisation that constantly strives for such a culture of enquiry is inheriting something from the therapeutic community tradition that is at the heart of that enterprise. The very fact of making this a central part of the joint undertaking will influence the activity of the children's home or residential service as a whole; if the staff come to see is as central then the widening and deepening of the communication and sense of 'I can cope' will feed into each other as reinforcing processes. It is my belief – and my current endeavour – that this can be translocated from the therapeutic community tradition to the statutory children's homes sector and be enriching – even transformative – where it takes root and flourishes.

CHAPTER 19

Developing Community Groupwork in a Secure Setting

David Hartman

The secure setting as a therapeutic community?

The principles associated with therapeutic communities are sometimes seen as incompatible with secure settings, in that the exercise of power and coercion over young people is seen as incompatible with the principle of democratization, which is central to therapeutic community thinking. On the other hand one could take the view that autonomy and democracy are relative, not absolute, virtues. Even in a secure setting one can seek to maximise the young person's sense of involvement and agency. The same can be said of the other essential therapeutic elements such as attachment, containment and communication (Haigh 1999), which are by no means exclusive to classic therapeutic communities, which clients enter of their own free will and leave when they choose. To put this more plainly, just because your doors are locked doesn't mean you can forget the basic principles of a therapeutic environment.

This chapter describes a particular kind of secure setting, namely a psychiatric intensive care unit (PICU) for adolescents. One way in which we tried to foster the therapeutic quality of our unit was through the introduction of community groups.

Psychiatric intensive care

The Psychiatric Intensive Care Unit is a specialised form of acute psychiatric care for patients who cannot be cared for in a standard general psychiatric ward because of violence, suicidal behaviour or absconding from hospital. As a rule PICUs are locked units with an emphasis on physical security and the use of psychotropic medication. The PICU is a problematic setting as it is often seen as a dumping ground for unwanted patients, is often inadequately resourced and has vague therapeutic aims (Beer, Paton and Pereira 1997; Gentle 1996). One key paper (Goldney *et al.* 1985) described treatment purely in terms of psychopharmacology, but a more recent text (Beer, Paton and Pereira 2001) noted the importance of a psychological treatment programme including skills-based therapies, recreational activities and expressive therapies such as art therapy. The authors described a typical programme which included a once-weekly community meeting, but they did not explore the function of the community meeting for the PICU. Likewise Rood (1988) described a PICU in the USA which utilised twice-daily ward meetings as part of the programme, but the rationale for the community meetings was not discussed. My own impression is that such approaches are exceptional, and that community groups are rarely used in PICUs.

The context

Our Adolescent PICU is part of a small specialist psychiatric hospital for adolescents in the private healthcare sector. There are five units in the hospital, two of which are locked psychiatric intensive care units. This account is concerned with the development of community meetings on one of these units, known as ICU2. The unit takes up to 11 patients between the ages of 13 and 19, although most patients are typically 15 to 17 years old. The patients are admitted for a diverse range of clinical problems, but most have the following in common: they are all detained under the Mental Health Act of England and Wales, and they have been referred to ICU2 after repeated attempts to treat or care for them in other settings. Many come from adult psychiatric ICUs, general adolescent units or adult acute admission wards, and some come from Social Services secure units or young offenders' institutions. Patients are referred because of a significant risk of suicide or violence or both, in the context of severe mental illness or personality disorder. Some patients are admitted for relatively brief periods, for example for 28 days' assessment under Section 2 of the Mental Health Act, but because of the complexity and severity of their difficulties most remain for longer periods: between six and nine months is not unusual. There is usually a slight excess of female patients.

   The overall treatment philosophy of the unit was not pre-planned but has evolved out of the different perspectives of the clinicians and management who have been part of its development. The foundation is the 'Medical Model' in its broadest sense, not merely in the belief that the patient's problems can be helped with drugs (although this is implicit), but also incorporating the Hippocratic ethics of benign responsibility for a patient who is temporarily incapacitated, with a professional responsibility to provide care, palliative and effective treatment. The Medical Model is inescapable in any setting which uses the Mental Health Act as its essential legal framework, as our authority to detain patients rests on the assertion that they have been diagnosed as suffering from a mental illness.

The nursing approach, based on Stuart's Stress-Adaptation Model (Thomas, Handy and Cutting 1997), can be broadly described as developmental and needs-adapted. According to this approach the goal of treatment is to facilitate patients' development from immature, maladaptive to mature, adaptive ways of coping with adversity. The model recognises the need for a highly structured and controlled environment for very distressed patients, and the need to allow the patient to regain a sense of autonomy and agency as he or she recovers from the crisis. Medication is used to help control distress and dangerous behaviour in the 'crisis' and 'acute' stages of patients' illnesses.

The clinical team includes a psychodynamic psychotherapist, a psychodynamic-trained psychologist, a family therapist and two psychiatrists with group therapeutic and systemic training. Accordingly, the therapeutic principles of the team have developed with a blend of psychodynamic and systemic flavours. This blend should be apparent in the content of this paper, and the way that we understand groupwork not only in the usual group- analytic way, but also in the context of narrative therapy and systemic thinking about language.

The general approach of the unit implicitly incorporates attachment theory in our understanding of our patients, in that behaviour problems such as violence or self-harm are understood as reflecting distorted attachment patterns resulting from childhood abuse or neglect, and that there is a recognition of the value of stable and rewarding relationships as part of the treatment process.

Having described the nature of this particular intensive care unit, it is worthwhile to point out what we aren't. First, despite the enthusiasms of certain key members of the team, we are not a therapeutic community. The economic imperatives of our parent organisation dictate that we must fill a niche market in the health marketplace, namely that of an adolescent psychiatric intensive care unit, and this places some limits on the way we approach our work: this is discussed further below. Second, we are not a psychotherapeutic unit. Our staff consists largely of untrained healthcare assistants (HCAs), and qualified nurses with widely ranging professional backgrounds and levels of experience. Training is a high priority for us, but developing a coherent therapeutic philosophy is still an ongoing process.

The patient's experience

The ICU may be regarded as an example of a 'Total Institution' as described by Goffman (1961), in that every aspect of the patient's life is potentially or actually subject to scrutiny, control and influence. Unlike a prison or a social services secure unit, the primary goal of the ICU is therapeutic rather than custodial, but from the patient's perspective the experience of incarceration can be summed up as one of alienation, fragmentation and powerlessness. Patients are alienated in that they are somewhere they do not want to be, for a purpose they do not subscribe to, and they find themselves in an 'us and them' relationship with staff. The staff have all the power and knowledge and control over the therapeutic setting, and patients have none. They are also alienated in that they are removed from their familiar environment of home, family and friends. Their experience is fragmented in that they encounter multiple carers: from different disciplines, on different shifts, with differing personalities and levels of skill. Staff members have different agendas in their interactions with the patients, depending on their role and personal inclination, such as to understand, to control, to influence, to comfort or to provide physical care. Staff members, furthermore, from time to time go on leave, go off sick or resign. Patients form relationships within a peer group not of their choosing, and their friends also come and go unpredictably as they are admitted and discharged. Their powerlessness is self-evident: they are detained under the Mental Health Act which removes their liberty to leave the building when they choose, obliges them to accept psychiatric treatment, and gives staff the authority to use force to control their behaviour.

These aspects of the patient's experience on the unit would be problematic at the best of times, but they are doubly problematic in that they resonate with experiences the patient will have had prior to admission to hospital. They have experienced alienation in that they often have months or years of living on the fringes of society: they have often been excluded or have dropped out of school, they have often been subject to increasing stigmatisation by their peers because of their mental health problems, and they might have had encounters with the law and periods of incarceration. Their lives and relationships have been fragmented by frequent changes of care in a sequence of foster placements and children's homes interspersed with periods back in chaotic and abusive family environments. The patient's internal world is itself a fragmented jumble of chaotic object relationships, consequent perhaps on chaotic and fragmented early experiences of care. They have experienced powerlessness to the extent that many have been victims of abuse at the hands of their parents or other carers, and have been subjected to the power of the social services' care system, benign in its intentions, but often imperfect.

The community group

The community group takes place five days a week, immediately following the morning staff handover meeting. All staff and all patients are expected to attend. The meeting takes place in the dining room, with staff and patients seated around the tables, with tea, toast, fruit juice and breakfast cereals available. The meeting is chaired by a designated staff member and this role is rotated between the charge nurse, the consultant psychiatrist, the social worker and the teacher. The chairperson is required to structure the meeting, elicit participation from patients and staff and minimise disruptive processes.

The agenda has a set structure with some variation from day to day. The chairperson asks a colleague to read through the ward diary, noting patient appointments such as therapy sessions, visits or planned outings. We read through the programmed activities for the day, such as education, social skills group, art group, individual exercise or sport sessions. Activities may be discussed in terms of who is expected to attend, which members of staff will be present, and what the possible benefits or challenges might be for particular patients. If certain activities (such as patient outings) are contingent on risk or behavioural reward, this too is discussed in the group. Finally, we have 'any other business' which is time for agenda items raised by patients or staff. Patients will often use this to make requests of staff, or to make complaints against staff or fellow patients. Staff will raise items relating to the treatment programme, for example re-scheduling group meetings or announcing patient appointments. Staff might also raise items relating to staff or patient membership of the unit, for example a staff member being off sick, a patient's planned discharge or the incipient admission of a new patient. Another typical staff agenda item is to bring a unit rule to the attention of colleagues and patients. It is a principle of the meeting to bring the patients' problems and the ward's management into the public domain as far as possible. Sometimes this seems unreasonable for reasons of confidentiality or because the issue concerns a staff member outside the group, and a topic is adjourned for discussion elsewhere. Similarly, legal and policy decisions must be made elsewhere although useful information can be sought in the community meeting.

The therapeutic tasks

Despite this bleak picture of a psychiatric intensive care unit, we believe that there are potentials for us to turn the patients' experience into something more humane and helpful. This chapter describes some of our attempts to do so, by developing certain structures for communication.

The therapeutic task is different for each patient depending on the nature of his or her difficulties, but there is a level at which all patients share in the same process. We see each patient as moving across an 'illness' to 'health' spectrum, each with their own 'priority needs' (or care plans) towards which staff interventions are geared. We see the core therapeutic task as facilitating a development from immature, maladaptive defence mechanisms to more mature and adaptive ways of coping, in other words to facilitate mature defences such as sublimation, altruism and reaction formation, and to contain 'primitive' defences such as splitting, projective identification, acting out and denial. We anticipated that the community group would help us to deal with acting out on a number of levels. On the level of social learning it allows for social feedback from staff and, probably more importantly, from peers. The community group allows us to use peers and the whole staff group to explore incidents on the ward and discover the meaning of an incident and the motivation of the various participants. Worthington (1990) has also commented on the value of the community group in helping staff understand dynamic processes in the patient group. As a staff group it helps us achieve a better understanding of the patients and their relationships, which can be put to work in other therapeutic settings.

We might think about the function of the group as a 'container'. The community group is able to metabolise projective identification by examining a concrete manifestation of the projective identification (say, a smashed window or a verbal utterance), enlarging the details of the incident, giving it meaning and generating some tentative alternative ways of understanding the relationships of the participants. It must be emphasised that this task does not take place only, or even mainly, in the community group, but the group is a pivotal point in the day when the problem can be amplified and identified, to be taken up later in different settings.

Psychiatrist: Anything from the staff?

Charge nurse: Yes, I think we should discuss the window that got broken last night. We should try and clarify exactly what happened, and the implications for everybody here of that kind of behaviour.

Psychiatrist: So what is the story about the broken window? Which window is it?

Charge nurse: It's one of the panes next to the schoolroom. It's boarded up now, but it was broken about 9 p.m. last night I believe. I think there are issues here about patient safety, and the effect this kind of behaviour has on other patients.

Chair: What happened exactly?

Charge nurse: What was handed over this morning is that Helen kicked it in, and then Nicola picked up some glass and wouldn't hand it over when requested to do so, and this resulted in her being restrained by the night staff for some time, and receiving intramuscular medication.

Katie: I was there. I saw Helen kick it in.

Psychiatrist: Why do you think she did that?

Katie: She was angry because her mother didn't come and see her yesterday. She'd been stamping around and shouting all afternoon.

Healthcare assistant: That is true about Helen being upset, but haven't you left something out, Katie?

Katie: No…what?

Healthcare assistant: One of the night staff mentioned to me this morning that you had put the idea in Helen's mind. You had suggested it to her, in fact.

Chair: Pity Helen's not here. Is that right, Katie?

Katie: (*laughs*) Yeah, I did put her up for it.

Charge nurse: Why did you do a thing like that then?

Katie: For a laugh…it was so boring here last night.

(The conversation moves on to why the unit is boring at night, and what can be done about it. The patients agree to use the evening community meeting to plan evening activities with help from the night staff.)

A major difficulty we face here as clinicians is that we are obliged to exert power over our patients for their own safety or the safety of others, but we run the risk of exposing them to a profoundly untherapeutic experience. We believe that the community group is a useful element in the ward environment in that it can mitigate the possible harmful experiences and create some useful experiences of its own. This is a theme that we have also noted in the literature on community groups and inpatient group psychotherapy. Yalom's now classic text (Yalom 1983), for example, maintains that one of the functions of the inpatient group on an acute ward is 'the alleviation of iatrogenic anxiety', in other words to alleviate the anxiety which arises not from the patient's mental illness, but from their admission to hospital. Worthington (1990) suggests that '...a crucial function of the community meeting is that of allaying and managing the constant level of anxiety which is shared by the community arising out of the resonance of individual behaviour and group issues'. The resonating issues of alienation, powerlessness and fragmentation have been described above, and we have no illusions that the 24-hour environment on our ward is entirely therapeutic. However, the therapeutic community meeting serves to alert the staff and patients to stresses and problems in the treatment process.

Chair: (*going through diary*) Katie, you've got a psychotherapy session with Anna at 4.30.

Gemma: (*mumbles*) Oh shit.

Chair: What was that?

Gemma: Well, we're in for trouble tonight, aren't we? Katie has therapy, and gets all stressed out, and the day staff go off duty, and she'll kick off, won't she? Get restrained, get injected.

Chair: Katie, is Gemma right?

Katie: Yeah, well… I know my therapy is important but it always gets me thinking about the past, and then I get flashbacks…

Nurse: I'll be around this evening. Maybe we could spend some time together, play some games? And maybe we should talk to Anna about the time of your sessions?

Katie: Yeah, that would be good.

One way of alleviating anxiety is to give patients some control over the therapeutic process, and a sense of belonging on the unit. In a secure setting such as ours, patients have made no voluntary and informed decision to participate in a therapeutic process, so one cannot aspire to the democratic principles of a classic therapeutic community. Nevertheless we can introduce an element of negotiation into their lives, while retaining ultimate responsibility for their care and safety. Successful groupwork might be considered to embody a central metaphor of the culture of the organisation as a whole (Goldberg, Evans and Hartman 2001). Perhaps the metaphor of the ICU, with its culture of infantile dependence, is the phrase 'I want', and the community group might aptly be termed the 'I want group', as the wishes and needs of the patients are a perennial source of conversation.

Gemma: OK, items for the agenda. Katie?

Katie: I want to go to Sainsbury's this afternoon.

Gemma: Jason?

Jason: I want to come off 'levels'.

Gemma: Sam?

Sam: I want someone to sort out my benefits. I need money for fags.

Gemma: Nicola?

Nicola: I want to be allowed out in the garden with just one member of staff.

We might think of the group as a large distressed baby, and the therapeutic task as the need to respond empathically to these needs as they are articulated in the group. The group plays a key part in the therapeutic task of helping patients find words for their formless, incoherent sense of wanting something. From a systemic perspective the purpose of therapy is to create a shared sense of meaning through the process of dialogue (Seikkula 1993). Our group of patients have a very limited capacity for dialogue (as a result of their illnesses and also of the ICU context), but the community meeting allows us to build dialogue from the basic building block of the 'I want X' utterance. We can move beyond a request and an affirmative or negative response to more complex and dialogical conversations, with replies such as, 'yes but I want Y from you first', or 'yes, and he and she want Y and Z, so…', and so on. In this way a more empathic and reflective conversation can be developed from very simple beginnings.

Jason: I want to come off 'levels'.

Chair: Can you say more about that?

Jason: I haven't hit anyone recently. I don't need to be on levels any more.

Nurse: Jason has been doing really well, but he's still quite threatening some-times. I think it's still necessary to keep him out of trouble and to keep the others safe.

Chair: How about if we ask Dr Thompson to see you tomorrow, and if you're doing OK he might review it?

Jason: Yeah, that's fine. I won't threaten anyone.

We can try to reconcile the patients' wishes for freedom, autonomy, privacy or stimulation with our own quasi-parental need to ensure their safety and ap-propriate development. Sometimes we have to simply say 'no', but the group setting allows us to explain our thinking to the whole patient group; this allows the patient group to have an experience of benign and thoughtful rather than arbitrary authority. Over other, smaller parts of their lives the patients are encouraged to exercise choice. In the community group patients are encouraged to articulate needs which we are able to meet, for example to be taken shopping for essential items, to see the doctor for a physical complaint, or to be given information about their treatment. In circumscribed areas they can express preferences, for example where they will go on an outing, or which film they are going to see at the cinema. Exercising autonomy in these small ways is, we believe, a powerful antidote to the help-lessness induced by the secure setting.

We attempt to minimise the sense of fragmentation of their existence by providing the patients with information to help them structure their experi-ence in the unit. We use the community group as an opportunity to share in-formation about impending staff absences due to leave, illness or resignation, and we also use the group to introduce new staff members and explain their role. Similarly we use the group to highlight anticipated patient admissions and discharges. The community group punctuates time on the ward by following a daily and weekly rhythm, and fixed agenda items which look forward to the day ahead. The day is planned by referring to the staff diary, for appointments and other arrangements, and reviewing the patient group's daily timetable of education, groups and other activities.

This function may be understood in terms of Bakhtin's idea of the 'chronotrope' as related to the world of psychiatry by Peter Good (Good 2001). One's sense of place and time in the world is defined by the system of language used in one's social environment, and the social network is recipro-cally defined by one's use of language. As a rule, patients and staff exist in separate, discontinuous worlds of language. Good describes the 'patient chronotrope' which is concerned with immediate visceral experience and has a defeated, circular sense of time; and the 'care chronotrope' of staff which is concerned with rationality and has a linear, forward-looking and optimistic sense of time. The community meeting is a place and time when these two language systems can come together, and an authentic dialogue can emerge. By learning the staff group's language and engaging with the care chronotope, patients can get a sense that life on the unit has a rational purpose, and that their activities form part of a coherent whole in which staff have invested thought and care. Conversely when staff learn and use the patients' language, their sense of connectedness and understanding of the patients is greatly enhanced.

This overlapping of language systems is best illustrated by the way that patients appropriate and adapt technical terms such as 'specials' (special nursing, i.e. one-to-one nursing) and 'levels' (levels of security such as Level 1, Level 2 and so on). Being 'specialled' takes on new connotations of being special and needing extra attention. Similarly, the ICU setting generates new words that have a shared and specific meaning for patients and staff, for example 'kicking off' (to ventilate your feelings by causing wilful damage to people and property), or 'cutting up' (deliberate self-mutilation).

The evolution of the group

We have been using the community group on this unit for about four years and during that time we have seen progressive changes in the way it is used by patients and staff. Initially patients were very passive in the group and the conversation was led and dominated by the chairperson, who was usually a doctor, senior nurse, teacher or social worker. Patients initially showed little enthusiasm for active participation in the group, and their contributions were usually limited to requests of the 'I want' type. We have gently encouraged patients to take more responsibility for example by noting the agenda items, and more recently by taking agenda items and effectively chairing the meeting with minimal assistance and guidance from the staff chairperson. It is in the nature of the ICU that if a patient is well enough to chair a community meeting he or she is probably well enough to be discharged, so patient participation at this level tends to be irregular and fleeting. Just as the patients' participation has evolved, so has the participation of staff. We have felt more confident in deviating from the set structure of the meeting when the situation demands it, for example when a current crisis requires more in-depth discussion. We have also seen that more 'junior' members of the staff team have become more able to assert themselves in the group and use it for their own purposes, rather than merely being spectators of an interaction between senior staff and patients.

The community group has generated a vast amount of content and we have realised that the set time of thirty minutes, five days a week, was not adequate to address all the issues that demanded discussion. As a result there have been a number of offshoots from this original group. The first innovation was a once-weekly community group in the evening, to help generate dialogue between the patients and the night staff, particularly around the issue of the night shift being seen as boring and unstructured. Further innovations included hour-long 'planning groups' on Mondays and Fridays, to allow staff and patients to plan the week ahead, and the forthcoming weekend. These groups were structured and task-based, and we recognised the need for more time for unstructured and free-flowing discussion of current issues, and as a result we started a 'psychotherapy group' which runs for an hour a week based on principles outlined by Yalom (1983). The most recent development has been to make the evening community groups daily rather than once a week.

This evolution of groupwork has led to a need for more effective team communication to link the groups together, so we started a once-weekly senior staff meeting (separate from the case-focused ward round) called the 'ward environment meeting'. Because the pace of work on the ICU is so fast and frenetic, it is close to impossible to create the time for all staff to reflect and link their work together, but the most recent development has been a 'work discussion group' for healthcare assistants and nurses.

Conclusion

As mentioned in the introduction, we have no aspirations to describe ourselves as a therapeutic community in the classical sense, but we have found that the development of a community-orientated approach to groupwork has helped us develop into a 'psychiatric milieu' as described by John Gunderson (Gunderson 1978) with its elements of containment, support, structure, involvement and validation. This old idea finds an echo in Rex Haigh's description of a 'therapeutic environment' (Haigh 1999), with the key component principles of attachment, containment, communication, involvement and agency.

Our experience of trying to develop the therapeutic ethos of our ICU has taught us that one does not need forcibly and comprehensively to re-shape a secure setting into the mould of a therapeutic community. Indeed such a sweeping change could destabilise an institution which is inherently fragile, with potentially calamitous results for staff and patients alike. Our impression is that one can introduce changes gradually, at a level in keeping with the skill levels of staff and the capacity of the patient group, and one can allow the changes to develop at a pace which the 'community' tolerates and evokes.

A psychiatric intensive care unit for adolescents is an unusual and highly specialised milieu but it is likely that the problems posed by this environment can be generalised to many other therapeutic and care settings where patients are subjected to degrees of power, constraint and coercion. This includes general acute psychiatric units, forensic secure units and social services secure units. Such units are inevitably coercive and are often harsh and frightening environments. This chapter has described the evolution of a therapeutic community approach to groupwork in this setting, and we hope that we have demonstrated that the humanising influence of therapeutic community principles can be brought to bear on secure treatment settings such as psychiatric ICUs, secure units and forensic wards. One simple measure which can help bring this about is a daily therapeutic community meeting, in which staff provide the structure and boundaries, but allow a space where patients can make their voices heard.

Conclusion

CHAPTER 20

Review, Reflection and Reading

Adrian Ward, Kajetan Kasinski, Jane Pooley and Alan Worthington

As editors our aim in producing this book was to provide in one volume an account of how the therapeutic community approach is applied to work with damaged children and adolescents, what informs it, how it arose, how it is practised, and how it is developing. To do this we chose to select and draw out what we considered to be a core of the key aspects of the work, and devote a chapter to each of them. Though there are many reasons why this is probably the best approach to making sense of a complex and what may in many ways seem to be an imprecise subject, it has two shortcomings.

The first is that it is difficult for such a format to reflect or do justice to what actually happens in a therapeutic community, to what the experience of this sort of approach is like, or to what it requires from those involved in it at whatever level. For example (with apologies to Nicholl 1998), on a certain afternoon the director of a particular therapeutic community was meeting with academic staff from a nearby university to discuss details of a shortly-to-be-established professional training course in residential work with young people. Soon after the meeting started it was interrupted by a noisy argument involving two staff and two adolescents in the corridor outside. No sooner had the director invited those involved into his office in order to try to defuse the situation, than he received a phone call from reception that the new deputy director of a social services department responsible for several children on the unit had just arrived, unannounced, and would like to introduce himself. What it is important to convey through such an example is not just that the events and interactions (and consequent levels of detail and meaning involved) that take place in and around such a work setting are all inevitably interwoven with everything else that is happening, but also that it is 'precisely the concatenation of events, their density' which constitute 'the peculiar flavour' of this sort of work.

A second shortcoming is that, as editors, we discovered that the further the book progressed the more we became aware of chapters and of themes that had been missed out. In the Introduction it was pointed out that we would like to have included more about the importance and meaning of individual relationships, of the physical environment, about the moral and ethical dilemmas that arise in the work, about the issues arising from the cultural, ethnic and gender identities of children and families, and about the organisational and management issues. We would also like to have included more detail on what the approach can offer to a wider context, particularly its relevance to children placed with other families, and also to the ways in which children might be supported in their own families. Indeed, within each of these areas, we are aware of existing practice and developments that deserve greater acknowledgement, and we are sorry not to have been able to include more about this.

Perhaps one of the inevitable shortcomings of any book that tries to make sense of something as complex as therapeutic community practice (or other settings in which work is undertaken with very troubled children), is that in taking any one cross-sectional view, the need for other perspectives or cross-sections remains. That would be the case whatever one's starting point. Indeed, this is something like the work itself: understanding what happens between people and in groups, incorporating elements of history and the present with anticipating the future, is something that comes about through a process of taking a number of perspectives and viewpoints and putting these together into some form of whole.

For this reason, it may be worth saying something finally about some of the central themes that have recurred throughout this book, beginning with the theoretical bases of the work and their implications.

Our view as editors of the importance of psychodynamic theory to therapeutic community practice will be evident, and is particularly underlined in relation to three areas of practice. One is to do with providing a framework for an understanding of the meaning and impact of early relationships and experience, and how this might be addressed in practice. The second is to do with the ways we (as practitioners) are enabled to process and work with the impact that these children have on us, as well as the ways in which the therapeutic community environment (but this applies to any group or institutional setting and includes what we as adults do) impacts on the children. The third is to do

with the importance of understanding what happens in groups and institutions, and the ways in which psychodynamic thinking enables groups to be
effective as therapeutic resources and to remain focused on their task. This
applies to different group and institutional settings.

Nevertheless, while we underline the centrality of psychodynamic
thinking to therapeutic community work, it is also important to acknowledge
its role as a complementary theory rather than one that is universal. In other
words, while it is our view that psychodynamic theory is essential to understanding key aspects of the child, the task and the work, it is also important to
acknowledge that therapeutic community practitioners have needed to
recognise and become more receptive to the importance of other theoretical
models, professional disciplines and research, across the fields of psychology
(and models of mind, development and behaviour), education, care and organisation. These are essential to understanding and working with aspects of
child development and organisational issues, as well as in planning and addressing the ways in which parallel primary tasks are undertaken (e.g. care and
education) within frameworks of good professional practice. So while it is
evident from this book that we offer the view that an absence of
psychodynamic thinking can at best provide only a partial understanding
either of the child or of the institutional setting, we also make the point that an
application of psychodynamic theory on its own will not provide a complete
understanding. This 'complementariness' is therefore a key aspect of how
psychodynamic theory within therapeutic community practice works. In
other words, good therapeutic community practice is not just about the implementation of psychodynamic or systemic principles, but is about good
multidisciplinary practice.

This notion of the bringing together of different perspectives is one of the
key themes of therapeutic community work and is, of course, underlined by
the importance of systems theory, i.e. that each individual, group, interaction,
or even institution is not only a part of a wider system and needs to be understood within the context of the wider environment (familial, social, political,
cultural, professional) but is also a part of different sub-systems and therefore
different simultaneous contexts. So, when we return to the notion that therapeutic communities are about the creation of the holding environment, we are
always underlining notions of wholeness, holding together, integration,
parallel primary tasks, and the essential multidisciplinary nature of the work.
This emerges in many ways throughout the book, and is something that
needs to be underlined even more when we think systemically about the
broader context in which we work. The tasks of social care, mental health and
education remain, within the overriding statutory frameworks, essentially

separate and distinct, bounded by discrete lines of authority and responsibility. So where the regulatory frameworks relating to education, care and mental health emphasise separateness and difference, therapeutic community practice is about reinforcing the essential wholeness and relatedness of these aspects of each child's life. One cannot separate the notion of care from its roots in any child's emotional or psychological development (as underlined by the implementation of models of psychosocial care as distinct from the broader social care framework that regulates practice), in the same way that educational standards or attainments, or indeed the ways in which education is delivered or made available to very troubled children cannot be separated from an appreciation of their capacities to manage the psychosocial context in which learning takes place.

Finally, we would like to address you, the reader of this book, in a more direct and personal way. Like the work itself, a book such as this invites you to be more than just a passive consumer. The success of this book can perhaps best be measured in terms of any feedback we receive, both from the users themselves, and from the wider context in which this work is located, as well as of any subsequent dialogue we can achieve with both groups. The user feedback will involve not only how what is in the book is used or processed into the experience of those involved in therapeutic community work with young people, but also whether and how this gets back to us as editors; we would greatly welcome such feedback. The 'wider context' result will probably best be judged by whether the importance of such work (and indeed all work which involves the everyday detail of caring, educating, and bringing up children, and not just those at the extreme edges end of the spectrum) is recognised through it receiving the support, training, and recompense it needs. Only such a realised commitment can give us the right to expect others to commit themselves to changing the patterns of their own and others' upbringing, and, we hope, the pattern of their and their future children's lives.

You may also wish to make contact with others in this field who will be able to share ideas or give more information, and for that purpose we have included the contact details of a number of key organisations in the UK involved in practice, training and development in the general field of therapeutic care for children and young people.

Key Professional Organisations in the United Kingdom

The following are organisations you might contact if you want to visit a therapeutic community, learn about training courses, contact and share ideas with professionals from similar backgrounds or interests or develop your working environment towards a therapeutic community way of working. Each website will explain in more detail the work undertaken by the organisations.

Charterhouse Group of Therapeutic Communities
Station House
150 Waterloo Road
London SE1 8SB
Tel: (+44) 0207 803 0550
Fax: (+44) 0207 261 1307
Email: chg@btclick.com
www.pettarchiv.org/uk/charterhouse/home.htm

Peper Harow Foundation
Station House
150 Waterloo Road
London SE1 8SB
Tel: (+44) 0207 928 7388
Fax: (+44) 0207 261 1307
Email: mail@peperharow.org.uk
www.peperharow.org.uk

Association of Therapeutic Communities
Barns Centre
Church Lane
Toddington
Nr Cheltenham
Gloucester GL54 5DQ
Tel/Fax: (+44) 01242 620077
Email: post@therapeuticcommunities.org
www.therapeuticcommunities.org/index.htm

Caldecott College
The Paddocks
Smeeth
Ashford
Kent TN25 6SP
Tel: (+44) 01303 814232
Fax: (+44) 01303 814621
Email: info@caldecottcollege.org
www.caldecottcollege.org

School of Health and Social Care
University of Reading
Bulmershe Court
Earley
Reading
Berks RG6 1HY
Tel: (+44) 0118 378 8853
Email: l.mcmahon@reading.ac.uk
www.rdg.ac.uk/AcaDepts/ec/

Planned Environment Therapy Trust
Church Lane
Toddington
Cheltenham
Gloucester GL5 5DH
Tel: (+44) 01242 620125
Email: trust@pettrust.org.uk
www.pettarchiv.org.uk

YoungMinds
102–108 Clerkenwell Road
London EC1M 5SA
Tel: (+44) 020 7336 8445
Fax: (+44) 020 7336 8446
Email: enquiries@youngminds.org.uk
www.youngminds.org.uk

Editor and Contributor Biographies

The Editors

Adrian Ward is a Senior Lecturer in Social Work at the University of East Anglia, and an experienced practitioner, teacher, writer and editor within the field of group care generally, and therapeutic work with children and young people in particular. He is the editor of the journal *Therapeutic Communities*, the author of *Working in Group Care. Social Work in Residential and Day Care Settings* (Venture Press 1993), and co-editor with Linnet McMahon of *Helping Families in Family Centres: Working at Therapeutic* Practice (Jessica Kingsley 2001) and *Intuition Is Not Enough: Matching Learning with Practice in Therapeutic Child Care* (Routledge 1998).

Kajetan Kasinski is a Consultant Child and Adolescent Psychiatrist and Family Therapist. He works at the Northgate Clinic, where he set up an inpatient unit for younger adolescents which used many therapeutic community ideas and practices. In addition to his psychiatric training at the Maudsley Hospital and later at the Tavistock Clinic, he has worked in various innovative residential educational and community settings. He is a visiting teacher at the Tavistock Clinic.

Jane Pooley is an organisational consultant and family psychotherapist currently working for the Tavistock Consultancy Service and in private practice. She has worked as Director of the Charterhouse Group and was, for many years, a clinician and manager in both health and social care settings. She consults and supervises staff in a variety of residential child care settings – in-patient units, young offenders institutes and therapeutic communities – and is developing her interest in the application of therapeutic community principles in her work with businesses and social development initiatives.

Alan Worthington is a Director of the Peper Harow Foundation. He is an experienced teacher, practitioner and manager and, over his career, has worked across the boundaries of education, social care and mental health, both in the UK and abroad. From 1985–1994 he was the first Director of Thornby Hall, a therapeutic community and special school for children and adolescents in Northamptonshire.

The Contributors

Jenny Carter is Director of the Midlands Children's Project for the Peper Harow Foundation. The project incorporates a small residential centre and a placement support project for local children in substitute care. Her professional background is in therapeutic communities and residential family centre work.

Andrew Collie is Vice-Principal of Caldecott College, which specialises in therapeutic child care training. He has a professional background in adult mental health, therapeutic communities and residential child care. His professional interests are in the application of psychodynamic theory to a variety of social work environments. As well as teaching, he is an organisational consultant and clinical supervisor to staff in therapeutic communities.

David Hartman was born in South Africa where he completed his medical training. He trained as a psychiatrist at St George's Hospital in London, and he currently works as an Adolescent Psychiatrist at Huntercombe Maidenhead Hospital in Berkshire. He has an interest in the hospital treatment of young people with severe mental illness including severe and complex post-traumatic stress disorder.

Monica Lanyado is a Child and Adolescent Psychotherapist who helped to found the Child and Adolescent Psychotherapy training in Scotland. She is now in private practice in London, a consultant to a Peper Harow therapeutic community and a training supervisor for the British Association of Psychotherapists. She is former co-editor of the *Journal of Child Psychotherapy* and joint editor with Anne Horne of the *Handbook of Child and Adolescent Psychotherapy: Psychoanalytic Approaches* (Routledge 1999).Her book *Treating Childhood Trauma: The Presence of the Therapist* will be published by Brunner Routledge in 2004.

Andy Lole began his work with children as a CSV volunteer, working in an assessment centre in London. He then trained as a primary school teacher in Nottingham, where he went on to teach in a mainstream school. He moved to the Cotswold Community, Wiltshire in 1986. In 1994 he became the Headteacher at the Mulberry Bush School, Oxfordshire.

Michael Maher worked in building, conservation and teaching before finding Peper Harow, where he worked for six years and became Deputy Director. He then trained as a group analyst and now works in Surrey heading the Residential Care and Support Unit for the county's children's homes and residential schools.

Linnet McMahon is a Lecturer in Social Work at the University of Reading and is the course leader of the MA in Therapeutic Child Care course. She has written *The Handbook of Play Therapy* (Routledge 1992) and with Adrian Ward co-edited *Helping Families in Family Centres: Working at Therapeutic Practice* (Jessica Kingsley 2001) and *Intuition Is Not Enough: Matching Learning with Practice in Therapeutic Child Care* (Routledge 1998).

Colette Richardson is a Principal Family Therapist at Northgate Clinic, an inpatient unit for adolescents. She is also a Visiting Lecturer at the Prudence Skinner Family Therapy Training Department, Springfield Hospital, London and co-director of a family therapy training progamme in Cluj-Napoca, Romania. Originally she trained as a children's and general nurse and worked for 12 years in a therapeutic community.

Phil Richardson is Head of Psychology Discipline and Director of the Psychotherapy Evaluation Research Unit, Tavistock and Portman NHS Trust. He is Professor of Clinical Psychology at the University of Essex and editor of the journal *Psychology and Psychotherapy: Theory, research and practice*.

Richard Rollinson joined the Peper Harow Foundation in September 2001. He qualified in Social Work at Oxford in 1983. He lectured on the Health and Social Work courses at Reading University for five years. From 1991 he was Director of the Mulberry Bush School in Oxfordshire. For much of that time he was Vice-Chair of the Charterhouse Group of Therapeutic Communities and Chair of its Research committee. He remains a Trustee. He has been a member of the Department of Health National Advisory Group on residential care and of the then DfEE National Advisory Group for the education of children with emotional and behavioural difficulties. Currently he is a Trustee of Bryn Melyn Foundation, Vice-Chair of Caring for Children and a member of the Mental Health Foundation Committee on the mental health needs of children at risk.

Philip Stokoe is a Senior Clinical Lecturer in Social Work at the Adult Department of the Tavistock Clinic and a psychoanalyst in private practice working with adults and couples. In addition he provides consultation to a wide range of organisations in the helping professions, particularly those working with adolescents.

Peter Wilson has been Director of YoungMinds, the children's mental health charity, for the last twelve years. He is a child psychotherapist, trained at the Anna Freud Centre and has had a wide range of experience in community child mental health services. He was Senior Clinical Tutor in the Institute of Psychiatry for several years and Director of the Brandon Centre, a centre for psychotherapy and counselling. In the residential field, he worked as a psychiatric social worker in Hawthorne Cedar Knolls School, a residential treatment centre in New York in the 1960s. He has also consulted to staff in several adolescent inpatient units and therapeutic communities in the UK.

John C. Wright is a consultant clinical psychologist and psychoanalytic psychotherapist currently working as a senior clinical lecturer and psychotherapist in Plymouth. Previous posts have included work in both outpatient and residential settings for children and young people. Research interests include studies in attachment theory, psychotherapy process and outcome studies.

References

Acheson, D. (1998) *Independent Enquiry into Inequalities in Health.* London: HMSO.

Ainsworth, F. and Salter, M.D. (1978) Patterns of Attachment. Hillside, NJ: Lawrence Erlbaum.

Andersen, T. (1987) 'The reflecting team: Dialogue and meta-dialogue in clinical work.' *Family Process 26,* 415–28.

Andersen, T. (1990) 'The reflecting team.' In T. Andersen (ed) *The Reflecting Team: Dialogues and Dialogues about the Dialogues.* Broadstairs, Kent: Borgmann.

Andersen, T. (ed) (1991) *The Reflecting Team.* New York: Norton.

Anderson, H. (1997) *Conversation, Language, and Possibilities.* New York: Basic Books.

Anderson, H. and Goolishian, H. (1988) 'Human systems as linguistic systems.' *Family Process 27,* 371–93.

Anderson, H., Goolishian, H. and Winderman, L. (1986) 'Problem determined systems: Towards transformation in family therapy.' *Journal of Strategic and Systemic Therapies 5,* 1–19.

Aries, P. (1962) *Centuries of Childhood.* New York: Jersey Books.

Ashby, R. (1956) *An Introduction to Cybernetics.* London: Chapman Hall.

Banks, S. (2000) *Ethics and Values in Social Work.* Basingstoke: Macmillan.

Barkham, M., Margison, F., Leach, C., Lucock, M., Mellor-Clark, J., Evans, C., Benson, L., Connell, J., Audin, K. and McGrath, G. (in press) 'The CORE-OM and benchmarking: Towards practice-based evidence in the psychological therapies.' *Journal of Consulting and Clinical Psychology.*

Bateson, G. (1972) *Steps to an Ecology of Mind.* New York: Balantine.

Beecham, J. (1998) 'Economic evaluation and child psychiatric inpatient services.' In J. Green and B. Jacobs (eds) *Inpatient Child Psychiatry.* Routledge: London.

Beecham, J., Knapp, M. and Asbury, M. (1996) 'Costs and children's mental health services.' In A. Netten and J. Dennett (eds) *Unit Costs of Health and Social Care Services 1996.* Canterbury: Personal Social Services Research Unit, University of Kent at Canterbury.

Beer, M.D., Paton, C. and Pereira, S. (1997) 'Hot beds of general psychiatry. A national survey of psychiatric intensive care units.' *Psychiatric Bulletin 21,* 142–44.

Beer, M.D., Paton, S. And Pereira, S.M. (2001) *Psychiatric Intensive Care.* London: Greenwich-Medical Media.

Bergan, J.R. and Kratochwill, T.R. (1990) *Behavioural Consultation and Therapy.* New York: Plenum Press.

Bettelheim, B. (1961) *The Informed Heart.* London: Paladin.

Bettelhem, B. (1966) 'Training the child care worker in a residential centre.' *American Journal of Ortho-Psychiatry, 36.*

Bettelheim, B. (1974) *A Home for the Heart.* New York: Alfred A Knopf.

Bickman, L., Noser, K. and Summerfelt, W.T. (1999) 'Long-term effects of a system of care on children and adolescents.' *Journal of Behavioural Health Services & Research 26,* 2, 185–202.

Bion, W.R. (1957) 'Differentiation of the psychotic from the non-psychotic personalities.' In *Second Thoughts.* London: Karnac Books.

Bion, W.R. (1959) 'Attacks on linking.' In *Second Thoughts.* London: Karnac Books.

Bion, W.R. (1961) *Experiences in Groups and Other Papers.* London, Tavistock and New York: Basic Books.

Bion, W.R. (1962; 1991) *Learning from Experience.* London: Karnac Books/Heineman.

Blotcky, M.J. and Dimperio, T.L. (1991) 'Outcome of inpatient treatment.' *Journal of the American Academy of Child and Adolescent Psychiatry 30,* 3, 507.

Bollas, C. (1990) *The Shadow of the Object.* London: Free Association Books.

Boscolo, L., Cecchin, G., Hoffman, L. and Penn, P. (1987) *Milan Systemic Family Therapy.* New York: Basic Books.

Bowlby, J. (1969) *Attachment,* Vol 1 of *Attachment and Loss.* London: Hogarth Press, New York: Basic Books, Harmondsworth: Penguin (1975).

Bowlby, J. (1973) *Separation: Anxiety and Anger,* Vol 2 of *Attachment and Loss.* London: Hogarth Press, New York: Basic Books, Harmondsworth: Penguin (1975).

Bowlby, J. (1980) *Loss: Sadness and Depression,* Vol 3 of *Attachment and Loss.* London: Hogarth Press, New York: Basic Books, Harmondsworth: Penguin.

Bowlby, J. (1984) *Attachment and Loss (Volume 1 – Attachment).* 2nd edition. London: Hogarth Press.

Bowlby, J. (1988) *A Secure Base. Clinical Applications of Attachment Theory.* London: Routledge.

Boxall, M. (2002) *Nurture Groups in School.* London: Paul Chapman.

Bridgeland, M. (1971) *Pioneer Work with Maladjusted Children.* London: Staples Press.

Broderick, C. and Schrader, S. (1991) 'The history of professional marriage and family therapy.' In S. Gurman and D. Kniskern (eds) *Handbook of Family Therapy Vol. 2,* New York: Brunner Mazel.

Brown, P. (1981) *The Cult of the Saints.* Chicago: University of Chicago Press.

Bruggen, P. and O'Brien, C. (1987) *Helping Families. Systems, Residential and Agency Responsibility.* London and Boston: Faber and Faber.

Burns, B.J. (1996) 'What drives outcomes for emotional and behavioural disorders in children and adolescents?' *New Directions for Mental Health Services 71,* 89–102.

Butlin, E. (1973) 'Institutionalisation, management structure and therapy in residential work with emotionally disturbed children.' *British Journal of Social Work 5*, 3, 283–95.

Byng-Hall, J. (1995) *Improvising Family Scripts: Improvisation and Systems Change.* New York: Guilford Press.

Campbell, D. and Draper, R. (eds) (1985) *Applications of Systemic Family Therapy: The Milan Approach.* London: Grune & Straton.

Campbell, D., Draper, R. and Huffington, C. (1988) *Teaching Systemic Thinking.* London: DC Associates.

Campling, P. and Haigh R. (1999) *Therapeutic Communities: Past Present and Future.* London: Jessica Kingsley Publishers.

Canham, H. (1998) 'Growing up in residential care.' *Journal of Social Work Practice 12*, 1, 65–75.

Cant, D. (2002) 'Joined-up psychotherapy' – the place of individual psychotherapy in residential provision for children.' (unpublished)

Caplan, G. (1964) *Principles of Preventative Psychiatry.* London: Tavistock.

Caplan, G. (1970) *The Theory and Practice of Mental Health Consultation.* London: Tavistock.

Carpenter, M. (1851) *Reformatory Schools for the Children of the Perishing and Dangerous Classes and for Juvenile Offenders.* London: Gilpin.

Cecchin, G. and Pirotta, S. (1988) 'The Milan training programme.' In H. Liddle., D. Bruenlin and R. Schwartz (eds) *Handbook of Family Therapy Training and Supervision.* New York: Guilford Press.

Cecchin, G., Lane, G. and Ray, W. (1992) *Irreverence: A Strategy for Therapists' Survival.* London: Karnac Books.

Cecchin, G., Lane, G. and Ray, W. (1994) *The Cybernetics of Prejudices in the Practice of Psychotherapy.* London: Karnac Books.

Chamberlain, P. and Reid, J.B. (1998) 'Comparison of two community alternatives to incarceration for chronic juvenile offenders.' *Journal of Consulting and Clinical Psychology 66*, 4, 624–33.

Chassaguet-Schmirgel, J. (1984) *The Ego Ideal.* New York: Norton.

Checkland, P. (1981) *Systems Thinking. Systems Practice.* New York: Wiley.

Clinton, H.R. (1996) *It Takes a Village to Raise a Child, and Other Lessons Children Teach Us.* New York: Simon & Schuster.

Cole, T., Visser, J. and Upton, G. (1998) *Effective Schooling for Pupils with Emotional and Behavioural Difficulties.* London: David Fulton.

Cooper, D. (1967) *Psychiatry and Anti-psychiatry.* London: Tavistock.

Cornsweet, C. (1990) 'A review of research on hospital treatment of children and adolescents.' *Bulletin of the Menninger Clinic 54*, 64–77.

Curry, J.F. (1991) 'Outcome research on residential treatment: Implications and suggested directions.' *American Journal of Orthopsychiatry 61*, 3, 348–57.

Curtis Report, The (1946) *Report of the Care of Children Committee.* London: HMSO.

Dallos, R. and Draper, R. (2000) *An Introduction to Family Therapy.* Buckingham: Open University Press.

Dare, C. (1982) 'Techniques of consultation: In consultation from child and adolescent psychiatric settings.' In C. Dare, R. Ryle, D. Steinberg and W. Yule (eds) *News of the Association for Child Psychology and Psychiatry,* 11, July.

Dawkins, R. (1976) *The Selfish Gene.* Oxford: Oxford University Press.

Department of Health (1991) *The Children Act 1989 Guidance and Regulations, Volume IV. Residential Children's Homes.* London: Stationery Office.

Department of Health (2002) *Children's Homes: National Minimum Care Standards.* London: Stationery Office.

Dockar-Drysdale, B. (1968) *Therapy in Child Care. Papers on Residential Work, Vol.3.* London: Longman.

Dockar-Drysdale, B. (1990) *The Provision of Primary Experience. Winnicottian Work with Children and Adolescents.* London: Free Association Books.

Dockar-Drysdale, B. (1993) *Therapy and Consultation in Child Care.* London: Free Association Books.

Ekstein, M.A. and Wallerstein, J. (1959) 'Counter transference in residential treatment of children.' In *The Psychoanalytic Study of the Child 14,* 186–217.

Eliot, T.S. (1940) *Four Quartets – East Coker* in *Collected Poems.* London: Faber & Faber.

Elton Report (1989) *Discipline in Schools.* Report of the committee of enquiry chaired by Lord Elton. DES and Welsh Office.

Erchul, W.P. and Martens, B.K. (1997) *School Consultation: Conceptual and Empirical Bases in Practice.* New York: Plenum.

Erikson, E. (1965) *Childhood and Society.* London: Hogarth Press.

Evans, C., Mellor-Clark, J., Margison, F., Barkham, M., McGrath, G., Connell, J. and Audin, K. (2000) 'Clinical outcomes in routine evaluation: The CORE-OM.' *Journal of Mental Health 9,* 3, 247–55.

Fahlberg, V. (ed) (1990) *Residential Treatment. A Tapestry of Many Therapies.* Indianapolis, IN: Perspectives Press.

Fanshel, D., Finch, S.J. and Grundy, J.F. (1990) *Foster Children In A Life Course Perspective.* New York: Columbia University Press.

Farnfield, S. and Kaszap, M. (1998) 'What makes a helpful grownup? Children's views of professionals in the mental health services.' *Health Informatics Journal 4,* 3–11.

Farquharson. G. (1991) 'Adolescents, therapeutic communities, and Maxwell Jones.' *International Journal of Therapeutic Communities 12,* 125–29.

Fonagy, P., Steele, M., Steele, H. and Higgit, A. (1992) 'The theory and practice of resilience.' *Journal of Child Psychology and Psychiatry 35,* 231–57.

Fonagy, P., Steele, H. and Steele, M. (1996) 'Associations among attachment classifications of mothers, fathers and their infants.' *Journal of Child Development 67,* 2, 541–55.

Fraiberg, S. (1980) *Clinical Studies in Infant Mental Health. The First Year of Life.* London: Tavistock.

Freedman, J. and Combs, G. (1996) *Narrative Therapy.* New York: Norton.

Freud, S. (1915) *The Unconscious.* Standard Edition 14, Pelican Freud Library 11.

Fruggeri, L., Telfner, U., Castellucci, A., Marsari, M.and Matteini, M. (1991) *New Systemic Ideas from the Italian Mental Health Movement.* London: Karnac Books.

Furnivall, J.M.R. (1991) 'Peper Harow Consultancy. A consumer's view.' In W.R. Silveira (ed) *Consultation in Residential Care.* Aberdeen: Aberdeen University Press.

Gatiss, S.J. (2001) 'Standards and criteria for therapeutic community childcare, health and education.' *Therapeutic Communities 22*, 3, 197–214.

Gentle, J. (1996) 'Mental health intensive care: The nurses' experience and perceptions of a new unit.' *Journal of Advanced Nursing 24*, 1194–1200.

Gergen, K. (1999) *An Invitation to Social Construction.* London: Sage.

Godfrey, M. (1996) 'User and carer outcomes in mental health.' *Outcome Briefing 8*, 17–20.

Goffman, E. (1961) *Asylums: Essays on the Social Situation of Mental Patients and Other Inmates.* Harmondsworth: Penguin.

Goldberg, D., Evans, P. and Hartman, D. (2001) 'How adolescents in groups transform themselves by embodying institutional metaphors.' *Clinical Child Psychology and Psychiatry 6*, 1, 93–107.

Goldney, R., Bowes, J., Spence, N., Czechowizz, A. and Hurley, R. (1985) 'The psychiatric intensive care unit.' *British Journal of Psychiatry 146*, 50–54.

Good, P. (2001) *Language for Those Who Have Nothing. Mikhail Bakhtin and the Landscape of Psychiatry.* New York: Kluwer Academic/Plenum.

Grady, P. (2000) 'Waiting for miracles to happen? A consideration of the use of a short term model of work in a long term residential unit.' MA in Therapeutic Child Care dissertation, University of Reading.

Greenhalgh, P. (1994) *Emotional Growth and Learning.* London: Routledge.

Gunderson, J. (1978) 'Defining the therapeutic process in psychiatric milieus.' *Psychiatry 41*, 327–35.

Haigh, R. (1999) 'The quintessence of a therapeutic environment. Five universal qualities.' In P. Campling and R. Haigh (eds) *Therapeutic Communities: Past, Present and Future.* London: Jessica Kingsley Publishers.

Hey, J., Leheup, R. and Almudevar, M. (1995) 'Family therapy with "invisible families".' *British Journal of Medical Psychology 68*, 125–33.

Hindle, D. and Vaciago Smith, M. (1999) *Lectures in Personality Development: A Psychoanalytic Perspective.* London: Routledge.

Hinshelwood, R.D. (1987) *What Happens in Groups. Psycho-analysis, the Individual and the Community.* London: Free Association Books.

HMSO (1999a) *Modernising Government.* London: Stationery Office (Cm 4310).

HMSO (1999b) *Professional Policy Making For The 21st Century.* London: Stationery Office.

HMSO (2000) *Adding It Up: Improving Analysis And Modelling In Central Government.* London: Stationery Office.

Hodges, J., Lanyado, M. and Andreou, C. (1994) 'Sexuality and violence: Preliminary hypotheses from the psychotherapeutic assessments in a research programme on young sexual offenders.' *Journal of Child Psychotherapy 20,* 3.

Holmes, J. (1993) *John Bowlby and Attachment Theory.* London: Routledge.

Holmes, J. (2002) 'Are poetry and psychotherapy too "wet" for serious psychiatrists?' *Psychiatric Bulletin 26,* 137–38.

Hopkins, J. (1999) 'Some contributions on attachment theory.' In M. Lanyado and A. Horne (eds) *The Handbook of Child and Adolescent Psychotherapy. Psychoanalytic Approaches.* London: Routledge.

Hopkins, J. (2000) 'Overcoming a child's resistance to late adoption: How one new attachment can facilitate another.' *Journal of Child Psychotherapy 26,* 3, 335–47.

Horne, A. (1999a) 'Normal emotional development.' In M. Lanyado and A. Horne (eds) *The Handbook of Child and Adolescent Psychotherapy: Psychoanalytic Approaches.* London: Routledge.

Horne, A. (1999b) 'Sexual abuse and sexually abusing behaviour in childhood and adolescence.' In M. Lanyado and A. Horne (eds) *The Handbook of Child and Adolescent Psychotherapy. Psychoanalytic Approaches.* London: Routledge.

Howe, D. (1996) 'Surface and depth in social work practice.' In N. Parton (ed) *Social Theory, Social Change and Social Work.* London: Routledge.

Howe, D. (1998) 'Relationship-based thinking and practice in social work.' *Journal of Social Work Practice 12,* 1, 45–56.

ICD10 (1992) *The ICD10 Classification of Mental and Behavioural Disorders.* Geneva: World Health Organisation.

Imrie, D. and Green, J. (1998) 'Research into efficacy and process of treatment.' In J. Green and B. Jacobs (eds) *Inpatient Child Psychiatry.* London: Routledge.

Jensen, P. S., Hoagwood, K. and Petti, T. (1996) 'Outcomes of mental health care for children and adolescents: II. Literature review and application of a comprehensive model.' *Journal of the Academy of Child and Adolescent Psychiatry 35,* 8, 1064–77.

Jones, E. (1993) *Family Systems Therapy.* Chichester: Wiley.

Keenan, C. (1991) 'Working within the life space.' In J. Lishman (ed) *Handbook of Theory for Practice Teachers.* London: Jessica Kingsley Publishers.

Kelly, G.A. (1955) *The Psychology of Personal Constructs.* Volumes 1 & 2. New York: Norton.

Kendell, R.E. (2002) 'The Distinction between Personality Disorder and Mental Illness.' *British Journal of Psychiatry 180,* 110–115.

Kennard, D. (1983) *An Introduction to Therapeutic Communities.* London: Jessica Kingsley Publishers.

Kennard, D. (1999) 'Therapeutic Communities in Europe.' In P. Campling and R. Haigh (eds) *Therapeutic Communities: Past, Present and Future.* London: Jessica Kingsley Publishers.

Kennard, D. and Lees, J. (2001) 'A checklist of standards for democratic therapeutic communities.' *Therapeutic Communities 22*, 2, 143–51.

Klein, M. (1946) 'Notes on some schizoid mechanisms.' *International Journal of Psycho-Analysis 26*, 137–42.

Kolvin, I., Muller, F.J., Scott, D., Gatzanis, S.R.M. and Fleeting M. (1990) *Continuities of Deprivation: The Newcastle 1000 Families Study.* Aldershot: Avebury.

Kraemer, S. (1999) 'Obstacles to therapeutic work in the residential care of children and adolescents.' *Therapeutic Communities 20*, 145–56.

Kroll, L. and Green, J. (1997) 'The therapeutic alliance in child inpatient treatment: Development and initial validation of a family engagement questionnaire.' *Clinical Child Psychology and Psychiatry 2*, 3, 431–47.

Langfeld, J. (2000) 'The development of therapeutic treatment in a small children's home – reflections of a manager.' MA in Therapeutic Child Care dissertation, University of Reading.

Lanyado, M. (1988) 'Working with anxiety in a residential special primary school.' *Maladjustment and Therapeutic Education 6*, 1 Spring, 36–48.

Lanyado, M. (1999). 'The treatment of traumatisation in children.' In M. Lanyado and A. Horne (eds) *The Handbook of Child Psychotherapy. Psychoanalytic Approaches.* London: Routledge.

Lanyado, M. (2001) 'Daring to try again: The hope and pain of forming new attachments.' *Therapeutic Communities 22*, 1.

Lanyado, M. (2002) 'Creating transitions in the lives of children suffering from "multiple traumatic loss".' *Clinical Psychology and Psychiatry* (in press).

Lanyado, M. (2004) *Treating Childhood Trauma: The Presence of the Therapist.* London: Brunner Routledge (in press).

Lanyado, M., Hodges, J., Bentovim, A., Andreou, C. and Williams, B. (1995) 'Understanding boys who sexually abuse other children: A clinical example.' *Psychoanalytic Psychotherapy 9*, 3.

Lees, J., Manning, N. and Rawlings, B. (1999) *CRD Report 17 – Therapeutic Community Effectiveness. A Systematic International Review of Therapeutic Community Treatment for People with Personality Disorders and Mentally Disordered Offenders.*

Lennhoff, F.G. (1960) *Exceptional Children.* London: Allen and Unwin.

Lewis, G. and Appleby, L. (1988) 'Personality Disorder: The patients psychiatrists dislike.' *British Journal of Psychiatry 153*, 44–49.

Little, M. (1995) *A Life Without Problems. Achievements of a Therapeutic Community.* Aldershot: Arena.

Little, M. (2000) 'Understanding the research.' In A. Hardwick and J. Woodhead (eds), *Loving, Hating and Survival. A Handbook for All who Work with Troubled Children and Young People.* Aldershot: Ashgate.

Maher, A. (1999) 'Using a therapeutic model of thought and practice.' In A. Hardwick and J. Woodhead (eds) *Loving, Hating and Survival: A Handbook for All who Work with Troubled Children and Young People.* Ashgate: Arena.

Maher, M. (2000) 'The compound I; the group self and the poetic self.' In *Group Analysis* *33*, 4, 519–530.

Main, M. (2000) 'The organized categories of infant, child, and adult attachment: Flexible vs. inflexible attention under attachment-related stress.' *Journal of the American Psychoanalytic Association 48*, 4, 1055–96.

Main, T. (1946) 'The hospital as a therapeutic institution.' *Bulletin of the Menninger Clinic 10*, 56–70.

Main, T. (1990) 'Knowledge, learning and freedom from thought.' *Psychoanalytic Psychotherapy 5*, 1, 59–78.

Main, T.F. (1989) *The ailment and other psycho-analytic essays.* London: Free Association Books.

Mason, B. (1989) *Handing Over. Developing Consistency Across Shifts in Residential and Health Care Settings.* London: Karnac Books.

Mattinson, J. (1975) *The Reflection Process in Casework Supervision.* London: Institute of Marital Studies.

McCann, J., James, A., Wilson, S. and Dunn, G. (1996) 'The prevalence of psychiatric disorder in young people in the care system.' *British Medical Journal 313*, 1529–30.

McMahon, L. and Ward, A. (2001) *Helping Families in Family Centres: Working at Therapeutic Practice.* London: Jessica Kingsley.

McRae, J. (2000) 'How can we hold the carers who hold the children, to prevent foster placement breakdown?' MA in Therapeutic Child Care dissertation, University of Reading.

Menzies-Lyth, I. (1988) *Containing Anxiety in Institutions. Selected Essays Volume 1.* London: Free Association Books.

Menzies-Lyth, I. (1989) *The Dynamics of the Social. Selected Essays Volume 2.* London: Free Association Books.

Miller, E.J. (1993) *Creating a Holding Environment: Conditions for Psychological Security.* London: Tavistock.

Miller, E.J. and Gwynne, E.V. (1972) *A Life Apart. A Study of Residential Institutions for the Physically Handicapped and the Young Chronic Sick.* London: Tavistock.

Minuchin, S. (1974) *Families and Family Therapy.* Cambridge, MA: Harvard University Press.

Mosley, J. (1996) *Quality Circle Time in the Primary Classroom.* Wisbech: LDA.

Neill, A.S. (1960) 'My scholastic life.' Journal of the Summerhill Society.

Nicholl, D. (1998) *The Testing of Hearts.* London: Darton, Longman & Todd.

Obholzer, A. (1994) 'Authority, power and leadership. Contributions from group relations training.' In Obholzer, A. and Roberts, V.Z. (eds) (1994) *The Unconscious at Work: Individual and Organisational Stress in the Human Services.* London: Routledge.

Obholzer, A.R. (ed) (1994) *Unconscious at Work: Individual and Organisational Stress in the Human Services.* London: Routledge.

Obholzer, A. and Roberts, V. Z. (1994) *The Unconscious at Work.* London: Routledge.

Ogden, T. (1982) *Projective Identification and Psychotherapeutic Technique.* London: Karnac Books.

Oxman, A.D. and Guyatt, G.H. (1988) 'Guidelines for reading literature reviews.' *Canadian Medical Association Journal 138*, 697–703.

Parsons, M. and Dermen, S. (1999) 'The violent child and adolescent.' In M. Lanyado and A. Horne (eds) *The Handbook of Child and Adolescent Psychotherapy. Psychoanalytic Approaches.* London: Routledge.

Peacock, S. (1997) 'Holding on: An exploration of the relevance of 'holding' and 'containment' in field social work with children.' MA in Therapeutic Child Care dissertation, University of Reading.

Perry, B., Pollard R., Blakley, T., Baker, W. and Vigilant, D. (1995) 'Childhood trauma, the neurobiology of adaptation and "user-dependent" development of the brain: How "states" become "traits".' *Infant Mental Health Journal 16*, 4 Winter, 271–91.

Pfeiffer, S.I. and Strzelecki, S.C. (1990) 'Inpatient psychiatric treatment of children and adolescents: A review of outcome studies.' *American Journal of Child and Adolescent Psychiatry 29*, 6, 847–53.

Pines, M. (1981) 'The frame of reference of group psychotherapy.' In *International Journal of Group Psychotherapy 31*, 3.

Polksy, H. (1962) *Cottage Six: The Social System of Delinquent Boys in Residential Treatment.* New York: Russel Sage Foundation.

Polnay and Ward (2000) 'Promoting the health of looked after children.' *British Medical Journal 320*, 661–2.

Rapoport, R.N. (1960) *Community as Doctor.* London: Tavistock.

Reber, A.S. and Reber, E. (2001) *The Penguin Dictionary of Psychology.* Harmondsworth: Penguin.

Redl, F. (1966) *When we Deal with Children.* New York: Free Press.

Redl, F. and Wineman, D. (1951) *Children Who Hate.* New York: Free Press.

Redl, F. and Wineman, D. (1957) *The Aggressive Child.* New York: Free Press.

Rice, A.K. (1963) *The Enterprise and its Environment.* London: Tavistock.

Rood, L. (1988) 'The intensive care unit.' *New Directions for Mental Health Services 39*, 41–47.

Rose, M. (1977) *'Residential Treatment – a Total Therapy.'* David Wills Lecture, Annual Windsor Conference of the Association of Therapeutic Communities.

Rose, M. (1990) *Healing Hurt Minds: The Peper Harow Experience.* London: Tavistock/Routledge.

Rowling, J.K. (1997) *Harry Potter and the Philosopher's Stone.* London: Bloomsbury.

Salzberger-Wittenberg, I. (1999) 'Different kinds of endings.' In I. Salzberger-Wittenberg, G. Williams and E. Osborne (eds) *The Emotional Experience of Learning and Teaching.* London: Karnac Books.

Secretary of State for Health (2000) *The NHS Plan.* London: Stationery Office.

Seikkula, J. (1993) 'The aim of therapy is to generate dialogue: Bakhtin and Vygotsky in the family session.' *Human Systems 4*, 33–48.

Selvini Palazzoli, M., Boscolo, L., Cecchin, G. and Prata, G. (1978) *Paradox and Counter Paradox*. New York: Aronson.

Seyegh, I. and Grizenko, N. (1991) 'Studies of the effectiveness of day treatment programs for children.' *Canadian Journal of Psychiatry 36*, 246–53.

Shahar, S. (1990) *Childhood in the Middle Ages*. London: Routledge.

Shohet, R. and Hawkins, P. (2000) *Supervision in the Helping Professions*. Oxford: Open University Press.

Silveira, W.R. (ed) (1991) *Consultation in Residential Care*. Aberdeen: Aberdeen University Press.

Sinason, V. (1992) *Mental Handicap and the Human Condition*. London: Routledge.

Sinclair, I. and Gibbs, I. (1998) *Children's Homes. A Study in Diversity*. Chichester: Wiley.

Skidelsky. R. (1969) *English Progressive Schools*. Harmondsworth: Penguin.

Skuse, D., Bentovim, A., Hodges, J., Stevenson, J., Andreou, C., Lanyado, M., Williams, B., New, M., McMillan, D. (1997) *The Influence of Early Experience of Sexual Abuse on the Formation of Sexual Preferences During Adolescence*. Commissioned Research Report for the Department of Health.

Social Services Inspectorate (1993) *Corporate Parents. Inspection of Residential Child Care Services in 11 Local Authorities, November 1992 – March1993*. London: Depertment of Health.

Sprincc, J. (2002) 'Developing containment: Psychoanalytic consultancy to a therapeutic community for traumatised children.' *Journal of Child Psychotherapy 28*, 2, 147–61.

Stern, D. (1985) *The Interpersonal World of the Infant*. New York: Basic Books.

Stiffman, A.R., Horwitz, S.M., Hoagwood, K. and Wadsworth, M.E. (2000) 'Adult and child reports of mental health services in the Service Assessment for Children and Adolescents (SACA).' *Journal of the Academy of Child and Adolescent Psychiatry 39*, 1032–39.

Stiles, W.B., Morrison, L.A., Haw, S.K., Harper, H., Shapiro, D.A. and Firth-Cozens, J. (1991) 'Longitudinal study of assimilation in exploratory psychotherapy.' *Psychotherapy 28*, 195–206.

Street, C. (2000) *Providing Residential Services for Children and Young People: A Multidisciplinary Perspective*. Aldershot: Ashgate.

Thomas, B., Handy, S. and Cutting, P. (eds) (1997) *Stuart and Sundeen's Mental Health Nursing: Principles and Practice*. London: Mosby.

Trieschman, A.E. (1969) 'Understanding the stages of a typical temper tantrum.' In A.E. Trieschman, J.K. Whittaker and L.K. Brendtro (eds) *The Other 23 Hours: Child-Care Work With Emotionally-Disturbed Children in a Therapeutic Milieu*. New York: Aldine.

Trieschman, A.,Whittaker, J. and Bendtro, L. (1969) *The Other 23 Hours: Child-Care Work with Emotionally Disturbed Children in a Therapeutic Milieu*. New York: Aldine.

Utting, D. (1995) *Family and Parenthood, Supporting Families, Preventing Breakdown*. York: Joseph Rowntree Foundation.

Utting, D. (ed) (1998) *Children's Services Now and in the Future.* York: Joseph Rowntree Foundation.

Valentine, M. (1994) 'The social worker as "bad object".' *British Journal of Social Work 24,* 71–86.

Van der Kleij, G. (1985) 'The group and its matrix.' *Group Analysis 18.*

von Bertalanffy, L. (1968) *General Systems Theory: Foundations, Development, Applications.* New York: Braziler.

von Foerster, H. (1981) *Observing Systems.* Seaside, CA: Intersystems Publications.

Waddell, M. (1998) *Inside Lives, Psychoanalysis and the Growth of the Personality.* London: Tavistock Clinic Series, Duckworth.

Ward, A. (1993) 'The large group: The heart of the system in group care.' *Groupwork 6,* 1, 63–77.

Ward, A. (1995) 'Opportunity led work: 1. Introducing the concept.' *Social Work Education 14,* 4, 89–105.

Ward, A. (1996) 'Opportunity led work: 2. The framework.' *Social Work Education 15,* 3, 40–59.

Ward, A. and McMahon, L. (1998) *Intuition is Not Enough. Matching Learning With Practice in Therapeutic Child Care.* London: Routledge.

Wardle, C.J. (1991) 'Historical influences on services for children and adolescents.' In H. Berrios and G. Freeman (eds) *One Hundred and Fifty Years of British Psychiatry.* London: Gaskell.

Watzlawick, P., Weakland, J. and Fisch, R. (1974) *Change, Principles of Problem Formation and Problem Resolution.* New York: Norton.

Weisz, J.R. (1998) 'Empirically supported treatments for children and adolescents. Efficacy, problems, and prospects.' In K.S. Dobson and K.D. Craig (eds) *Empirically Supported Therapies. Best Practice in Professional Psychology.* London: Sage, 66–92.

Weisz, J.R., Donenberg, G.R., Han, S.S. and Weiss, B. (1995) 'Bridging the gap between laboratory and clinic in child and adolescent psychotherapy.' *Journal of Consulting and Clinical Psychology 63,* 688–701.

Whitwell, J. (2001) 'Therapeutic child care.' In K. White (ed) *Reframing Children's Services. National Council of Voluntary Child Care Organisations Annual Review Journal 3,* London.

Wiener, N. (1950) *The Human Use of Human Beings.* New York: Avon Books.

Wills, D. (1945) *The Barns Experiment.* London: Allen and Unwin.

Wills, D. (1960) *Throw Away Thy Rod.* London: Gollancz.

Wilson, P. (1991) 'Consultation to institutions: Questions of role and orientation'. In S. Ramsden (ed) *Occasional Papers No. 6 Psychotherapy – Pure and Applied.* Association of Child Psychology and Psychiatry.

Wilson, P. (1999) 'Therapy and consultation in residential care.' In M. Lanyado and A. Horne (eds) *The Handbook of Child and Adolescent Psychotherapy: Psychoanalytic Approaches.* London: Routledge.

Winnicott, D.W. (1956) 'Primary maternal preoccupation.' In D.W. Winnicott (1958) *Collected Papers. Through Paediatrics to Psycho-Analysis.* London: Tavistock.

Winnicott, D.W. (1958) 'The capacity to be alone.' In D.W. Winnicott (1965) *The Maturational Processes and the Facilitating Environment.* London: Hogarth Press and the Institute of Psycho-Analysis.

Winnicott, D.W. (1960) 'The theory of the parent–infant relationship.' In D.W. Winnicott (1965) *The Maturational Processes and the Facilitating Environment.* London: Hogarth Press and the Institute of Psycho-Analysis.

Winnicott, D.W. (1964) *The Child, The Family and The Outside World.* Harmondsworth: Penguin.

Winnicott, D.W. (1965) *The Maturational Processes and the Facilitating Environment.* London: Hogarth Press.

Woodhead, J. (1999) 'Containing care.' In J. Woodhead and A. Hardwick (eds) *Loving, Hating and Survival.* Aldershot: Ashgate.

Woods, S. (2000) 'Towards an understanding of the developing relationship between a newly placed adoptive child and his adoptive parents – a case study.' MA in Therapeutic Child Care dissertation, University of Reading.

Woolfenden, S.R., Williams, K. and Peat, J. (2001) 'Family and parenting interventions in children and adolescents with conduct disorder and delinquency aged 10–17 (Cochrane Review).' *The Cochrane Library, Issue 2.* Oxford: Update Software.

Worthington, A. (1990) 'The function of the community meeting in a therapeutic community for pre- and young adolescents.' *International Journal of Therapeutic Communities 11*, 2, 95–102.

Wright-Watson, J. (1990) 'The function of play in a therapeutic community for children and adolescents.' *International Journal of Therapeutic Communities 11*, 2, 77–86.

Yalom, I.D. (1983). *Inpatient Group Psychotherapy.* New York: Basic Books.

Subject Index

Author Index

Printed in Great Britain
by Amazon.co.uk, Ltd.,
Marston Gate.